THE

PASCAL

HANDBOOK

THE
PASCAL
HANDBOOK

JACQUES TIBERGHIEN

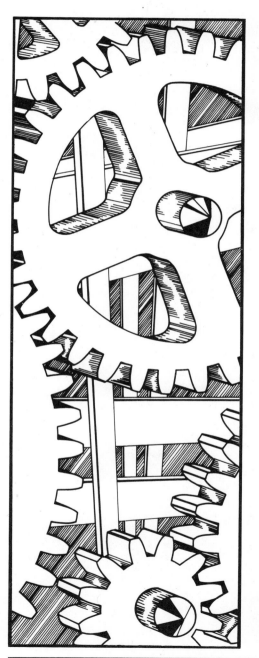

Every effort has been made to supply complete and accurate information. However, Sybex assumes no responsibility for its use, nor for any infringements of patents or other rights of third parties which would result.

Library of Congress Card Number: 80-53283
ISBN 0-89588-053-9
Printed in the United States of America
10 9 8 7 6 5 4 3 2

Acknowledgements

Valuable contributions by many persons and organizations have made this book possible. The author is pleased to be able to acknowledge certain of them here.

Control Data, Hewlett Packard, Intel, Apple Computer, Microsoft, IBM, Oregon Minicomputer Software, University of California at San Diego and The Pascal User's Group provided important and timely information about the various Pascal implementations.

Eric Novikoff and Joseph Faletti were responsible for a detailed review of the work and many valuable improvements to the final manuscript.

Joseph Kalash and Charles Koester furnished valuable assistance in the development and verification of the program examples.

A. Winsor Brown of POINT 4 Data Corporation contributed many valuable revisions to the second printing of this book.

Julie Sickert and Janet Rampa supervised the manuscript and the editorial process, constantly contributing to the book's improvement.

Roger Gottlieb, Guy Orcutt, Karl Sterne and Rodnay Zaks provided guidance and support throughout the development and production of this book.

The entire Sybex staff accomplished the design, editing and timely production of THE PASCAL HANDBOOK in a most efficient and helpful manner.

Contents

Preface

When originally defined by Niklaus Wirth in 1971, Pascal was seen as a coherent, powerful and well-defined language and quickly gained wide acceptance. However, the very success of, and enthusiasm for, Pascal has led to the development of multiple and incompatible versions. These multiple versions have, in turn, created a worldwide effort at defining a new standard, the ISO (International Standards Organization) Standard. Despite this effort at standardization, new extensions are still being implemented.

As a result, most Pascal versions available today display some incompatibilities, and programs written in one version may not execute in another. When writing a Pascal program, a programmer must frequently verify and cross-check the definitions and effects of specific features being used.

Drawing together information scattered until now among diverse sources, this handbook has been written as a single reference manual designed to facilitate the use of Pascal by all Pascal users. Every feature of Pascal is explained in a convenient format for some major Pascal dialects including Jensen and Wirth's original definition, with the CDC implementation, the proposed ISO Standard, UCSD Pascal, Pascal 1000 (HP 1000), OMSI Pascal-1, and Pascal/Z. Compiler options are not included.

Organized alphabetically, this book is designed for ease in retrieving and understanding all features of the language. As such, it is a comprehensive and indispensible tool for the Pascal user.

Each significant feature of Pascal is a separate entry. Separate entries are found for:

— *symbols*, including:

reserved words	such as **PROGRAM, BEGIN** and **END**
operators	such as + — and *
delimiters	such as ; . ' and ( ).

— *predefined identifiers*, including:

types	such as REAL, INTEGER, CHAR
functions	such as ABS, SIN, SQR
procedures	such as READ, WRITE, GET
constants	such as MAXINT, TRUE, FALSE

— *concepts*, such as "global", "assignment" and "statement".

In order to provide easy access to information, a format with a quick-reference heading and up to four main sections has been consistently applied to the description of each entry.

The *heading* of each entry shows:

1. the feature being described in large, clear type with a brief definition
2. a chart indicating
   — whether the feature is a symbol, identifier, or concept
   — which versions of Pascal implement this feature.

The *description* of each entry is presented in four sections:

1. SYNTAX: a diagram showing how the entry may be legally used
2. DESCRIPTION: what it is, what it does
3. IMPLEMENTATION-DEPENDENT FEATURES: any differences between the various implementations, including appropriate syntax diagrams
4. EXAMPLES: whenever necessary, typical examples that clarify the use or meaning of the entry are presented.

The "Standard" referred to in this handbook is the *proposed ISO Standard* as published at this time (see reference list at the end of this book), not the original Jensen and Wirth definition of Pascal. This standard has not, however, been finalized and some features may still be modified. The author has therefore used his own judgment in the few cases where features were still under discussion. For example, *conformant arrays* are not described here, as they will probably not be included in the final standard.

Another practical problem that the author faced was to select the implementations to be described in this book. Some recent implementations are not widely used and some depart significantly from Standard Pascal. The author has selected widely used implementations that he feels conform to the original spirit of Pascal.

This book should provide a comprehensive and practical reference for Pascal programmers, whether novices or experienced users. By using a consistent and carefully organized format for the description of all Pascal features, this book will:

   — encourage the use of all features of the language
   — ease the programming process
   — facilitate learning the language
   — assist in the translation of programs from one version of Pascal into another.

The author hopes to have captured the current spirit of Pascal within the pages of this book and welcomes comments and suggestions for improvement.

HOW TO READ THIS BOOK

entry

A brief definition of the Pascal entry or feature is given here for quick reference.

☐ **SYMBOL**   ☐ **STANDARD**   ☐ **J & W/CDC**   ☐ **PASCAL/Z**

☐ **IDENTIFIER**   ☐ **HP 1000**   ☐ **OMSI**   ☐ **UCSD**

☐ **CONCEPT**

1
SYNTAX

The formal syntax of the entry is presented in diagram form or described in words. A syntax diagram illustrates the correct use of the word or symbol and reflects the rules for combining it with other legal constructs in a program. (See the next section for How to Read a Syntax Diagram.)

2
DESCRIPTION

What the entry means, what it is used for, and its effect in a program.

3
IMPLEMENTATION-DEPENDENT FEATURES

Enhancements or restrictions to the use of the entry that are specific to the various implementations of Pascal.

4
EXAMPLE

Whenever required, an example program featuring the Pascal entry is presented in order to:

— illustrate the correct syntax of the entry within an actual program
— show how it works with other elements of a program to accomplish a specific task.

ABOUT THE HEADING:

THE ENTRY BOX

The type-face used for the term in the entry box has a specific meaning:

BOLDFACE UPPERCASE	means that the term is a reserved word.
UPPERCASE	means that it is a predefined identifier or directive.
lowercase	means that it is a concept.

Note: Codes for ASCII characters are given in decimal.

THE CHART

1. The first column of the chart below the definition of the entry indicates the *type* of entry.

    SYMBOL refers to reserved words, symbols (operators and delimiters) or directives (context-dependent words) that have a fixed, predefined meaning in Pascal and cannot be redefined by the user.

    IDENTIFIER refers to words that have a predefined meaning in Pascal, but may be redefined by the programmer to take a different meaning. These include predefined program parameters, constants, types, procedures and functions.

    CONCEPT refers to general terms that describe or define the syntax and operation of the Pascal language. Unlike symbols and identifiers, concepts do not appear in programs.

entry

☐ **STANDARD**   ☐ **J & W/CDC**   ☐ **PASCAL/Z**

☐ **HP 1000**   ☐ **OMSI**   ☐ **UCSD**

2. The last three columns of the chart indicate in which *versions* of Pascal the entry has been implemented.

> **STANDARD** is the proposed ISO Standard (DP 7185, first version).

> **HP 1000** refers to Pascal 1000 which was developed by Hewlett Packard for the HP 1000.

> **J&W/CDC** refers to Jensen and Wirth's original definition of Pascal implemented on CDC 6000 series machines.

> **OMSI** refers to OMSI Pascal-1, developed by Oregon Minicomputer Software, Inc. for the PDP-11.

> **PASCAL/Z** is a Pascal compiler for Z-80 microcomputers distributed by Ithaca Intersystems, Inc.

> **UCSD** refers to the II.0 Pascal system and language developed at the University of California, San Diego, for mini-micro-computer applications. Apple Pascal (1.0) is highly compatible with UCSD Pascal II.0.

HOW TO
READ A SYNTAX DIAGRAM

A box with rounded edges is used to represent predefined words including both reserved words **(BOLDFACE UPPERCASE)** and predefined identifiers (UPPERCASE). No blanks are permitted within such words.

A circle is used to represent reserved symbols (non-alphanumeric characters). No intervening blanks are permitted between the non-alphanumeric characters of a symbol.

A rectangle encloses syntax elements that are defined elsewhere in their own diagram. A qualifier, e.g., for type, may also be included.

Lines and arrows indicate authorized paths and are used to show the correct sequence of elements in the diagram. Except where noted in the text, blanks, comments and ends-of-lines may appear along the lines connecting enclosed words, symbols, and referenced syntax diagrams.

For example, the syntax for a VARiable declaration is drawn as follows:

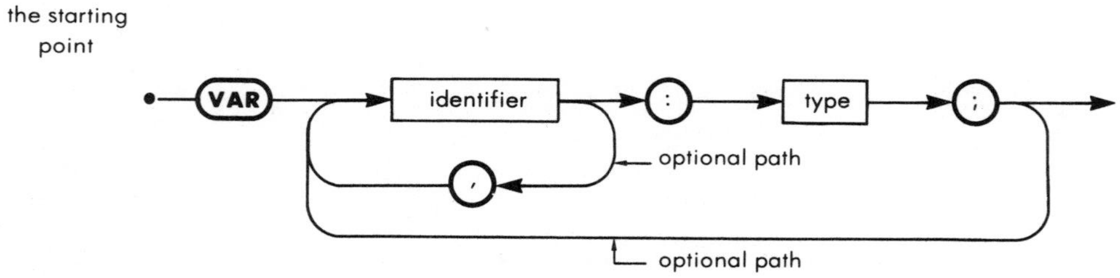

the starting
point

VAR → identifier → : → type → ; →

optional path

,

optional path

The correctness of the declaration

VAR A,B,C : INTEGER;

can be verified by tracing through the syntax diagram. The diagram that follows is a step-by-step illustration of the way in which the VAR declaration is constructed (or verified) by following the syntax rules specified in the syntax diagram.

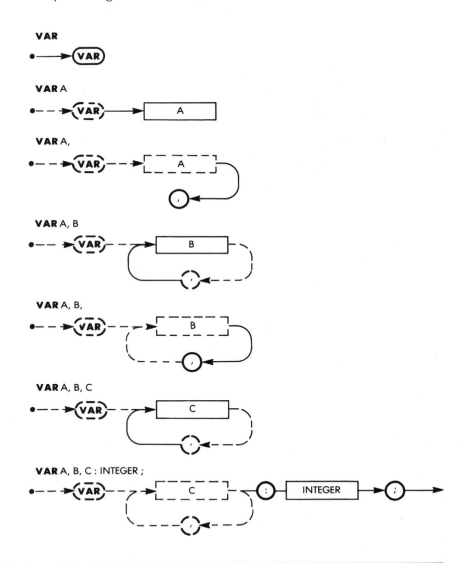

ABS is a standard function that returns the absolute value of its parameter.

☐ **SYMBOL**　　　■ **STANDARD**　　　■ **J & W/CDC**　　　■ **PASCAL/Z**
■ **IDENTIFIER**　　■ **HP 1000**　　　　■ **OMSI**　　　　　■ **UCSD**
☐ **CONCEPT**

1
SYNTAX

Factor containing the ABS function:

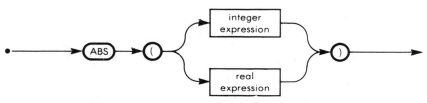

2
DESCRIPTION

The function ABS has one REAL or INTEGER parameter. The returned value is of the same type as the parameter, and is equal to the absolute value of the parameter.

3
IMPLEMENTATION-DEPENDENT FEATURES

3.1 HP 1000　　The parameter of the ABS function can also be of type LONGREAL, in which case the returned value is also of type LONGREAL.

ABS

3.2 J & W/CDC   None known.

3.3 OMSI   Fails to give correct result for the value $(-MAXINT-1)$, but does not indicate error.

3.4 Pascal/Z   None known.

3.5 UCSD   Fails to give correct result for the value $(-MAXINT-1)$, but does not indicate error.

4
EXAMPLE

```
PROGRAM ABSVAL(INPUT,OUTPUT);
VAR T : CHAR;
       IVAL : INTEGER;
       RVAL : REAL;
BEGIN
       WRITELN('TYPE I FOLLOWED BY A SPACE AND AN INTEGER NUMBER,');
       WRITELN('OR R FOLLOWED BY A SPACE AND A REAL NUMBER');
       READ(T);
       IF T = 'I'
           THEN BEGIN
                    READLN(IVAL);
                    WRITELN('ABSOLUTE VALUE OF ',IVAL:1,' IS : ',ABS(IVAL):1)
                END
           ELSE BEGIN
                    READLN(RVAL);
                    WRITELN('ABSOLUTE VALUE OF ',RVAL:10:3,' IS : ',
                            ABS(RVAL):10:3)
                END
END.
```

ALFA

ALFA is a non-standard predefined type describing strings of characters.

☐ SYMBOL	☐ STANDARD	■ J & W/CDC	☐ PASCAL/Z
■ IDENTIFIER	☐ HP 1000	■ OMSI	☐ UCSD
☐ CONCEPT			

1
SYNTAX

Type ALFA:

2
DESCRIPTION

The possible values of a variable of type ALFA are all of the strings with exactly ten characters. The type ALFA is defined as a Packed Array [1..10] of CHAR.

Variables of type ALFA can be used in relational expressions. The ordering of unequal values is done according to the ordering of the characters. When one side of a relational expression is of type ALFA, the other side can be any ten-character string, or a variable of type ALFA.

ALFA can be defined by the user in standard Pascal by:

```
TYPE
    ALFA = PACKED ARRAY [1..10] OF CHAR;
```

ALFA

3
IMPLEMENTATION-DEPENDENT FEATURES

The type ALFA is only implemented in OMSI and J & W/CDC Pascals.

4
EXAMPLE

```
PROGRAM ALFAEX(OUTPUT);
(* DEMONSTRATE USE OF TYPE ALFA *)
VAR
      ALF1,ALF2 : ALFA;
BEGIN
      ALF1 := 'TODAY          ';
      ALF2 := 'TOMORROW    ';
      IF ALF1 > ALF2
            THEN WRITELN(ALF2,ALF1)
            ELSE WRITELN(ALF1,ALF2)
END.
```

AND

The Boolean operator AND is used to obtain the logical conjunction of two Boolean factors.

- ■ SYMBOL
- □ IDENTIFIER
- □ CONCEPT

- ■ STANDARD
- ■ HP 1000

- ■ J & W/CDC
- ■ OMSI

- ■ PASCAL/Z
- ■ UCSD

1
SYNTAX

Refer to the expression heading.

2
DESCRIPTION

When the AND operator appears between two Boolean factors, first their value is computed, and then the logical conjunction of their values is computed. The value of the logical conjunction as a function of the value of its factors is given in the following table.

LEFT FACTOR \ RIGHT FACTOR	true	false
true	true	false
false	false	false

AND

When using Boolean expressions, it is important to remember the order of precedence of Boolean operators:

NOT, AND, OR, relational operators.

(For more details, see the expression heading.)

3
IMPLEMENTATION-DEPENDENT FEATURES

3.1 HP 1000   None known.

3.2 J & W/CDC   None known.

3.3 OMSI   As a radical extension, the operator AND can be used with two INTEGER factors. The resulting expression is of type INTEGER, and is equal to the bitwise Boolean conjunction of the operands. That is, each bit in the result is formed by ANDing the corresponding bits in the operands.

3.4 Pascal/Z   None known.

3.5 UCSD   None known.

4
EXAMPLE

```
PROGRAM ANDTEST(OUTPUT);
VAR I,J,K : INTEGER;
BEGIN
    I := 2; J := 3; K := 4;
    IF (I < = J) AND (J < = K)
        THEN WRITELN('J INSIDE [I,K]')
        ELSE WRITELN('J OUTSIDE [I,K]')
END.
```

APPEND

APPEND is a non-standard predefined procedure that opens an existing file in order to append data to it. See also APPEND for Pascal/Z.

See also APPEND for Pascal/Z.

☐ SYMBOL ☐ STANDARD ☐ J & W/CDC ☐ PASCAL/Z
■ IDENTIFIER ■ HP 1000 ☐ OMSI ☐ UCSD
☐ CONCEPT

1
SYNTAX

APPEND statement:

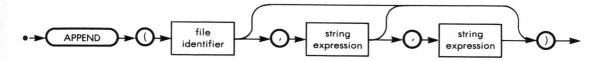

2
DESCRIPTION

The effect of the statement APPEND(F) can be described as follows:

— The file F is opened in the sequential write-only mode.

— All information present on F is skipped.

— The function EOF(F) becomes TRUE.

— Subsequent PUT(F), WRITE(F) OR WRITELN(F) are allowed.

The first parameter of the APPEND statement is the name of the file. The second parameter is a string containing the name of an external file, in the format required by the RTE operating system. The possible values of the third parameter are given by the following syntax diagram.

APPEND

Options string:

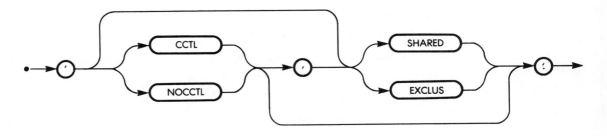

The meaning of the third parameter is as follows:

'CCTL':   The external file has carriage control.

'NOCCTL':   The external file has no carriage control.

'SHARED':   The external file can be open to several programs simultaneously.

'EXCLUS':   The external file cannot be open to several programs simultaneously.

The options CCTL and NOCCTL are only applicable to textfiles. They are ignored when used with other files.

A textfile with carriage control is a file associated with a printing device that uses the first character of each line to control the motion of the paper. (See paragraph 2.2 of the OUTPUT heading.)

The second and third parameters of the APPEND procedure provide an alternative method of associating Pascal files with external files. This method is more versatile than the method using program parameters.

3
IMPLEMENTATION-DEPENDENT FEATURES

APPEND (as described under this heading) is only implemented in HP 1000 Pascal.

4
EXAMPLE

```
PROGRAM APPENDFILES(INPUT,OUTPUT,OLDFILE);
(* HP 1000 ONLY *)
VAR OLDFILE : TEXT;
     C : CHAR;
BEGIN
     APPEND(OLDFILE);
     WHILE NOT EOF DO
         BEGIN
             READLN(C);
             WRITELN(OLDFILE,C)
         END
END.
```

APPEND

APPEND is a non-standard predefined procedure that appends one string to another. See also APPEND for HP 1000.

☐ SYMBOL   ☐ STANDARD   ☐ J & W/CDC   ■ PASCAL/Z
■ IDENTIFIER   ☐ HP 1000   ☐ OMSI   ☐ UCSD
☐ CONCEPT

1
SYNTAX:

APPEND statement:

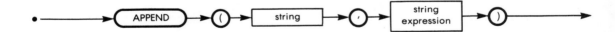

2
DESCRIPTION

The procedure APPEND has two parameters: both are strings, but the first is a variable parameter while the second is a value parameter. When APPEND is executed, the second string is appended to the first.

3
IMPLEMENTATION-DEPENDENT FEATURES

APPEND (as described under this heading) is only implemented in Pascal/Z.

ARCTAN

ARCTAN is a standard REAL function that returns the value of an angle whose tangent is equal to the parameter of the function.

- ☐ SYMBOL
- ■ IDENTIFIER
- ☐ CONCEPT

- ■ STANDARD
- ■ HP 1000

- ■ J & W/CDC
- ■ OMSI

- ■ PASCAL/Z
- ■ UCSD

1
SYNTAX

Factor containing the ARCTAN function:

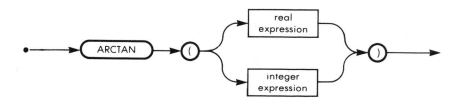

2
DESCRIPTION

The function ARCTAN(X) computes the value of an angle Φ such that:

$$\tan\Phi = X$$

and

$$-\pi/2 < \Phi < \pi/2,$$

Φ being expressed in radians. X may be REAL or INTEGER, but the value of ARCTAN(X) is always REAL.

ARCTAN

3
IMPLEMENTATION-DEPENDENT FEATURES

3.1 HP 1000 The parameter of the ARCTAN function can be of type LONGREAL, in which case the returned value is also of type LONGREAL.

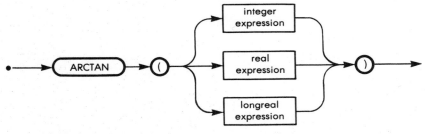

3.2 J & W/CDC None known.

3.3 OMSI None known.

3.4 Pascal/Z None known.

3.5 UCSD The function ARCTAN is named ATAN.

Note: in the APPLE implementation, ATAN is part of the TRANSCEND library.

4
EXAMPLE

```
PROGRAM ATGVAL(INPUT,OUTPUT);
CONST PI = 3.1415927;
VAR X : REAL;
BEGIN
    WRITELN('TO OBTAIN THE ARC TANGENT OF A NUMBER, JUST TYPE IT');
    READLN(X);
    WRITELN(X,' IS THE TANGENT OF ',ARCTAN(X)*180/PI,' DEGREES')
END.
```

ARRAY

An ARRAY is a structured type, with a fixed number of elements that are all of the same type.

- ■ **SYMBOL**
- □ **IDENTIFIER**
- ■ **CONCEPT**

- ■ **STANDARD**
- ■ **HP 1000**

- ■ **J & W/CDC**
- ■ **OMSI**

- ■ **PASCAL/Z**
- ■ **UCSD**

1
SYNTAX

1.1 Array Type

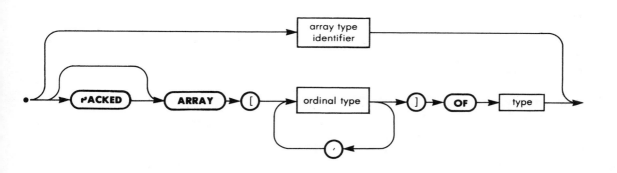

Since an array is itself a type,

    A: **ARRAY** [1..10] **OF ARRAY** [−5..5] **OF** BOOLEAN;

is an equivalent (and preferred) form of

    A: **ARRAY** [1..10, −5..5] **OF** BOOLEAN;

ARRAY

1.2 Variable Referenced as Part of an Array

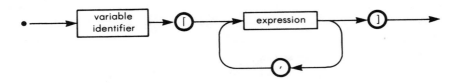

The array identifier is a variable identifier or a field identifier of type ARRAY.

Using the above example of equivalency,

    A[2] [3]

is equivalent to

    A[2,3]

independent of the form of the declaration. This is because A[2] is itself an array with components of type ARRAY [– 5..5] OF BOOLEAN.

2
DESCRIPTION

An array has a fixed number of components, all of the same type. These components are called the base type of the array. Each component can be directly referenced by the name of the array identifier and the index. The base type can be any type, while the index has to be of an ordinal type.

3
IMPLEMENTATION-DEPENDENT FEATURES

The maximum size and dimensionality are implementation defined, but usually very large (typically limited only by MAXINT or the available storage).

4
EXAMPLE

```pascal
PROGRAM HISTOGRAM(INPUT,OUTPUT);
CONST MAX = 100;
VAR INDEX : 0..MAX;
    HISTO : ARRAY[0..MAX] OF INTEGER;
    VALUE : INTEGER;
BEGIN
    FOR INDEX := 0 TO MAX DO HISTO[INDEX] := 0;
    WHILE NOT EOF DO
        BEGIN
            READ(VALUE);
            IF VALUE IN [0..MAX]
                THEN
                    BEGIN
                        INDEX := VALUE;
                        HISTO[INDEX] := HISTO[INDEX] + 1
                    END
                ELSE
                    WRITELN('VALUE OUT OF RANGE: ',VALUE)
        END;
    FOR INDEX := 0 TO MAX DO
        WRITELN(HISTO[INDEX],'NUMBERS HAD VALUE: ',INDEX)
END.
```

assignment

The assignment is used to give a value to a variable or to specify the value to be returned by a function.

☐ SYMBOL   ■ STANDARD   ■ J & W/CDC   ■ PASCAL/Z
☐ IDENTIFIER   ■ HP 1000   ■ OMSI   ■ UCSD
■ CONCEPT

1
SYNTAX

Assignment statement:

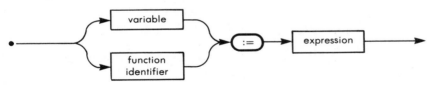

2
DESCRIPTION

The variable or the function whose identifier appears to the left of the := sign is given (or returns) the value of the expression on the right side.

The type of the left side of an assignment must be identical to the type of the right side, except in the following situations:

1. When the left side is REAL, the right may be INTEGER, or a subrange thereof.
2. One side may be a subrange of the other, provided that the value to be assigned is in the range of the left side.
3. Assignment between different SET types is possible, as long as all of the members of the right set can be members of the left.

Variables of type FILE, or structured types containing files, cannot be assigned.

---

assignment

3
IMPLEMENTATION-DEPENDENT FEATURES

3.1 HP 1000

3.1.1 Longreals In assignments, LONGREALs are allowed wherever REALs are allowed.

3.1.2 Structured Types Assignments between structured types are allowed, even when one side is packed and the other is normal.

3.1.3 Strings A shorter string can be assigned to a longer string. Trailing blanks are added in the longer string.

A longer string cannot be assigned to a shorter string. Since strings are packed arrays of CHAR, assignments between strings and packed or normal arrays of CHAR are allowed.

3.2 J & W/CDC   None known.

3.3 OMSI   None known.

3.4 Pascal/Z   None known.

3.5 UCSD

3.5.1 Long Integers

— INTEGERs can be assigned to long integers.

— REALs cannot be assigned to long integers.

— Long integers can be assigned to REALs (not in all implementations).

— Long integers cannot be assigned to INTEGERs. (See the TRUNC heading.)

3.5.2 Structured Types Assignments between structured types are allowed only if both sides are packed or normal.

3.5.3 Strings STRINGs of different lengths can be assigned, provided that the maximum declared length is not exceeded by such an assignment. The length of the string is automatically adjusted. Strings can be

assignment

assigned to packed arrays of CHAR but not to arrays of CHAR. (This restriction will be removed in future releases of the compiler.) Arrays can never be assigned to strings, since strings contain a length parameter which does not exist in an array.

4
EXAMPLE

Examples of assignments can be found under almost all headings.

ATAN

ATAN is the name given to the ARCTAN function in most of the implementations of UCSD Pascal.

☐ SYMBOL   ☐ STANDARD   ☐ J & W/CDC   ☐ PASCAL/Z
■ IDENTIFIER   ☐ HP 1000   ☐ OMSI   ■ UCSD
☐ CONCEPT

Refer to the ARCTAN heading for details about ATAN.

BEGIN

The reserved word BEGIN is used with the reserved word END to delimit a compound statement or the body of a block.

- ■ **SYMBOL**
- □ **IDENTIFIER**
- □ **CONCEPT**

- ■ **STANDARD**
- ■ **HP 1000**

- ■ **J & W/CDC**
- ■ **OMSI**

- ■ **PASCAL/Z**
- ■ **UCSD**

1
SYNTAX

Compound statement:

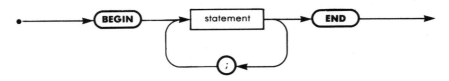

2
DESCRIPTION

BEGIN signals to the Pascal compiler that a compound statement or the body of a block follows.

3
IMPLEMENTATION-DEPENDENT FEATURES

None known.

4
EXAMPLE

```
PROGRAM EO2(INPUT,OUTPUT);
(* PROGRAM TO COMPUTE THE ROOTS OF A SECOND ORDER EQUATION
A * SQR(X) + B * X + C = 0 *)
VAR A,B,C,D,X1,X2 : REAL;
BEGIN
      READLN(A,B,C);
      D := SQR(B) − 4.0 * A * C;
      IF D < 0
            THEN WRITELN('NO REAL ROOTS')
            ELSE
                  BEGIN
                        X1 := (−B + SQRT(D))/(2.0 * A);
                        X2 := (−B − SQRT(D))/(2.0 * A);
                        WRITELN('ROOTS ARE : ',X1,X2)
                  END
END.
```

Additional examples of the use of BEGIN can be found under almost all headings.

block

A block is a syntactic entity containing declarations that define objects, and statements that manipulate them.

☐ SYMBOL ■ STANDARD ■ J & W/CDC ■ PASCAL/Z
☐ IDENTIFIER ■ HP 1000 ■ OMSI ■ UCSD
■ CONCEPT

1
SYNTAX

Block:

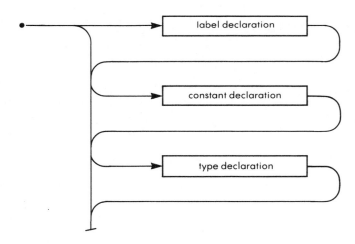

block

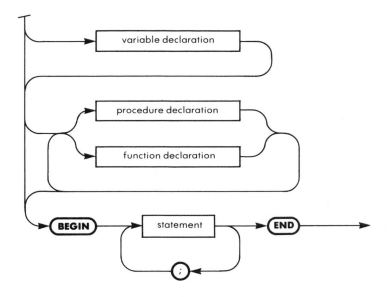

2
DESCRIPTION

A block can be conceptually divided into two parts: the declaration part, and the executable part. Since procedure and function definitions also contain blocks, blocks can be nested. All objects manipulated in the executable part have to be defined in the declaration of the same or an enclosing block.

Objects declared in a block are accessible from inner blocks, but not from outer blocks. If the same identifier is used to define different objects in nested blocks, then the innermost definition prevails.

3
IMPLEMENTATION-DEPENDENT FEATURES

3.1 HP 1000   The syntax of a block does not require a strict ordering of the declarations.

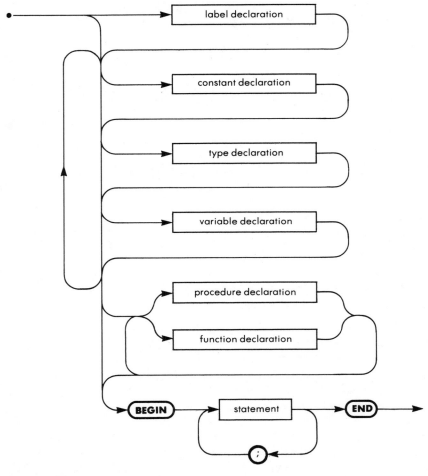

3.2 J & W/CDC   None known.

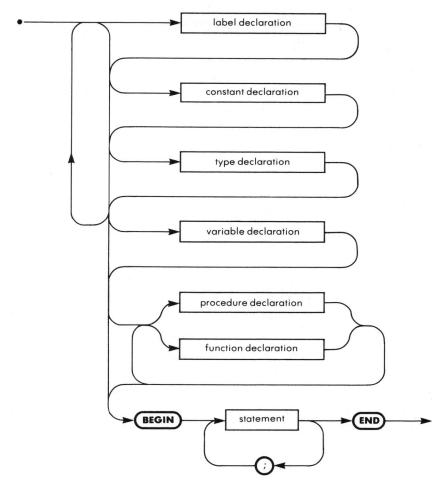

block

3.3 OMSI   The syntax of a block does not require a strict ordering of declarations.

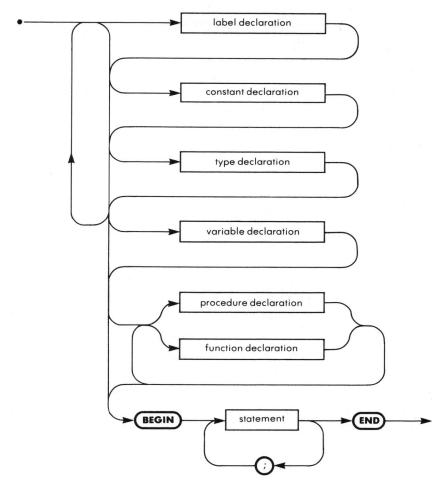

3.4 Pascal/Z   None known.

3.5 UCSD   The PROGRAM block may contain the UNIT and/or USES extensions which relax the order of declaration. See UNIT and USES.

BLOCKREAD

BLOCKREAD is a non-standard predefined integer function that transfers data from a disk file to an array.

☐ SYMBOL   ☐ STANDARD   ☐ J & W/CDC   ☐ PASCAL/Z
■ IDENTIFIER   ☐ HP 1000   ☐ OMSI   ■ UCSD
☐ CONCEPT

1
SYNTAX

BLOCKREAD function:

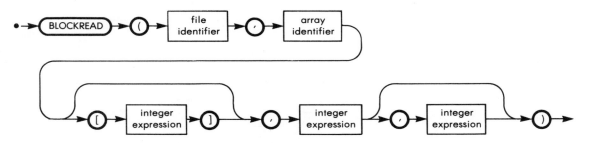

2
DESCRIPTION

BLOCKREAD is an integer function which has three or four parameters. The first parameter, F, is the name of an untyped file. The second parameter, A, is the name of an array. An integer index, I, may be added to the array name. The third parameter, N, is a positive integer expression. The fourth (optional) parameter, B, is also a positive integer expression:

    BLOCKREAD(F,A[I],N,B)

BLOCKREAD

BLOCKREAD transfers N blocks of 512 bytes from the file F to the array A, starting at the Ith element. If I is omitted, the transfer starts at the first element of the array.

B is the number relative to the beginning of the file of the first block to be transferred. The first block of a file has the number 0. If B is not present, then the transfer will be started at the current position of the file window.

The value returned by the function is the actual number of blocks transferred.

3
IMPLEMENTATION-DEPENDENT FEATURES

BLOCKREAD is only implemented in UCSD Pascal.

4
EXAMPLE

```
PROGRAM BREAD(FD,OUTPUT);
VAR
      FD : FILE;
      BUFFER : ARRAY[1..512] OF CHAR;
BEGIN (* BREAD *)
      RESET(FD);
      IF  BLOCKREAD(FD, BUFFER, 1)  <>  1 THEN
          WRITELN('ERROR');
END (* BREAD *).
```

BLOCKWRITE

BLOCKWRITE is a non-standard predefined integer function that transfers data from an array to a disk file.

☐ SYMBOL   ☐ STANDARD   ☐ J & W/CDC   ☐ PASCAL/Z
■ IDENTIFIER   ☐ HP 1000   ☐ OMSI   ■ UCSD
☐ CONCEPT

1
SYNTAX

BLOCKWRITE function:

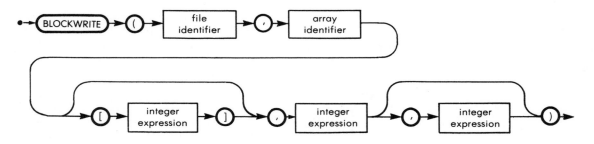

2
DESCRIPTION

BLOCKWRITE is an integer function which has three or four parameters. The first parameter, F, is the name of an untyped file. The second parameter, A, is the name of an array. An integer index, I, can be added to the array name. The third parameter, N, is a positive integer expression. The fourth (optional) parameter, B, is also a positive integer expression:

    BLOCKWRITE(F,A[I],N,B)

BLOCKWRITE

BLOCKWRITE transfers N blocks of 512 bytes from the array A, beginning at the Ith element, to the file F. If I is omitted, the transfer starts from the first element of A.

B gives the position in the file where the first transferred block must be written. Block positions are numbered starting from 0. If B is not given, writing starts at the current position of the file window. The value returned by the function is the actual number of blocks transferred.

3
IMPLEMENTATION-DEPENDENT FEATURES

BLOCKWRITE is only implemented in UCSD Pascal.

4
EXAMPLE

```
PROGRAM BWRITE(FD,OUTPUT);
VAR
       FD : FILE;
       BUFFER : ARRAY[1..512] OF CHAR;
BEGIN (* BWRITE *)
       REWRITE(FD);
       BUFFER[1] := 'H';
       BUFFER[2] := ';';
       IF BLOCKWRITE(FD, BUFFER, 1) <> 1 THEN
            WRITELN('ERROR');
END (* BWRITE *).
```

BOOLEAN

The type BOOLEAN is a predefined ordinal type representing logical data.

☐ SYMBOL   ■ STANDARD   ■ J & W/CDC   ■ PASCAL/Z
■ IDENTIFIER   ■ HP 1000   ■ OMSI   ■ UCSD
☐ CONCEPT

1
SYNTAX

1.1 Boolean Type

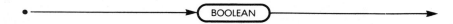

1.2 Boolean Constant

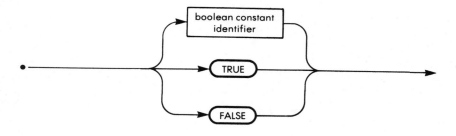

2
DESCRIPTION

2.1 Values   The Boolean type is predefined by the implicit type
declaration:

BOOLEAN

BOOLEAN = (FALSE,TRUE)

This implies that in relational expressions false < true.

2.2 Boolean Operators The operators applicable to Boolean operands are:

NOT	logical negation
AND	logical conjunction
OR	logical disjunction

When expressions are evaluated, the NOT operations are performed first, followed by the ANDs, which are followed by the ORs, except when parentheses modify this rule of precedence.

2.3 Relational Operators All relational operators yield Boolean values, whatever their operands are. The relational operators are:

=	equal to
<>	not equal to
<	less than
>	greater than
<=	less than or equal to, or set contained
>=	greater than or equal to, or set containing
IN	member of set

2.4 Standard Functions The standard functions yielding a Boolean value are:

ODD(X)	TRUE if the integer expression X is odd.
EOLN(F)	TRUE if end of line is encountered on file F.
EOF(F)	TRUE if end-of-file is encountered on file F.

The standard functions PRED(X) and SUCC(X) could be applied to Boolean expressions:

PRED(X)	FALSE if X is TRUE
	undefined if X is FALSE.
SUCC(X)	TRUE if X is FALSE
	undefined if X is TRUE.

BOOLEAN

3
IMPLEMENTATION-DEPENDENT FEATURES

None known.

4
EXAMPLE

```
PROGRAM BOOL(OUTPUT);
VAR A,B : BOOLEAN;
BEGIN
     FOR A : = FALSE TO TRUE DO
     FOR B : = FALSE TO TRUE DO
          BEGIN
               WRITELN(A:6,' AND ',B:6,' IS ',A AND B:6);
               WRITELN (A:6,' OR ',B:6,' IS ',A OR B:6)
          END
     END.
```

BREAK

BREAK is a non-standard predefined procedure that forces the operating system to transmit data from partially filled buffers.

☐ SYMBOL   ☐ STANDARD   ☐ J & W/CDC   ☐ PASCAL/Z
■ IDENTIFIER   ☐ HP 1000   ■ OMSI   ☐ UCSD
☐ CONCEPT

1
SYNTAX

BREAK statement:

2
DESCRIPTION

For efficiency, data is buffered before the actual transmission to peripheral devices. In some circumstances, it is necessary to force transmission, even if the buffer is not yet filled. The procedure BREAK is used for this purpose.

3
IMPLEMENTATION-DEPENDENT FEATURES

BREAK is only implemented in OMSI Pascal.

BUFFERREAD

BUFFERREAD is a non-standard predefined integer function that transfers blocks of arbitrary length from disk to memory.

□ SYMBOL   □ STANDARD   □ J & W/CDC   □ PASCAL/Z
■ IDENTIFIER   □ HP 1000   □ OMSI   ■ UCSD
□ CONCEPT

1
SYNTAX

BUFFERREAD function:

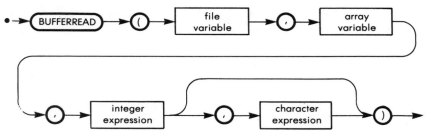

2
DESCRIPTION

BUFFERREAD has three or four parameters. The first parameter, F, is the name of an untyped file. The second parameter, A, is the name of a packed array of CHAR. The third parameter, LENGTH, is a positive integer expression, and the fourth (optional) parameter, S, is an expression yielding a CHAR value:

    BUFFERREAD(F,A LENGTH,S)

BUFFERREAD

BUFFERREAD transfers a block of LENGTH bytes from the untyped disk file F to the array A. If the parameter S is specified, the transfer will stop after a byte containing the value of S is encountered.

The value returned by BUFFERREAD is equal to the number of bytes transferred.

3
IMPLEMENTATION-DEPENDENT FEATURES

BUFFERREAD is only implemented in the Intel version of UCSD Pascal.

BUFFERWRITE

BUFFERWRITE is a non-standard predefined integer function that transfers blocks of arbitrary length from disk to memory.

☐ SYMBOL   ☐ STANDARD   ☐ J & W/CDC   ☐ PASCAL/Z

■ IDENTIFIER   ☐ HP 1000   ☐ OMSI   ■ UCSD

☐ CONCEPT

1
SYNTAX

BUFFERWRITE function:

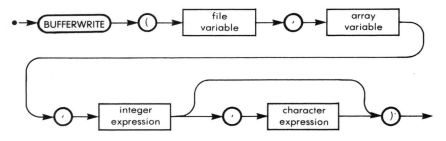

2
DESCRIPTION

BUFFERWRITE has three or four parameters. The first parameter, F, is the name of an untyped file. The second parameter, A, is the name of a packed array of CHAR. The third parameter, LENGTH, is a positive integer expression, and the fourth (optional) parameter, S, is an expression yielding a CHAR value.

    BUFFERWRITE(F,A,LENGTH,S)

BUFFERWRITE

BUFFERWRITE transfers a block of LENGTH bytes from the array A to the untyped file F. If the parameter S is specified, the transfer will stop after a byte containing the value of S is encountered.

The value returned by BUFFERWRITE is equal to the number of bytes transferred.

3
IMPLEMENTATION-DEPENDENT FEATURES

BUFFERWRITE is only implemented in the Intel version of UCSD Pascal.

CARD

CARD is a non-standard predefined function that returns the cardinality of a set.

☐ SYMBOL   ☐ STANDARD   ■ J & W/CDC   ☐ PASCAL/Z
■ IDENTIFIER   ☐ HP 1000   ☐ OMSI   ☐ UCSD
☐ CONCEPT

1
SYNTAX

CARD function:

2
DESCRIPTION

The CARD function has one parameter, an expression of type SET, and returns an INTEGER value equal to the cardinality of (i.e., the number of elements in) the parameter.

3
IMPLEMENTATION-DEPENDENT FEATURES

CARD is only implemented in J & W/CDC Pascal.

CASE

The CASE statement uses the value of an ordinal expression to select one statement among several for execution. The CASE variant part of a RECORD field list uses the type of the selector to specify how many alternatives there are.

■ SYMBOL   ■ STANDARD   ■ J & W/CDC   ■ PASCAL/Z
□ IDENTIFIER   ■ HP 1000   ■ OMSI   ■ UCSD
□ CONCEPT

1
SYNTAX

CASE statement:

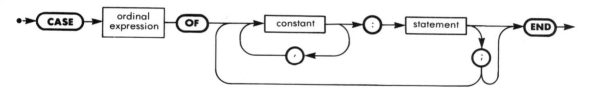

2
DESCRIPTION

The word CASE is used within two different contexts:

1. In the CASE statement.
2. In the declaration of a RECORD with variants (see the RECORD heading).

In a CASE statement, the different alternative statements are preceded by constants that are called "case-constants." (These constants are essentially different from those declared by the LABEL declaration, and cannot appear in GOTO statements). Several different case-constants may precede a statement, but all case-constants within a CASE statement must be distinct.

The value of the ordinal expression following the word-symbol CASE

CASE

is called the "selector." When the CASE statement is executed, the value of the selector is evaluated and compared to the different case labels. If the selector is found equal to one of the case labels, the corresponding instruction is executed; otherwise, the result of the CASE statement is to cause an error.

3
IMPLEMENTATION-DEPENDENT FEATURES

3.1 HP 1000   Two extensions to the syntax of CASE statements are provided:

— A list of consecutive values can be replaced by the first and last values separated by the .. symbol.
— When the selector does not match any of the labels, the statement following the OTHERWISE symbol is executed.

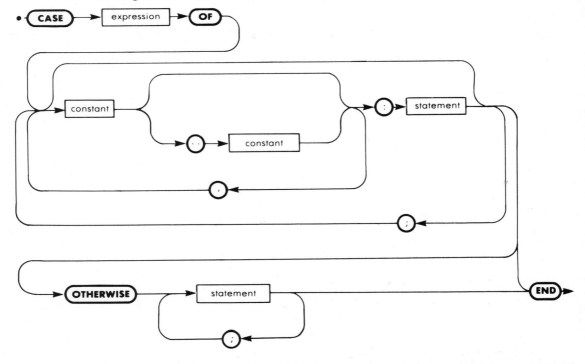

3.2 J & W/CDC   None known.

3.3 OMSI   The CASE statement has been extended with an ELSE clause. The ELSE symbol introduces a statement which should be executed if the selector does not match any of the statement labels.

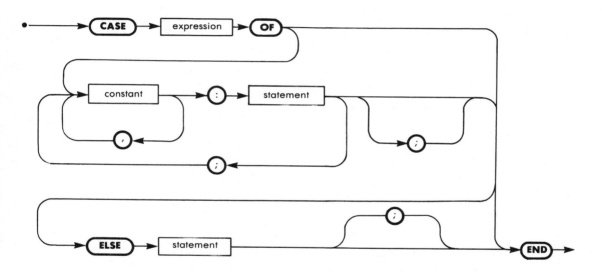

If the ELSE clause is not present, and if none of the statement labels are matched by the selector, then nothing is done by the CASE statement.

3.4 Pascal/Z   The CASE statement has been extended in a manner identical to that described in paragraph 3.3 of this heading.
Compiler options allow the programmer to optimize the code generated for CASE statements. (Such options are not described in this handbook.)

3.5 UCSD   If the selector does not match any of the labels, then nothing is done by the CASE statement.

CASE

4
EXAMPLE

```
PROGRAM VOLUMEW(INPUT,OUTPUT);
(* THIS PROGRAM COMPUTES THE VOLUME OF SPHERICAL OR CYLINDRICAL
CONTAINERS. TWO FORMATS OF INPUT DATA ARE ACCEPTED:
        "SPHERE"        RADIUS
        "CYLINDER"      RADIUS      HEIGHT
THE LAST TWO LETTERS OF THE WORD CYLINDER CAN BE OMITTED.
RADIUS AND HEIGHT ARE EXPRESSED IN METERS. *)
TYPE SHAPE = (SPHERE,CYLINDER);
            CONTAINER = RECORD
                                CASE TAG : SHAPE OF
                                    SPHERE : (RADS : REAL);
                                    CYLINDER : (RADC, HEIGHT : REAL)
                        END;
VAR CNTNR : CONTAINER;
PROCEDURE READSHAPE(VAR S : SHAPE);
    LABEL 1;
    VAR INP : PACKED ARRAY[1..6] OF CHAR;
        I : 1..6;
    BEGIN
    1 : FOR I := 1 TO 6 DO READ(INP[I]);
        READLN;
        IF INP = 'SPHERE'
            THEN S := SPHERE
            ELSE
                IF INP = 'CYLIND'
                    THEN S := CYLINDER
                    ELSE BEGIN WRITELN('INPUT ERROR'); GOTO 1 END
    END;
```

```
FUNCTION VOL(C : CONTAINER) : REAL;
    CONST PI = 3.1416;
    BEGIN
        WITH C DO
            BEGIN
                CASE TAG OF
                    SPHERE : VOL := PI * SQR(RADS) * RADS * 4.0/3.0;
                    CYLINDER : VOL := PI * SQR(RADC) * HEIGHT
                END
            END
    END;
BEGIN
    WITH CNTNR DO
        BEGIN
            READSHAPE(TAG);
            CASE TAG OF
                SPHERE : READLN(RADS);
                CYLINDER : READLN(RADC, HEIGHT)
            END
        END,
        WRITLELN('THE VOLUME IS : ',VOL(CNTNR),' M3')
END.
```

CHARacter

The type CHAR is a predefined ordinal type representing characters used for communication between the computer and the outside world.

☐ SYMBOL   ■ STANDARD   ■ J & W/CDC   ■ PASCAL/Z
■ IDENTIFIER   ■ HP 1000   ■ OMSI   ■ UCSD
■ CONCEPT

1
SYNTAX

1.1 Char Type

1.2 Char Constant

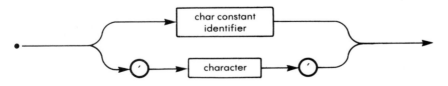

1.3 Character

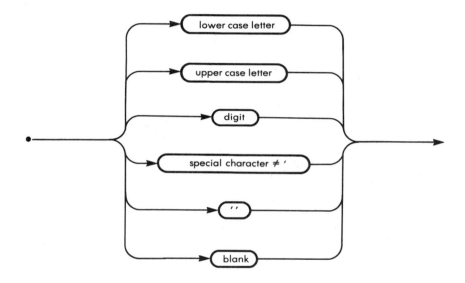

1.4 Remarks

1. Lower case letters are unacceptable in some implementations, upper case letters in others.

2. The set of special characters is implementation-dependent.

3. The character value single quote (') (ASCII 39) is denoted by two single quotes in quotes: ('''').

2

DESCRIPTION

2.1 Values   In each computer system, an ordered set of characters is defined. These sets of characters can differ significantly from one machine to another, however, and, on the same machine, from one installation to another.

CHARacter

All character sets have the following minimal common properties:

— they contain at least one ordered set of Latin letters: 'A'..'Z' or 'a'..'z'

— they contain the ordered set of decimal digits '0'..'9', which have consecutive values

— they contain the blank character.

2.2 Standard Functions Pascal provides two standard functions to ease the problems resulting from a lack of standardization of character sets. These standard functions allow a given set of characters to be mapped onto a subset of natural numbers (called the ordinal numbers of the character set), and vice versa.

ORD(C)   yields the value of the ordinal number of the character C.

CHR(I)   yields the character with the ordinal value I.

The functions PRED(C) and SUCC(C), which are applicable to all ordinal types, are also applicable to the CHAR types. They should be used with caution, since their result can be implementation-dependent. Some characters will have no predecessor or successor in a given set, yielding an undefined value for the corresponding function.

3
IMPLEMENTATION-DEPENDENT FEATURES

3.1 HP 1000 The syntax of a character constant is extended.

When the character # (ASCII 35) is followed by an unsigned integer I, it represents the ASCII character of which the ordinal number equals I.

When the character # is followed by a letter, or any of the characters @, [, \,], ↑, or __, it corresponds to the character generated by an ASCII keyboard when the control key and a letter or a special character key are struck.

CHAR constant (HP 1000):

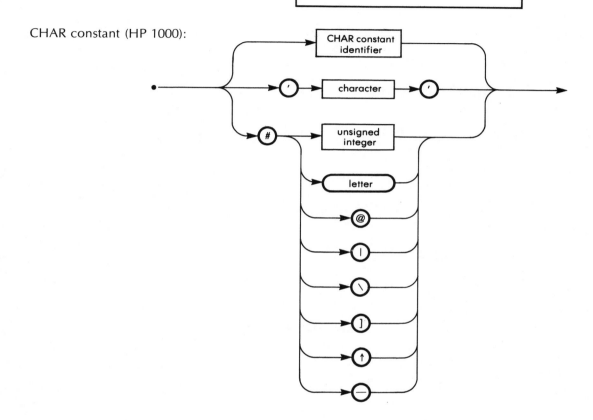

3.2 J & W/CDC   CDC machines do not use the ASCII character set. Since the character set is limited to 63 or 64 characters, lower case letters are not available.

The ordinal numbers of the characters range from 0 to 63.

3.3 OMSI   All ASCII characters are legal. Their ordinal numbers range from − 128 to + 127.

3.4 Pascal/Z   All ASCII characters are legal, and their ordinal numbers range from 0 to 255.

3.5 UCSD   All ASCII characters are legal, and their ordinal numbers range from 0 to 255.

CHARacter

4
EXAMPLE

```
PROGRAM LOW(INPUT,OUTPUT);
(* THIS PROGRAM CONVERTS A FILE CONTAINING UPPER AND LOWER
CASE LETTERS INTO A FILE CONTAINING ONLY UPPER CASE LETTERS.
ALL OTHER CHARACTERS ARE LEFT UNCHANGED. *)
VAR LET : CHAR;
    OFFSET : INTEGER;
BEGIN
    OFFSET := ORD('A') - ORD('a');
    WHILE NOT EOF DO
        IF NOT EOLN
            THEN
                BEGIN
                    READ(LET);
                    IF LET IN ['a'..'z'] THEN
                        LET := CHR(OFFSET + ORD(LET));
                    WRITE(LET)
                END
            ELSE
                BEGIN
                    READLN;
                    WRITELN
                END;
    WRITELN
END.
```

CHR

CHR is a standard character function that returns a character whose ordinal number is given.

☐ SYMBOL ■ STANDARD ■ J & W/CDC ■ PASCAL/Z
■ IDENTIFIER ■ HP 1000 ■ OMSI ■ UCSD
☐ CONCEPT

1
SYNTAX

Factor containing the CHR function:

2
DESCRIPTION

The function CHR has an integer parameter. The returned value is of type CHAR, and is equal to the character which has an ordinal number equal to the value of the parameter of the function CHR (independent of whether the character has a graphic symbol). The function CHR is undefined for all values of the parameter corresponding to characters that are undefined in a particular implementation, or outside the range of ordinal values of CHAR.

3
IMPLEMENTATION-DEPENDENT FEATURES

None known.

CHR

4
EXAMPLE

```
PROGRAM CHRTEST(INPUT,OUTPUT);
VAR N : INTEGER;
BEGIN
      WRITELN('TYPE ONE INTEGER NUMBER');
      READLN(N);
      WRITELN('THE CHARACTER WITH ORDINAL NUMBER ',N:1,' IS ',CHR(N))
END.
```

Another example can be found under the CHAR heading.

CLOCK

CLOCK is a non-standard predefined INTEGER function that returns the central processor time used by a job.

☐ SYMBOL   ☐ STANDARD   ■ J & W/CDC   ☐ PASCAL/Z
■ IDENTIFIER   ☐ HP 1000   ☐ OMSI   ☐ UCSD
☐ CONCEPT

1
SYNTAX

CLOCK function:

2
DESCRIPTION

The function CLOCK has no parameters. It returns an integer value equal to the number of milliseconds of central processor time that the job has already used. The job encompasses all tasks that have been executed since the operating system identified the user's account. To know the number of seconds a Pascal program has used the central processor, the function CLOCK should be called at the beginning and at the end of the program, and the difference between the two results computed.

3
IMPLEMENTATION-DEPENDENT FEATURES

The function CLOCK is only implemented in J & W/CDC.

4
EXAMPLE

See the program GLOBALS under the global heading.

CLOSE

CLOSE is a non-standard predefined function that closes a file. A closed file cannot be accessed for data transfers.

☐ SYMBOL   ☐ STANDARD   ☐ J & W/CDC   ☐ PASCAL/Z
■ IDENTIFIER   ■ HP 1000   ■ OMSI   ■ UCSD
☐ CONCEPT

1
SYNTAX

See paragraph 3 under this heading.

2
DESCRIPTION

The effect of the statement CLOSE(F) can be described as follows:

— No subsequent executions of PUT(F) or GET(F) are allowed (i.e., the file F may not be read from or written to), unless they are preceded by a statement that opens F, such as the RESET or REWRITE statements.

— The function EOF(F) becomes TRUE.

3
IMPLEMENTATION-DEPENDENT FEATURES

3.1 HP 1000

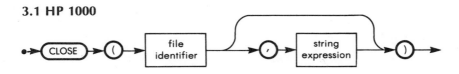

The first parameter is the name of the file that must be closed. The second parameter tells the RTE operating system what must be done with the file F. The acceptable strings are:

'SAVE':   the file is retained as a permanent file
'PURGE': the file is removed from permanent storage.

If no second parameter is present, then the operating system will save the file if it has been asssociated with an external filename by the program parameters, or by the optional parameters in one of the functions RESET, REWRITE, APPEND or OPEN; otherwise the file will be purged.

If the SAVE parameter is present but the file does not have an external filename, a default filename is generated by the system.

3.2 OMSI

3.3 UCSD

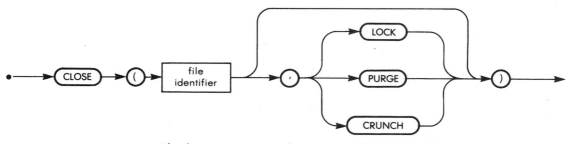

The first parameter is the name of the file that must be closed. The option that can follow the name of the file tells the operating system what should be done with the file:

— If no option is specified, a normal close is done, i.e., the status of the file is set to closed, and, if the file is a disk file and was opened with a REWRITE statement, the file is then deleted.

CLOSE

- LOCK: If the file is on a directory-organized device, and was opened by a REWRITE statement, then the file is made permanent. Otherwise, a normal CLOSE is done.

- PURGE: The TITLE associated with the file in a directory will be deleted. If the file was on a device that has no directory, then the device will go off-line.

- CRUNCH: This option is similar to LOCK, except that only the part of the file located before the actual position of the file window is kept. (This option is not yet available on all implementations.)

4
EXAMPLE

```
PROGRAM INTFILE;
(* UCSD ONLY *)
(* PRINT THE LAST NUMBER IN THE FILE, AND CHANGE THE MIDDLE
ONE TO 43 *)
VAR F : FILE OF INTEGER;
     SIZE : INTEGER
BEGIN
     RESET(F,'INTEGERFILE');
     SIZE : = 255;
     SEEK(F,SIZE);
     GET(F);
     WRITELN('THE LAST ENTRY OF THE FIRST BLOCK IS ',F↑ : 1);
     IF ODD(SIZE)
         THEN SEEK(F,SIZE DIV 2 + 1)
         ELSE SEEK(F,SIZE DIV 2);
     F↑ : = 43;
     PUT(F);
     CLOSE(F,'LOCK')
END.
```

comment

Comments are sequences of characters inserted in programs to document and explain their operation.

☐ **SYMBOL**　　　■ **STANDARD**　　　■ **J & W/CDC**　　　■ **PASCAL/Z**

☐ **IDENTIFIER**　　■ **HP 1000**　　　■ **OMSI**　　　　　■ **UCSD**

■ **CONCEPT**

1
SYNTAX

Comment:

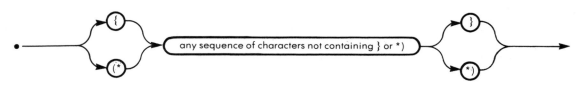

any sequence of characters not containing } or *)

2
DESCRIPTION

Comments are essential elements of well-written programs. Effective use of comments can greatly simplify program debugging and maintenance.

Comments are separators. Replacing them by another separator, such as a blank, does not alter the meaning of the program.

Errors that are extremely difficult to find can be introduced into programs by omitting a } or *) symbol; this causes all of the code between the missing symbol and the next comment to be treated as a comment.

In many implementations, compiler directives have the same syntax as Pascal comments. These directives allow the programmer to select options from the compiler. They are not described in this handbook.

3

IMPLEMENTATION-DEPENDENT FEATURES

3.1 HP 1000   The syntax requires that a comment beginning with {
should be terminated by }, and that a comment beginning with (*
should be terminated by *).

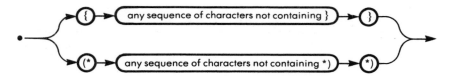

This syntax allows nested comments, which are very useful since they
allow the programmer to transform parts of a program not yet debugged
into comments, even if they already contain comments.

3.2 J & W/CDC   None known.

3.3 OMSI   The symbols /. and ./ can be used instead of { and }.

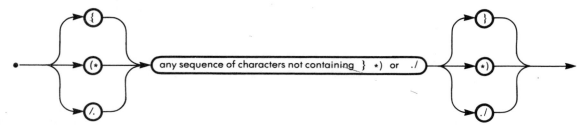

PDP11 assembly code can be intermixed with Pascal programs, in the
form of Pascal comments.

3.4 Pascal/Z   None known.

3.5 UCSD   Comments in the UCSD implementations have the same
syntax as in the HP 1000 implementation. (See paragraph 3.1 of this
heading.)

CONCAT

CONCAT is a non-standard predefined function that concatenates any number of string parameters.

□ SYMBOL   □ STANDARD   □ J & W/CDC   □ PASCAL/Z
■ IDENTIFIER   □ HP 1000   □ OMSI   ■ UCSD
□ CONCEPT

1
SYNTAX

The CONCAT function:

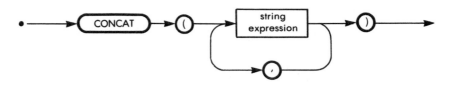

2
DESCRIPTION

The function CONCAT has an arbitrary number of arguments, all of the type STRING. The returned value is a string formed by a concatenation of all of the actual strings, in the order in which they appear in the parameter list.

3
IMPLEMENTATION-DEPENDENT FEATURES

CONCAT is only implemented as a predefined function in UCSD Pascal.

CONCAT

4
EXAMPLE

```
PROGRAM STRING4;
(* UCSD ONLY *)
VAR ST1,ST2,ST3 : STRING;
BEGIN
      ST1 := 'ONE';
      ST2 := 'THREE';
      ST3 := CONCAT(ST1,',TWO,',ST2);
      IF ST3 = 'ONE,TWO,THREE'
           THEN WRITELN('''',ST3,''' OK !')
           ELSE WRITELN('''',ST3,''' STRANGE !')
END.
```

CONSTants are named data items whose value is established at compile time, and cannot be changed.

■ SYMBOL   ■ STANDARD   ■ J & W/CDC   ■ PASCAL/Z

□ IDENTIFIER   ■ HP 1000   ■ OMSI   ■ UCSD

■ CONCEPT

1
SYNTAX

1.1 Constant Declaration

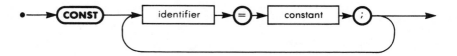

1.2 Constant

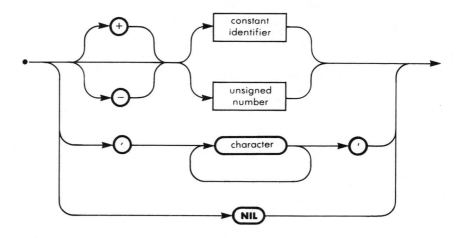

CONSTant

2
DESCRIPTION

A constant identifier has a fixed value. This value cannot be changed during program execution, since a constant identifier may not appear in the left side of an assignment or as an actual VAR parameter.

A constant identifier can be of any simple type, or can be a pointer. Constant identifier do not have to appear in a type declaration, since their type can be derived from their value. A problem may arise when defining a constant identifier to have the same value as an identifier used in an enumeration. Since constant declarations have to precede the type declaration, such constant identifiers cannot be declared at the same level as the enumerated type definition.

Unfortunately, Pascal does not allow structured constants. For example, an array with constant values has to be declared as a variable, and cannot be initialized at compile time.

3
IMPLEMENTATION-DEPENDENT FEATURES

3.1 HP 1000

3.1.1 Enumerated Types   Since type declarations may precede a constant declaration, it is possible to define constant identifiers to have the same value as an identifier used in an enumeration in the same block where the type has been defined.

3.1.2 Structured Constants   HP 1000 Pascal allows definition of structured constants.

Constant declaration:

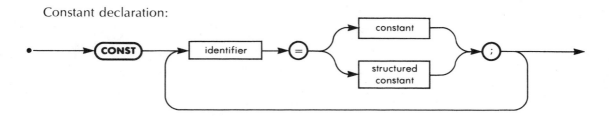

Structured Constant:

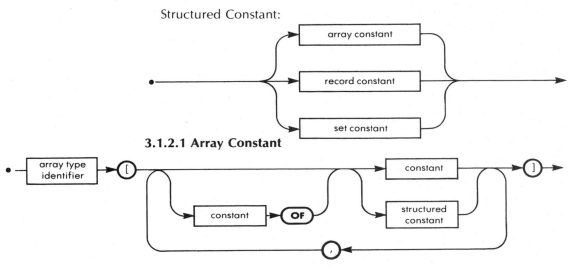

3.1.2.1 Array Constant

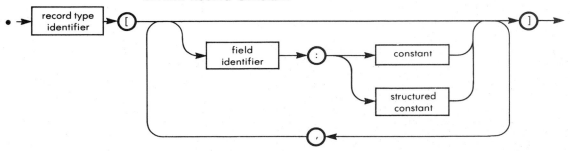

The array type identifier is followed by a list of values which are to be included in the constant array. The construction N **OF** X where N is a constant and X a constant or a structured constant is equivalent to a list containing N times X.

3.1.2.2 Record Constant

The record type identifier is followed by a list of the values to be assigned, each value being preceded by the name of the field it initializes. If the record type has variants, then the tag fields must be initialized before any variant field is initialized. If no tag field exists, but the record has variants, then the initialization of any variant field determines which variant is in use.

CONSTant

3.1.2.3 Set Constant   The set type identifier is followed by a list of values which are to be included in the constant set. Two values separated by the .. symbol (ASCII 46,46) are equivalent to the list of all values in the interval defined by the two values.

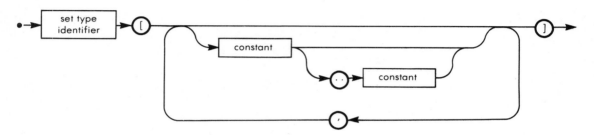

3.1.3 Constant   Due to the existence of structured constants, and constant expressions, a constant can take many more forms than those defined in the standard.

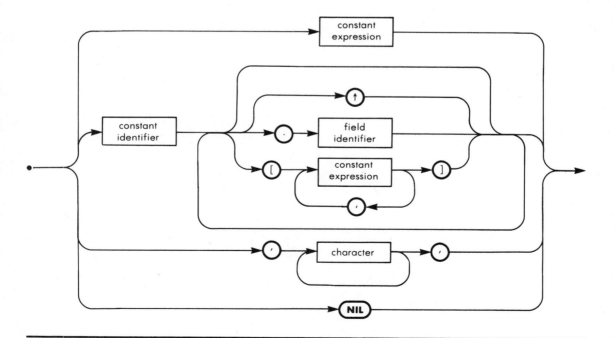

CONSTant

A constant expression is any expression which contains only previously declared constant identifiers or unsigned numbers, so that its value can be evaluated during the compilation.

3.1.4 Example of Constant Declaration (HP 1000)

```
(* HP 1000 CONSTANTS *)
TYPE ROWT = ARRAY [1..3] OF REAL;
     MATRIXT = ARRAY [1...3]OF ROWT;
     STRINGT = PACKED ARRAY [1..20] OF CHAR;
     ADDRESST = RECORD
                      NAME : STRINGT;
                      NUMBER : INTEGER;
                      STREET : STRINGT;
                      TOWN : STRINGT;
                      ZIP : INTEGER
               END;
     CHARSET = SET OF CHAR;
CONST
     IDENTITY = MATRIXT [ROWT[1.0, 0.0, 0.0],
                         ROWT[0.0, 1.0, 0.0],
                         ROWT[0.0, 0.0, 1.0]];
     MYADDRESS = ADDRESST [NAME : 'MY NAME',
                           NUMBER : 1234,
                           STREET : 'MY STREET',
                           TOWN : 'MY TOWN',
                           ZIP : 56789];
     LETTERS = CHARSET ['a'..'z','A'..'Z'];
     PI = 3.1415926;
     TWOPI = PI * 2.0;
```

3.2 J & W/CDC   None known.

3.3 OMSI   Since type declarations may precede a constant declaration, it is possible to define constant identifiers to have the same value as an

identifier used in an enumeration in the same block where the type has been defined.

3.4 Pascal/Z   A limited number of constant expressions are allowed in constant definitions.

Constant:

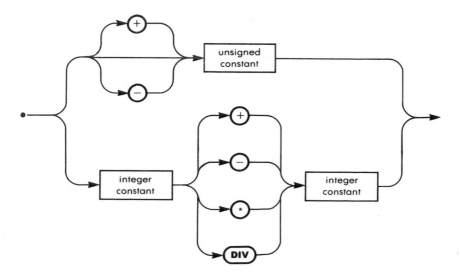

3.5 UCSD   An integer constant identifier whose value is outside the range − 32768, + 32767 is automatically treated as a long integer constant.

COPY

COPY *is a non-standard predefined function which returns a STRING obtained by copying from another STRING, starting at a specified position.*

☐ SYMBOL   ☐ STANDARD   ☐ J & W/CDC   ☐ PASCAL/Z
■ IDENTIFIER   ☐ HP 1000   ☐ OMSI   ■ UCSD
☐ CONCEPT

1
SYNTAX

The COPY function:

2
DESCRIPTION

The function COPY has three parameters: the first, called Source, is of type STRING. The second parameter, called Index, is a positive integer, and the third parameter, called Size, is also a positive integer. The returned value is a STRING with length Size, copied from Source, starting at the Index'th character in Source:

COPY(Source, Index, Size);

3
IMPLEMENTATION-DEPENDENT FEATURES

COPY is only implemented in UCSD Pascal.

COPY

4
EXAMPLE

```
PROGRAM STRING6;
(* UCSD ONLY *)
VAR ST1,ST2 : STRING;
BEGIN
    ST1 := 'ONE,TWO,THREE';
    ST2 := COPY(ST1,POS(',',ST1)+1,3);
    IF ST2 = 'TWO'
        THEN WRITELN('''',ST2,'''',OK !')
        ELSE WRITELN('''',ST2,'''',STRANGE !')
END.
```

COS

COS is a standard REAL function that returns the cosine of its parameter.

☐ SYMBOL   ■ STANDARD   ■ J & W/CDC   ■ PASCAL/Z
■ IDENTIFIER   ■ HP 1000   ■ OMSI   ■ UCSD
☐ CONCEPT

1
SYNTAX

Factor containing the COS function:

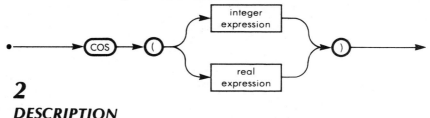

2
DESCRIPTION

The function COS has one INTEGER or REAL parameter, which is an angle, expressed in radians (90° = $\pi/2$ radians). COS returns the cosine of that angle as a REAL value.

In some implementations, the accuracy of the COS function is degraded when the parameter has a value outside of the -2π, $+2\pi$ interval.

3

IMPLEMENTATION-DEPENDENT FEATURES

3.1 HP 1000 The parameter of the COS function can be of type LONGREAL, in which case the returned value is also of type LONGREAL.

COS

COS function (HP 1000):

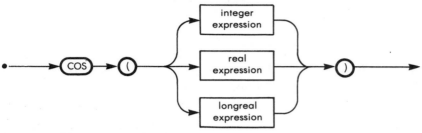

3.2 J & W/CDC   None known.

3.3 OMSI   None known.

3.4 Pascal/Z   None known.

3.5 UCSD   None known.

Note: in the APPLE implementation, COS is part of the TRANSCEND library.

4
EXAMPLE

```
PROGRAM COSVAL(INPUT,OUTPUT);
CONST PI = 3.1415927;
VAR DEG,MIN,SEC : INTEGER;
    RAD : REAL;
BEGIN
    WRITELN('TYPE THE VALUE OF AN ANGLE IN DEGREES, MINUTES AND
            SECONDS,');
    WRITELN('EACH SEPARATED BY AT LEAST ONE SPACE');
    READLN(DEG,MIN,SEC);
    RAD := PI * (DEG + MIN/60 + SEC/3600)/180;
    WRITELN('THE COSINE OF ',DEG:2,' DEG. ',MIN:2,' MIN. ', SEC:2,
            'SEC. IS : ',COS(RAD):10:5)

END.
```

DATE

DATE is a non-standard predefined procedure that assigns the current date to a variable.

☐ SYMBOL   ☐ STANDARD   ■ J & W/CDC   ☐ PASCAL/Z
■ IDENTIFIER   ☐ HP 1000   ☐ OMSI   ☐ UCSD
☐ CONCEPT

1
SYNTAX

DATE statement:

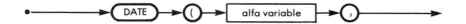

2
DESCRIPTION

The procedure DATE has one parameter of type ALFA. After the procedure DATE has been executed, this parameter contains the current date.

3
IMPLEMENTATION-DEPENDENT FEATURES

Date is only implemented in J & W/CDC Pascal.

DATE

EXAMPLE

```
PROGRAM TESTDATE(OUTPUT);
(* J & W ONLY *)
VAR A : ALFA;
BEGIN
      DATE(A);
      WRITELN('TODAY IS : ',A)
END.
```

DELETE

DELETE is a predefined non-standard procedure that removes a specified number of characters from a string.

☐ SYMBOL   ☐ STANDARD   ☐ J & W/CDC   ☐ PASCAL/Z
■ IDENTIFIER ☐ HP 1000   ☐ OMSI   ■ UCSD
☐ CONCEPT

1
SYNTAX

DELETE statement:

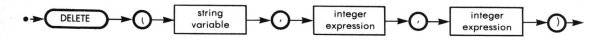

2
DESCRIPTION

The procedure DELETE has three parameters. The first, a VAR parameter called Source, is a string. The second parameter, called Index, is a positive integer. The third parameter, called Size, is also a positive integer. In the string Source, Size characters, starting at the Index'th character in Source, are removed:

DELETE(Source,Index,Size);

3
IMPLEMENTATION-DEPENDENT FEATURES

DELETE is only implemented as a predefined procedure in UCSD Pascal.

DELETE

EXAMPLE

```
PROGRAM STRING3;
(* UCSD ONLY *)
VAR ST : STRING;
BEGIN
      ST : = 'ONE,TWO,THREE';
      DELETE(ST,POS('TW',ST),4);
      IF ST = 'ONE,THREE'
          THEN WRITELN('''',ST,'''',OK !')
          ELSE WRITELN('''',ST,'''',STRANGE !')
END.
```

DISPOSE

DISPOSE is a standard procedure which allows memory space that is no longer needed for dynamic variables to be freed.

☐ SYMBOL ■ STANDARD ■ J & W/CDC ☐ PASCAL/Z
■ IDENTIFIER ■ HP 1000 ■ OMSI ☐ UCSD
☐ CONCEPT

1
SYNTAX

DISPOSE statement:

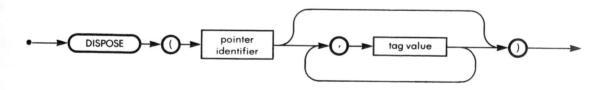

2
DESCRIPTION

The standard procedure DISPOSE(p) informs the heap manager that the space used by the variable p↑ is no longer needed, and can therefore be used when new dynamic variables are to be created. Calling DISPOSE(p) when the value of p is undefined or NIL results in an error. After execution of DISPOSE(p), the value of p is undefined.

If, when the dynamic variable p↑ was created, the procedure NEW was used with tag parameters, then identical tag parameters must be used with the DISPOSE procedure.

DISPOSE

3
IMPLEMENTATION-DEPENDENT FEATURES

3.1 HP 1000 The procedure DISPOSE behaves as described in the standard; however, heap management can be obtained by using the procedures MARK and RELEASE if a simple stack management scheme is adequate (refer to the corresponding headings).

3.2 J & W/CDC None known.

3.3 OMSI Tag values can be given when DISPOSE is called, but they are ignored.

3.4 Pascal/Z The procedure DISPOSE does not exist. The procedures MARK and RELEASE should be used to manage the heap (refer to the corresponding headings).

3.5 UCSD The procedure DISPOSE does not exist. The procedures MARK and RELEASE should be used to manage the heap (refer to the corresponding headings).

4
EXAMPLE

For an example of the use of DISPOSE, see procedure DELETE in the program DELNAME under the pointer heading.

DIV

The operator DIV is used to compute the integer quotient of two integer factors.

- ■ SYMBOL
- ☐ IDENTIFIER
- ☐ CONCEPT

- ■ STANDARD
- ■ HP 1000

- ■ J & W/CDC
- ■ OMSI

- ■ PASCAL/Z
- ■ UCSD

1
SYNTAX

Refer to the expression heading.

2
DESCRIPTION

When the reserved word DIV appears between INTEGER (or subranges thereof) factors in a term, the values of these factors are first evaluated, and then the left factor is divided by the right factor. The INTEGER portion of the quotient is returned as the result. Division by the value zero is an error.

3
IMPLEMENTATION-DEPENDENT FEATURES

3.1 HP 1000   None known.

3.2 J & W/CDC   None known.

3.3 OMSI   DIV by powers of two may give incorrect results for negative numbers.

3.4 Pascal/Z   None known.

DIV

3.5 UCSD Long integer factors are allowed with the DIV operator. If one or both factors of a quotient are long integers, then the quotient is a long integer.

4
EXAMPLE

```
PROGRAM DIVTEST(OUTPUT);
    CONST I = 5; J = 2;
    VAR K : INTEGER;
    BEGIN
        K := I DIV J;
        IF K = 2 THEN WRITELN('DIV WORKS AS EXPECTED')
                ELSE WRITELN('WHAT HAPPENS ?')
    END.
```

DOWNTO

The reserved word DOWNTO is a part of the FOR statement, and is used when the loop parameter has to take decreasing values.

■ SYMBOL   ■ STANDARD   ■ J & W/CDC   ■ PASCAL/Z
□ IDENTIFIER   ■ HP 1000   ■ OMSI   ■ UCSD
□ CONCEPT

1
SYNTAX

FOR statement:

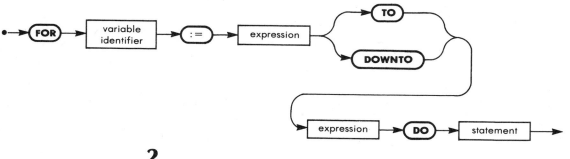

2
DESCRIPTION

See the FOR heading.

3
IMPLEMENTATION-DEPENDENT FEATURES

None known.

DOWNTO

4
EXAMPLE

```
PROGRAM FORLOOP(OUTPUT);
VAR
     I : INTEGER;
BEGIN
     WRITELN('THIS IS A COUNTDOWN :');
     FOR I := 10 DOWNTO 0 DO
          WRITELN(I)
END.
```

The reserved word ELSE is a part of the IF statement.

■ SYMBOL   ■ STANDARD   ■ J & W/CDC   ■ PASCAL/Z
□ IDENTIFIER   ■ HP 1000   ■ OMSI   ■ UCSD
□ CONCEPT

1
SYNTAX

IF statement:

2
DESCRIPTION

See the IF heading.

3
IMPLEMENTATION-DEPENDENT FEATURES

3.1 HP 1000   None known.

3.2 J & W/CDC   None known.

3.3 OMSI   The ELSE symbol can also appear in the CASE statement.

ELSE

CASE statement (OMSI):

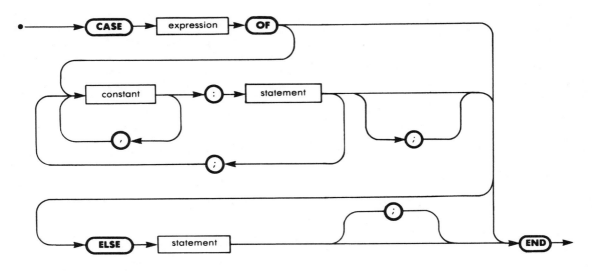

3.4 Pascal/Z The ELSE symbol can also appear in the CASE statement.
(See paragraph 3.3 under this heading, and the CASE heading.)

3.5 UCSD None known.

END

The reserved word END is used as a terminator in compound statements, blocks, record declarations and case statements.

- ■ SYMBOL
- □ IDENTIFIER
- □ CONCEPT

- ■ STANDARD
- ■ HP 1000

- ■ J & W/CDC
- ■ OMSI

- ■ PASCAL/Z
- ■ UCSD

1
SYNTAX

1.1 Compound Statement

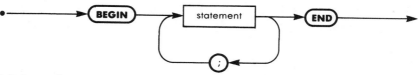

1.2 Record Type Declaration

1.3 Case Statement

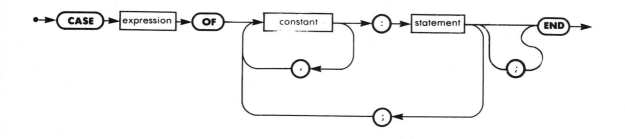

END

2
DESCRIPTION

The reserved word END is a closing delimiter of compound statements, blocks, record declarations and case statements. The END which terminates the outermost program block is always followed by a period.

3
IMPLEMENTATION-DEPENDENT FEATURES

None known.

4
EXAMPLE

```
PROGRAM VOLUMEW(INPUT,OUTPUT);
(* THIS PROGRAM COMPUTES THE VOLUME OF SPHERICAL OR
CYLINDRICAL CONTAINERS. TWO FORMATS OF INPUT DATA ARE
ACCEPTED:
        "SPHERE"        RADIUS
        "CYLINDER"      RADIUS      HEIGHT
THE TWO LAST LETTERS OF THE WORD CYLINDER CAN BE OMITTED.
RADIUS AND HEIGHT ARE EXPRESSED IN METERS. *)
TYPE SHAPE = (SPHERE,CYLINDER);
     CONTAINER = RECORD
                 CASE  TAG : SHAPE OF
                       SPHERE : (RADS : REAL);
                       CYLINDER : (RADS,HEIGHT : REAL)
                 END;
VAR CNTNR : CONTAINER;
PROCEDURE READSHAPE(VAR S : SHAPE);
     LABEL 1;
     VAR INP : PACKED ARRAY[1..6] OF CHAR;
         I : 1..6;
     BEGIN
```

```
1 :   FOR I := 1 TO 6 DO READ(INP[I]);
      READLN;
      IF INP = 'SPHERE'
            THEN S := SPHERE
            ELSE
                  IF INP = 'CYLIND'
                        THEN S := CYLINDER
                        ELSE
                              BEGIN
                                    WRITELN('INPUT ERROR');
                                    GOTO 1
                              END
      END;
      FUNCTION VOL(C : CONTAINER) : REAL;
            CONST PI = 3.1416;
            BEGIN WITH C DO
                  CASE TAG OF
                        SPHERE : VOL := PI * SQR(RADS) * RADS * 4.0/3.0;
                        CYLINDER : VOL := PI * SQR(RADS) * HEIGHT
                  END
            END;
      BEGIN WITH CNTNR DO
            BEGIN  READSHAPE(TAG);
                  CASE TAG OF
                        SPHERE : READLN(RADS);
                        CYLINDER : READLN(RADC, HEIGHT)
                  END
            END;
            WRITLELN('THE VOLUME IS: ',VOL(CNTNR),' M3')
      END.
```

Additional examples of the use of END can be found under almost all
headings.

EOF

EOF is a standard Boolean function that becomes TRUE when the end of a file is reached.

☐ SYMBOL   ■ STANDARD   ■ J & W/CDC   ■ PASCAL/Z
■ IDENTIFIER ■ HP 1000   ■ OMSI   ■ UCSD
☐ CONCEPT

1
SYNTAX

EOF function:

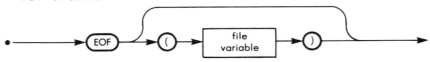

2
DESCRIPTION

The Boolean function EOF(F) has the value TRUE when no data on the file F appear under the file window. The Boolean function EOF(F) has the value FALSE when data on the file F appear under the file window.

When the name of the file F is omitted, the name INPUT is implied.

3
IMPLEMENTATION-DEPENDENT FEATURES

3.1 HP 1000   If the specified file F is closed, EOF(F) is TRUE.

3.2 J & W/CDC   None known.

3.3 OMSI   Due to particularities of the operating systems RT11 and RSTS11, the EOF function is very inaccurate, and cannot be used to detect the end of a file. This problem does not apply to textfiles.

3.4 Pascal/Z   None known.

3.5 UCSD   The behavior of the EOF function is different from the standard when used with INTERACTIVE files. EOF(F) does not become TRUE when the last component of F has been read, but only when the EOF mark itself has been read. The corresponding parameter of the READ or READLN procedures is left undefined when EOF becomes TRUE.

4
EXAMPLE

See the program LINESCAN under the EOLN heading.

EOLN

EOLN is a standard Boolean function that becomes TRUE when an end of line is reached in a text file.

☐ SYMBOL   ■ STANDARD   ■ J & W/CDC   ■ PASCAL/Z
■ IDENTIFIER   ■ HP 1000   ■ OMSI   ■ UCSD
☐ CONCEPT

1
SYNTAX

EOLN function:

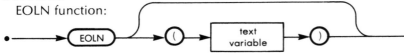

2
DESCRIPTION

The Boolean function EOLN(F) has the value TRUE when an end of line mark appears under the window of the text file F. If the end of line mark does not appear under the window on the text file F, then the Boolean function EOLN(F) is FALSE.

When EOLN(F) has the value TRUE, the value of the buffer variable F↑ is defined to be a blank.

When the name of the file F is omitted, the name INPUT is implied.

3
IMPLEMENTATION-DEPENDENT FEATURES

3.1 HP 1000   Since a line on a text file always has an even number of characters, one blank that has never been written can be found on a file before the end of line mark.

3.2 J & W/CDC   As a consequence of the obsolete character set used, blanks that have never been written can be found on a file before the end of line mark. Programs should never rely on the number of characters per line in a CDC text file.

3.3 OMSI   None known.

3.4 Pascal/Z   None known.

3.5 UCSD   As a consequence of the differences in the effects of the procedures READ and READLN (when used with INTERACTIVE files rather than TEXT files), the behavior of the EOLN function differs from that described in the standard.

If the file F is of type TEXT, EOLN will be TRUE when the last character before the end of line has been read, and whenever EOF is TRUE.

If the file F is of type INTERACTIVE, EOLN will be TRUE when the end of line character itself has been read, or when EOF is TRUE. When an end of line character has been detected, the value of F↑ is set to blank until a READLN is completed.

4

EXAMPLE

```
PROGRAM LINESCAN(INPUT,OUTPUT,INTFILE);
VAR INTFILE : TEXT;
        ANUMBER, ONLINE : INTEGER;
BEGIN
        RESET(INTFILE);
        WHILE NOT EOF(INTFILE) DO
            BEGIN
                ONLINE := 0;
                WHILE NOT EOLN(INTFILE) DO
                    BEGIN
                        READ(INTFILE, ANUMBER);
                        WRITE(ANUMBER);
                        ONLINE := ONLINE + 1
                    END;
                WRITELN;
                WRITELN(' THERE WERE ',ONLINE,' NUMBERS ON LAST LINE.');
                READLN(INTFILE)
            END
END.
```

EXIT

EXIT is a non-standard predefined procedure that can be used to leave a part of a program or the program itself.

■ SYMBOL   □ STANDARD   □ J & W/CDC   □ PASCAL/Z
■ IDENTIFIER □ HP 1000   ■ OMSI   ■ UCSD
□ CONCEPT

1
SYNTAX

See paragraphs 3.1.1 and 3.2.1 of this heading.

2
DESCRIPTION

See paragraphs 3.1.2 and 3.2.2 of this heading.

3
IMPLEMENTATION-DEPENDENT FEATURES

3.1 OMSI

3.1.1 Syntax

EXIT statement:

3.1.2 Description   The EXIT statement terminates the loop immediately enclosing it. Loops that can be terminated by the EXIT statement are the WHILE, REPEAT and FOR loops.

3.2 UCSD

EXIT

3.2.1 Syntax

EXIT statement:

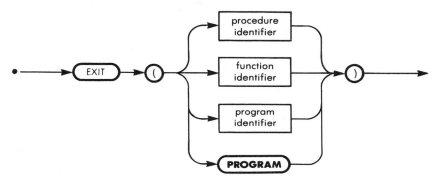

3.2.2 Description The procedure EXIT allows the programmer to terminate a procedure, a function or a program. EXIT has one parameter, the name of the procedure, function, or program to be terminated. When a program is to be terminated, the reserved word PROGRAM can be used instead of the name of the program.

3.2.2.1 Program Termination EXIT can be used to terminate the execution of a program. The name of the program or the reserved word PROGRAM must be used as the actual parameter for the EXIT procedure.

3.2.2.2 Procedure and Function Termination EXIT can be used to leave a procedure or a function in an orderly fashion. This procedure or function does not have to be the one which contains the EXIT statement. When an EXIT statement is encountered, the procedure EXIT follows the trail of procedure or function calls back to the procedure or function specified. Each procedure or function encountered is terminated. If the specified procedure or function is recursive, only the most recent invocation will be terminated.

Note: it is not necessary to use the EXIT statement to terminate the execution of a procedure, function or program. When the END of a procedure, function or program block is reached, termination is automatic.

EXIT should only be used in exceptional cases as it can make program flow difficult to follow.

EXP

EXP is a standard REAL function that returns the natural exponential function of its parameter.

☐ SYMBOL	■ STANDARD	■ J & W/CDC	■ PASCAL/Z
■ IDENTIFIER	■ HP 1000	■ OMSI	■ UCSD
☐ CONCEPT			

1
SYNTAX

Factor containing the EXP function:

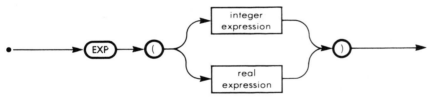

2
DESCRIPTION

The function EXP(X) computes the value of e^X. X may be INTEGER or REAL. The value of EXP(X) is always REAL.

e is the base of the natural logarithm; its value is 2.718281828.... The exponential function and the natural logarithmic function are inverse functions. (See the LN heading.)

3
IMPLEMENTATION-DEPENDENT FEATURES

3.1 HP 1000 The parameter of the EXP function can be of type LONGREAL, in which case the returned value is also of type LONGREAL.

EXP function (HP 1000):

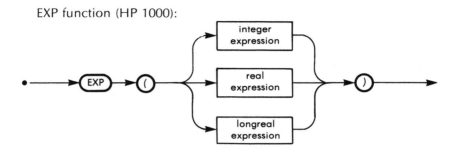

3.2 J & W/CDC   None known.

3.3 OMSI   None known.

3.4 Pascal/Z   None known.

3.5 UCSD   None known.

Note: in the APPLE implementation, EXP is part of the TRANSCEND library.

4
EXAMPLE

```
PROGRAM EXPVAL(INPUT,OUTPUT);
VAR X,Y : REAL;
BEGIN
    WRITELN('TO OBTAIN THE VALUE OF X TO THE POWER Y,');
    WRITELN('TYPE THE VALUES OF X AND Y, SEPARATED BY',
            'ONE SPACE');
    READLN(X,Y);
    WRITELN(X,' TO THE POWER ',Y,' IS : ',EXP(Y * LN(X)))
END.
```

EXP10

EXP10 is a non-standard predefined REAL function that returns the value of 10 raised to the value of its parameter.

☐ SYMBOL   ☐ STANDARD   ☐ J & W/CDC   ☐ PASCAL/Z
■ IDENTIFIER   ☐ HP 1000   ■ OMSI   ☐ UCSD
☐ CONCEPT

1
SYNTAX

EXP10 function:

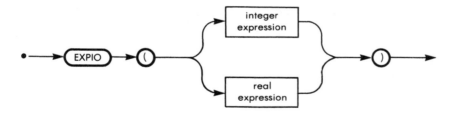

2
DESCRIPTION

The function EXP10(X) computes the value of 10^X. X can be REAL or INTEGER. The value of EXP10(X) is always REAL.

3
IMPLEMENTATION-DEPENDENT FEATURES

EXP10 is only implemented in OMSI Pascal.

4
EXAMPLE

```
PROGRAM EXP10VAL;
(* OMSI ONLY *)
VAR X : REAL;
BEGIN
      WRITELN('TO OBTAIN THE EXPONENTIAL IN BASE 10 OF X, TYPE THE VALUE',
             'OF X');
      READLN(X);
      WRITELN('10 TO THE POWER ',X,' IS : ', EXP10(X))
END.
```

EXPO

EXPO is a non-standard predefined function that returns the value of the exponent of a REAL number.

☐ SYMBOL   ☐ STANDARD   ■ J & W/CDC   ☐ PASCAL/Z
■ IDENTIFIER   ☐ HP 1000   ☐ OMSI   ☐ UCSD
☐ CONCEPT

1
SYNTAX

EXPO function:

2
DESCRIPTION

The function EXPO has one REAL parameter X, and returns an integer value which is equal to the exponent of the internal representation of X.

$$EXPO(X) = TRUNC(\log_2 |X|)$$

3
IMPLEMENTATION-DEPENDENT FEATURES

EXPO is only implemented in J & W/CDC Pascal.

An expression is a description of operations to be performed on constants or variables. An expression has a type and, after evaluation, a value.

☐ SYMBOL   ■ STANDARD   ■ J & W/CDC   ■ PASCAL/Z
☐ IDENTIFIER   ■ HP 1000   ■ OMSI   ■ UCSD
■ CONCEPT

1
SYNTAX

1.1 Expression

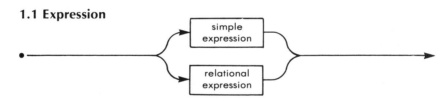

1.2 Relational Expression

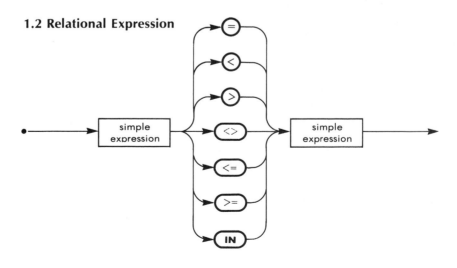

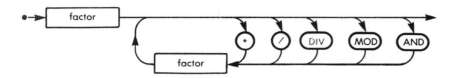

expression

1.3 Term

1.4 Factor

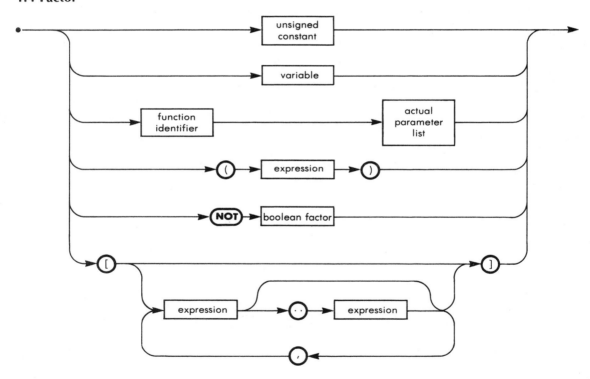

expression

1.5 Simple Expression

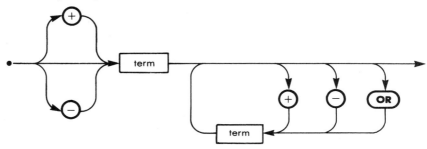

2
DESCRIPTION

2.1 Types of an Expression Relational Expressions are of type Boolean.

The type of a simple expression, which is determined by its constituents, can be one of the following:

> ordinal (this includes INTEGER and Boolean)
>
> REAL
>
> SET

2.2 Types in Relational Expressions The operators =, <> , > , < , >= , and <= can be used between simple expressions of compatible types:

REAL is compatible with INTEGER, and subranges thereof.

Ordinal types are compatible if their values belong to the same enumerations.

The same operators =, <> , > , < , >= , and <= can be used between strings of the same size. A string is a packed array of characters.

2.3 Evaluation of Expressions Expressions are evaluated by following the rules of operator precedence:

NOT, (applied to Boolean)	has the highest precedence
*, /, DIV, MOD, AND	come next, followed by

expression

+, −, OR	and, finally, the relational
=, <> , > , < , <=, >=, IN	operators

In other words, first the factors are evaluated, then the terms, followed by the simple expressions, and, finally, the expressions. When no rules of precedence apply, the order of evaluation is implementation-dependent.

3
IMPLEMENTATION-DEPENDENT FEATURES

3.1 HP 1000

3.1.1 Syntax   Due to extensions in the syntax of SET constants, and to the possibility of defining functions of a structured type, the syntax of a factor is modified. (See syntax diagram on following page.)

3.1.2 Types of an Expression   A simple expression can also be of type LONGREAL.

A simple expression containing LONGREALs is LONGREAL.

A LONGREAL expression can contain REALs, INTEGERs, or subranges thereof.

3.1.3 Types in a Relational Expression   LONGREAL is compatible with REAL, INTEGER and subranges thereof.

The relational operators = and <> can be used with all structured types except files, or structured types containing files.

3.2 J & W/CDC   None known.

3.3 OMSI

3.3.1 Boolean Operators With Integer Operands   The operators AND, OR and NOT can be used with INTEGER operands, yielding an INTEGER result.

Factor (HP 1000):

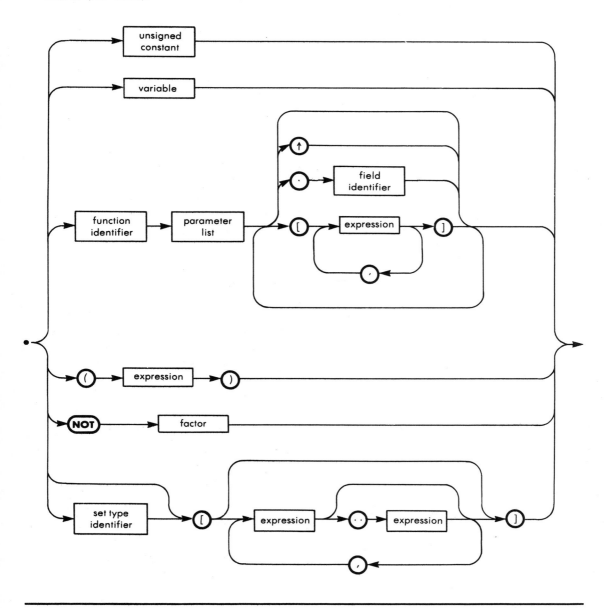

expression

3.3.2 Address Operator An additional operator @ is defined. Applied to a variable of any type, @ yields a result of pointer type, and is equal to the address of the operand.

The syntax of a factor is extended as follows.

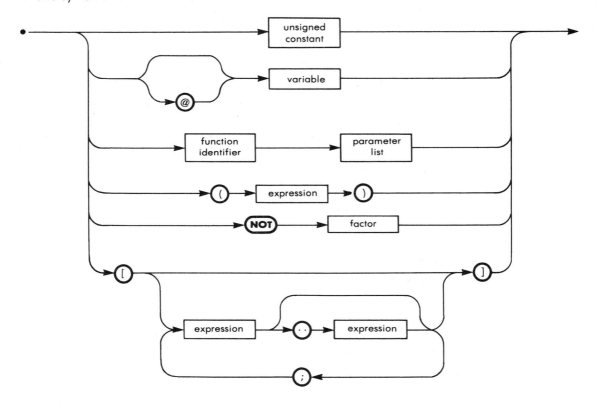

3.4 Pascal/Z None known.

3.5 UCSD

3.5.1 Type of an Expression A simple expression can also be of type long integer.

A simple expression containing long integers is long integer.

A long integer expression can contain INTEGERs and subranges thereof, but no REALs.

expression

An INTEGER or a REAL expression cannot contain long integers. Long integer expressions cannot contain the MOD operator.

3.5.2 Types in Relational Expressions   Long integer is compatible with INTEGERs and subranges thereof.

The relational operators = and <> can be used with all structured types except files, or structured types containing files.

4
EXAMPLES

```
PROGRAM NUMEX(OUTPUT);
CONST I = 2; J = 3;
      A = 2.0; B = 3.0;
VAR C : REAL;
    K : INTEGER;
    U,V : BOOLEAN;
BEGIN
    C := (A/B) * B;
    (* REAL OPERATIONS OFTEN CAUSE ROUNDING ERRORS *)
    K := (I DIV J) * J;
    (* INTEGER OPERATIONS YIELD EXACT RESULTS *)
    (* BUT DIV DROPS THE REMAINDER *)
    U := A = C;
    V := I = K;
    IF U THEN WRITELN('(A/B) * B = A');
    (* THIS LINE SHOULD NOT BE PRINTED *)
    IF V THEN WRITELN('(I DIV J) * J = I');
    (* THIS LINE SHOULD NOT BE PRINTED *)
    IF NOT (U AND V) THEN WRITELN('THIS IS A REAL WORLD',
                                  ' COMPUTER')
END.
```

expression

```
PROGRAM COUNTUP(INPUT,OUTPUT);
     VAR NUPPER : INTEGER;
          LETTER : CHAR;
          UPPER : SET OF 'A'..'Z';
BEGIN
     UPPER := ['A'..'Z'];
     NUPPER := 0;
     WHILE NOT EOF DO
          BEGIN
               READ(LETTER);
               IF LETTER IN UPPER THEN NUPPER := NUPPER + 1
          END;
     WRITELN('NBR OF UPPER CASE LETTERS WAS ',NUPPER)
END.
```

EXTERNAL or EXTERN is a non-standard directive used when it is necessary to reference a function or a procedure that is not part of the program.

■ SYMBOL   □ STANDARD   ■ J & W/CDC   ■ PASCAL/Z
□ IDENTIFIER   ■ HP 1000   ■ OMSI   ■ UCSD
□ CONCEPT

1
SYNTAX

EXTERNAL procedure or function declaration:

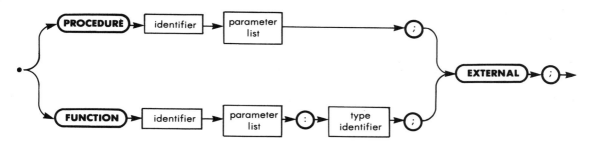

2
DESCRIPTION

Sometimes it is necessary to include in a Pascal program functions or procedures written in another language, such as an assembler language. Such procedures or functions are declared in a Pascal program by their heading alone, followed by the EXTERNAL symbol.

When using external procedures or functions, it is the responsibility of the programmer to make sure that the external procedures or functions pass parameters as Pascal procedures or functions do.

EXTERNAL
EXTERN

3
IMPLEMENTATION-DEPENDENT FEATURES

3.1 HP 1000   None known.

3.2 J & W/CDC   The symbol EXTERN should be used instead of EXTERNAL.
   An additional directive, FORTRAN, is provided, and is used to declare external procedures or functions written in Fortran.

3.3 OMSI   An additional directive, FORTRAN, is provided, and is used to declare external procedures or functions written in Fortran.

3.4 Pascal/Z   None known.

3.5 UCSD   In the heading of a procedure declared as EXTERNAL, a VAR parameter can be declared without any type.

FALSE

FALSE is a predefined Boolean constant, equal to the Boolean value false.

☐ SYMBOL ■ STANDARD ■ J & W/CDC ■ PASCAL/Z
■ IDENTIFIER ■ HP 1000 ■ OMSI ■ UCSD
☐ CONCEPT

1
SYNTAX

False is a Boolean constant identifier. Refer to the CONSTant heading.

2
DESCRIPTION

FALSE is a predefined Boolean constant, equal to the Boolean value false.

3
IMPLEMENTATION-DEPENDENT FEATURES

None known.

FALSE

4
EXAMPLE

```
PROGRAM TRUTHTABLE(OUTPUT);
FUNCTION BOOLTOINT(BOOL : BOOLEAN) : INTEGER;
BEGIN
    CASE BOOL OF
        TRUE : BOOLTOINT := 1;
        FALSE : BOOLTOINT := 0
    END
END;
BEGIN
    WRITELN('TRUTH TABLE FOR BOOLEAN AND FUNCTION');
    WRITELN('WHERE 1 = TRUE AND 0 = FALSE');
    WRITELN('---------------');
    WRITELN(1 : 1, 'I' : 2,BOOLTOINT(TRUE AND TRUE) : 5,BOOLTOINT(TRUE AND FALSE) : 8);
    WRITELN(0 : 1, 'I' : 2,BOOLTOINT(FALSE AND TRUE) : 5,BOOLTOINT(FALSE AND FALSE) : 8)
END.
```

A FILE is a sequence of data items, all of the same type, usually physically stored in the peripheral equipment of the computer.

- ■ SYMBOL
- □ IDENTIFIER
- ■ CONCEPT

- ■ STANDARD
- ■ HP 1000

- ■ J & W/CDC
- ■ OMSI

- ■ PASCAL/Z
- ■ UCSD

1
SYNTAX

1.1 File Type

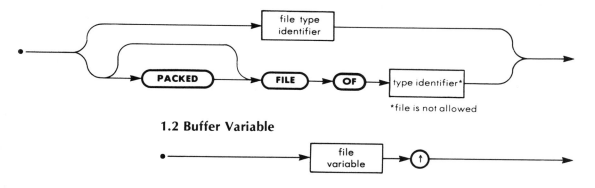

*file is not allowed

1.2 Buffer Variable

2
DESCRIPTION

Files are a method of structuring data, e.g., variable-length sequences of characters. Files are usually used for communication between the outside world and a program or between different programs, or to temporarily store large volumes of data.

Data items in a file are called components; they can be of any type, except files or structured types containing files. Standard Pascal files are sequential files, i.e., the components must be read in the same order in which they were written.

FILE

2.1 File Length The number of components in a file (known as the length of the file) is not fixed by the file declaration. Since files generally reside on secondary storage devices such as disks or tapes, the length of a file can often be much longer than a data structure residing in primary memory. However, the time required to access components of a file will be much longer than the access time of other data types.

A file with zero length is considered empty.

2.2 Buffer Variable Whenever a file variable is created, a buffer variable of the same type as the components of the file is created. Buffer variables provide the only pathway for data transfer between a file and the program. They can be assigned, and can appear in an expression. Transfers between files and their buffer variables are performed by the standard functions GET and PUT, or functions derived from them, such as READ and WRITE.

2.3 File Window A ''window'' exists between the file structure and the buffer variable, through which all data transfers are performed. This window can be moved forward along the components of the file, one at a time.

2.4 Opening and Closing of a File Before any data can be transferred between a file and a buffer variable, a file must have been opened by the standard procedures RESET or REWRITE. Depending on which of these procedures has been used, the file will be open only for READ operations or only for WRITE operations.

A file which is already open can be closed and reopened by the procedures RESET and REWRITE if it is necessary to change the direction of the data transfers.

No procedure is provided by standard Pascal to close a file. When the execution of the block in which the file is defined is terminated, the file is automatically closed.

2.5 Standard Procedures and Functions

RESET: opens a file so that it can be read from.

REWRITE: opens a file so that it can be written on (all components previously written on the file are lost).

GET: transfers one component of a file to the associated buffer variable.

PUT: appends the contents of a buffer variable to its file.

READ: assigns values found on a file to variables (with conversion to the internal form from a textual representation of integers or reals if the file is of type TEXT).

WRITE: appends the textual-representation values to a file (with conversion of integer, real and Boolean values to a textual representation if the file is of type TEXT).

EOF: a Boolean function that is TRUE when no component is available under the file window.

EOLN: a Boolean function that is TRUE when an end-of-line is reached in a text file.

2.6 Scope of a File Declaration   Files can be local to a program, or to a procedure. Files local to a procedure exist as long as the block in which they are declared is activated. Such files are used for temporary storage of data, and cannot be used to exchange data between programs, or between a program and the external world.

External files are used to exchange data between programs, or between a program and the external world. External files can exist in the file system of the computer before the program is executed, and can survive afterwards. A file is declared as an external file by mentioning its name as a parameter in the program statement.

A mechanism similar to the substitution of formal parameters by actual parameters in procedure calls is generally provided by the operating system under which the Pascal programs are executed. This mechanism translates the names of the files declared inside the program to the names of the files managed by the file system of the operating system.

2.7 Files of Characters   Files of characters have special properties, and special procedures and functions are provided to handle them. Refer to the TEXT heading for a description of the properties of files of characters.

FILE

3
IMPLEMENTATION-DEPENDENT FEATURES

3.1 HP 1000

3.1.1 Access Mode   Depending upon the procedure used to open it, a file can be accessed in read-only mode, in write-only mode, or in direct mode. In direct mode, which is only available on disk files, both READ and WRITE operations can be made in an arbitrary order.

3.1.2 Association Between Pascal and External Files   The association between Pascal files and external files managed by the RTE operating system can be performed by one of two methods:

— through the program parameters, as described in the standard.

— through additional parameters, in the procedures used to open and close files.

3.1.3 Procedures to Open and Close Files

RESET:	opens a file in the read-only mode.
REWRITE:	opens a new file in the write-only mode.
APPEND:	opens an existing file in the write-only mode.
OPEN:	opens a file in the direct mode.
CLOSE:	closes a file.

3.1.4 Non-Standard Procedures and Functions

READDIR:	positions the file window and then performs a READ operation.
WRITEDIR:	positions the file window and then performs a WRITE operation.
SEEK:	positions the file window.
POSITION:	returns the actual position of the file window.
MAXPOS:	returns the maximal value the function POSITION can ever take for a given file.

FILE

3.2 J & W/CDC An additional file type exists: the segmented file. Segmented files are not described in this handbook.

3.3 OMSI

3.3.1 Access Mode Files opened by RESET or REWRITE are always open for both READ and WRITE operations. The SEEK procedure allows access to the records on the file in a random rather than sequential order.

3.3.2 Association Between Pascal and External Files The association between Pascal files and files managed by the operating system is made by the RESET or REWRITE procedures.

3.3.3 Non-Standard Procedures and Functions

BREAK:	causes the system's file buffer to be emptied.
CLOSE:	closes a file.
SEEK:	positions the file window.

3.4 Pascal/Z

3.4.1 Access Mode Files can be opened for sequential READ and WRITE operations by the procedures RESET and REWRITE respectively. If the direct access formats of the READ and WRITE operations are used, then both operations are allowed, regardless of how the file has been opened.

3.4.2 Association Betwen Pascal and External Files The association between Pascal files and files managed by the operating system is made by the RESET and REWRITE procedures.

3.4.3 Buffer Variables and the Put and Get Procedures Buffer variables and the PUT or GET procedures are not explicitly available. All I/O has to be done using the READ, READLN, WRITE and WRITELN procedures.

3.5 UCSD

3.5.1 Typed and Untyped Files Two kinds of files exist: those organized in components, as described by the standard, and those containing raw binary data. The second kind of file is declared by the identifier

FILE

FILE, without any specification of the type of the components. They are called "untyped files."

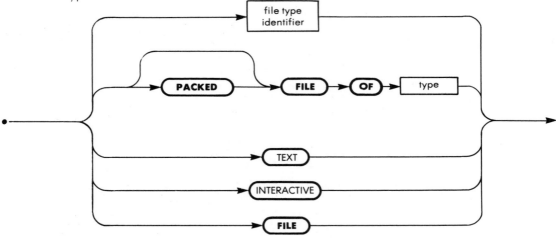

Untyped files do not have an associated buffer variable. Both typed and untyped files can be accessed in random or sequential order.

3.5.2 Association Between Pascal and External Files The association between Pascal files and files managed by the operating system can only be made through additional parameters in the procedures used to open and close the files.

3.5.3 Procedures to Open and Close Files

> RESET: opens an existing file.
>
> REWRITE: opens a new file.
>
> CLOSE: closes a file.

3.5.4 Non-standard Procedures and Functions Applicable to Typed Files

> SEEK: positions the file window.

3.5.5 Procedures and Functions Applicable to Untyped Files

> BUFFERREAD: transfers data from disk to memory in variable-sized blocks (Intel only).

BUFFERWRITE:	transfers data from memory to disk in variable-sized blocks (Intel only).
BLOCKREAD:	transfers data from disk to memory in fixed-size blocks.
BLOCKWRITE:	transfers data from memory to disk in fixed-size blocks.
EOF:	Boolean function which becomes true when no more data is available in the file.

3.5.6 Files as Actual Parameters Files cannot be actual parameters of procedures or functions.

4
EXAMPLE

```
PROGRAM MERGEAB(OUTPUT,FILEA,FILEB,FILEC);
(* PROGRAM TO MERGE TWO INTEGER FILES *)
(* THE FILES FILEA AND FILEB BOTH CONTAIN INTEGER NUMBERS IN INCREASING
ORDER. AFTER EXECUTION OF MERGEAB THE FILEC WILL CONTAIN ALL THE
NUMBERS FROM FILEA AND FILEB, IN INCREASING ORDER. *)
VAR FILEA,FILEB,FILEC : FILE OF INTEGER;
    LASTELEMENT : BOOLEAN;
BEGIN
    RESET(FILEA);
    RESET(FILEB);
    REWRITE(FILEC);
    LASTELEMENT : = EOF(FILEA) OR EOF(FILEB);
(* TAKE ONE COMPONENT FROM FILEA OR FILEB AND PUT IT ON FILEC. THIS
OPERATION IS REPEATED UNTIL THE END OF ONE OF THE FILES FILEA OR FILEB IS
REACHED. *)
    REPEAT
        IF FILEA↑ <= FILEB↑ THEN
```

FILE

```
    BEGIN
        FILEC↑ := FILEA↑;
        GET(FILEA);
        LASTELEMENT := EOF(FILEA)
    END
ELSE
    BEGIN
        FILEC↑ := FILEB↑;
        GET(FILEB);
        LASTELEMENT := EOF(FILEB)
    END;
    PUT(FILEC);
UNTIL LASTELEMENT;
(* IF THERE ARE STILL COMPONENTS AVAILABLE ON FILEA COPY THEM ON FILEC *)
    WHILE NOT EOF(FILEB) DO
    BEGIN
        FILEC↑ := FILEB↑;
        PUT(FILEC);
        GET(FILEB)
    END;
(* IF THERE ARE STILL COMPONENTS AVAILABLE ON FILEB COPY THEM ON FILEC *)
    WHILE NOT EOF(FILEA) DO
    BEGIN
        FILEC↑ := FILEA↑;
        PUT(FILEC);
        GET(FILEA)
    END
END.
```

FILLCHAR

FILLCHAR is a non-standard predefined procedure that fills a specified number of bytes with a specified character.

☐ SYMBOL   ☐ STANDARD   ☐ J & W/CDC   ☐ PASCAL/Z
■ IDENTIFIER   ☐ HP 1000   ☐ OMSI   ■ UCSD
☐ CONCEPT

1
SYNTAX

FILLCHAR statement:

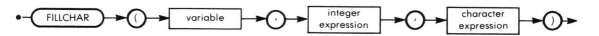

2
DESCRIPTION

The procedure FILLCHAR has three parameters. The first parameter, Destination, is a variable of any type except file. The second parameter, Count, is a positive integer expression, and the third parameter, Character, is an expression yielding a CHAR value:

FILLCHAR(Destination,Count,Character);

FILLCHAR assigns the value of Character to Count successive bytes, starting where the variable Destination is stored.

3
IMPLEMENTATION-DEPENDENT FEATURES

FILLCHAR is only implemented in UCSD Pascal.

FILLCHAR

4
EXAMPLE

```
PROGRAM FILL(OUTPUT);
VAR
    STR : ARRAY[1..10] OF CHAR;
BEGIN (* FILL *)
    FILLCHAR(STR, SIZEOF(STR), '*');
    WRITE('YOU SHOULD NOW SEE * TEN TIMES');
    WRITELN(STR)
END (* FILL *).
```

The FOR loop is used when a statement has to be repeated a predefined number of times.

- ■ SYMBOL
- □ IDENTIFIER
- □ CONCEPT

- ■ STANDARD
- ■ HP 1000

- ■ J & W/CDC
- ■ OMSI

- ■ PASCAL/Z
- ■ UCSD

1
SYNTAX

FOR statement:

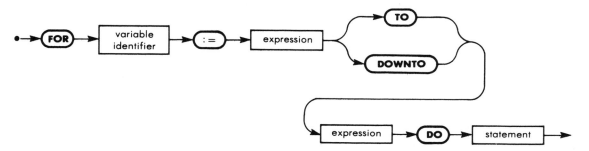

The variable and the two expressions must be of the same ordinal type (or a subrange thereof). The control variable must be simple (not part of a structured data type) and locally declared (i.e., within the block containing the loop). The control variable may not be changed inside the loop.

2
DESCRIPTION

The loop:

FOR I := A **TO** B **DO** statement

can be implemented according to the following flowchart:

FOR

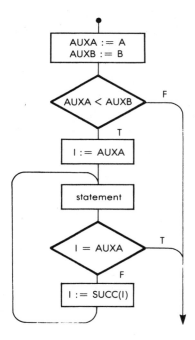

The auxiliary variables AUXA and AUXB do not exist explicitly in the program.

The loop

FOR I := A **DOWNTO** B **DO** instruction

can be implemented according to the same flowchart but with the following substitutions:

$$AUXA < AUXB \rightarrow AUXA > AUXB$$

and

$$I := SUCC(I) \rightarrow I := PRED(I)$$

The statement inside the loop may not modify the value of the loop variable I.

The value of I, after the execution of the FOR statement, is undefined.

3

IMPLEMENTATION-DEPENDENT FEATURES

None of the implementations detect violations of the restrictions (i.e., that a variable must be local and simple, and may not be assigned to inside the loop).

3.1 HP 1000   See general comment above.

3.2 J & W/CDC   The loop variable does not have to be local.

3.3 OMSI   May not work for A or B near MAXINT.

3.4 Pascal/Z   See general comment above.

3.5 UCSD   May not work for A or B near MAXINT.

4

EXAMPLE

```
PROGRAM FLOOP(OUTPUT);
VAR I : INTEGER;
BEGIN
    FOR I := 1 TO 10 DO
        WRITELN('LINE TO BE PRINTED 10 TIMES')
END.
```

FORTRAN

The non-standard directive FORTRAN is used to declare external procedures and functions written in FORTRAN.

■ SYMBOL □ STANDARD ■ J & W/CDC □ PASCAL/Z
□ IDENTIFIER □ HP 1000 ■ OMSI □ UCSD
□ CONCEPT

Refer to the EXTERNAL heading for more information.

FORWARD

FORWARD is a directive used when it is necessary to declare a function or a procedure before its body can be defined.

- ■ SYMBOL
- □ IDENTIFIER
- □ CONCEPT

- ■ STANDARD
- ■ HP 1000

- ■ J & W/CDC
- ■ OMSI

- ■ PASCAL/Z
- ■ UCSD

1
SYNTAX

1.1 Forward Procedure or Function Declaration

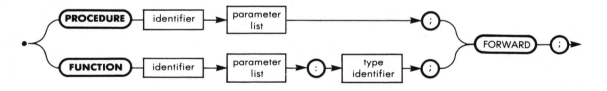

1.2 Definition of a Procedure or Function Announced Previously by a Forward Declaration

Note that the parameter list and FUNCTION type declaration appear only in the FORWARD declaration.

FORWARD

2
DESCRIPTION

It is necessary to define a procedure or function by a FORWARD declaration if this procedure or function has to be referenced before it can be defined completely. This situation occurs when two procedures or functions reference each other recursively.

FORWARD is a directive, not a reserved word. It is, however, a symbol (it may not have embedded blanks, and it need not be declared). It may only appear following a function or procedure heading.

3
IMPLEMENTATION-DEPENDENT FEATURES

FORWARD is a reserved word in Pascal/Z.

4
EXAMPLE

A program illustrating the use of the FORWARD directive can be found under the recursion heading.

FUNCTION

A FUNCTION is a group of statements that has a name and executes a specific task or algorithm. The function identifier has a type and, after execution, returns a value. A FUNCTION block is the part of a program defined by a FUNCTION declaration.

- ■ SYMBOL
- □ IDENTIFIER
- ■ CONCEPT

- ■ STANDARD
- ■ HP 1000

- ■ J & W/CDC
- ■ OMSI

- ■ PASCAL/Z
- ■ UCSD

1
SYNTAX

1.1 Function Declaration

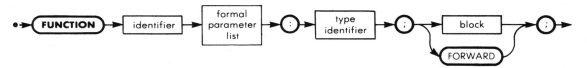

1.2 Formal Parameter List

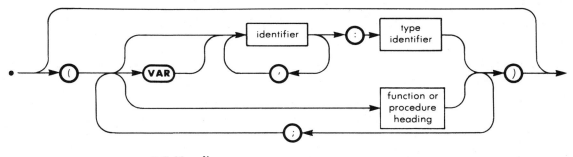

1.3 Heading

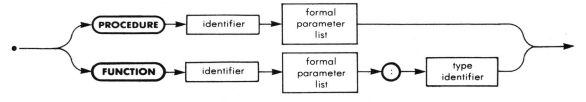

FUNCTION

1.4 Factor Containing a Function Reference (See the expression heading for a complete syntax of factors.)

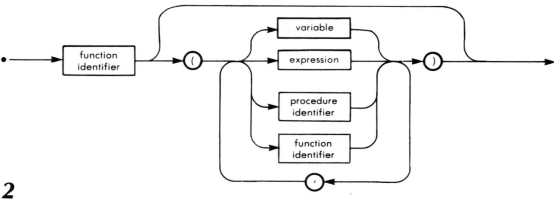

2
DESCRIPTION

Functions are used to avoid repetition of identical pieces of code, and to enhance the clarity of programs by encouraging modularity.

2.1 Scope of Identifiers The identifiers declared in the parameter list and in the declaration part of the block following the function heading are valid only inside that block. These identifiers are local to the function.

A function declaration is itself part of a block. Identifiers defined in this outer block are also valid inside the block of the function. These identifiers are global to the function.

If a local identifier is identical to the global identifier, then the local declaration prevails.

2.2 Function Activation A function is activated (its statements are executed) when a factor containing the function reference is evaluated.

When the function has completed execution, its value is used for the factor containing the function reference.

In many implementations, memory for local variables is made available upon activation and released upon completion of activation.

2.3 Parameters Data can be exchanged between a function and the block in which that function is activated (called) by means of global

FUNCTION

variables, parameters to the function, and the value returned by the function.

The value to be returned by the function is assigned by an assignment statement to the function identifier in the executable part of the function. A function cannot return a structured type; i.e., sets, arrays, records, or files are not allowed.

A list of formal parameters can be declared in the function heading. These variables are local to the function.

A list of actual parameters can be mentioned in the function call. These parameters are substituted for the formal parameters when the function is activated. The correspondence between the actual and formal parameters is established by their positions in both lists.

Four different kinds of parameters exist: value, variable, function and procedure.

2.3.1 Value Parameters

Formal value parameters are variables local to the function. Actual value parameters are expressions of a type compatible with their corresponding formal parameters. When the function is activated, the values of the actual parameters are evaluated and assigned to the corresponding parameters.

Note: the value of actual parameters cannot be affected by any assignment made to the formal parameters.

Although value parameters minimize interaction between different modules of a program, and are most efficiently accessed in a function, structured value parameters may waste memory space (actual and formal parameters occupy distinct places in memory) and processor time (each time that a function is activated, all of the value parameters have to be copied into the corresponding formal parameters) in some implementations.

Variables of type FILE cannot be passed as value parameters.

2.3.2 Variable Parameters

Lists of formal variable parameters in the function heading are preceded by the word VAR.

The substitution mechanism used for variable parameters is such that any reference to a formal parameter is replaced by a reference to the actual parameter. Therefore, all actual parameters must be variables (constants and expressions are not allowed as actual parameters).

The value of actual parameters is affected by assignments made to the formal parameters.

FUNCTION

Components of packed structures cannot be used as actual variable parameters.

2.3.3 Function and Procedure Parameters Formal function and procedure parameters have the same syntax as function and procedure headings. The formal parameter names that appear inside formal function and procedure declarations are meaningless, and their scope is limited to the heading in which they are used. Whenever a formal function or procedure parameter is referenced, the corresponding actual parameter is activated. Procedures and functions that are used as parameters to other procedures or functions can only have value parameters, and must have been declared in the program block.

2.4 Recursion Inside a function, an expression can contain that same function. This is called a recursive function activation and is allowed in Pascal.

Another form of recursion occurs when function A contains a reference to a function or procedure B, which itself contains a reference to the function A. This form of recursion is also allowed, but causes a syntactical problem: a procedure or function will be referenced before it is declared. This difficulty is solved by using a FORWARD declaration, which allows the programmer to announce in advance that a procedure's or function's body will be defined later.

2.5 Side Effects A side effect occurs when the value of a global variable or a VAR parameter is changed by a function. If this variable is used in an expression that contains a reference to the function, then the value of the expression depends upon the order of evaluation of the factors.

To avoid side effects, a function should not make assignments to global variables, and should not use variable parameters.

3

IMPLEMENTATION-DEPENDENT FEATURES

3.1 HP 1000

3.1.1 Directives An additional directive, EXTERNAL, is provided.

FUNCTION

Directives (HP 1000):

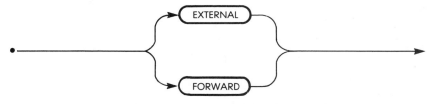

The EXTERNAL directive is used to include functions written in other languages in a Pascal program. Refer to the EXTERNAL heading for more information.

Only the first five characters of a procedure or function identifier are significant due to limitations in the present versions of the RTE operating system and the relocating loader.

3.1.2 Type of Functions Functions can have any type which can be assigned, i.e., all types except files, or structured types containing files.

Factor containing a function:

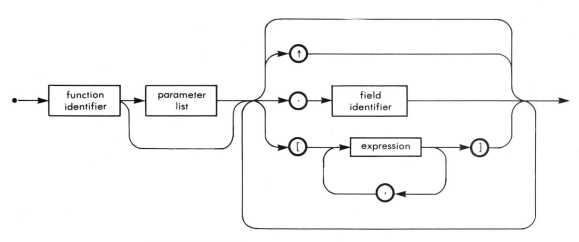

3.2 J & W/CDC

3.2.1 Syntax The syntax of the parameter list differs with respect to procedure and function parameters.

FUNCTION

Parameter list (J & W/CDC):

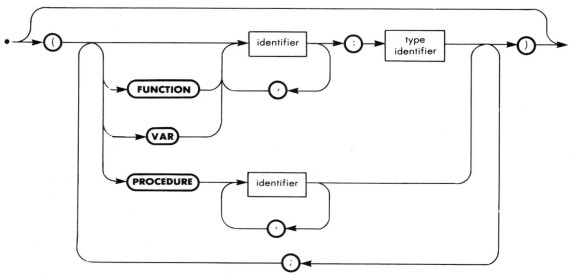

Predefined procedures and functions are not permitted as parameters.

3.2.2 Directives Two additional directives, EXTERN and FORTRAN, are provided. They are used to include functions written in other languages in a Pascal program.

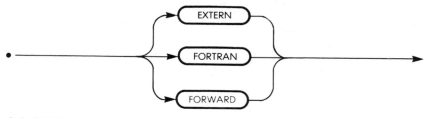

3.3 OMSI

3.3.1 Syntax The syntax of the formal parameter list is as described in paragraph 3.2.1 in this section.

Predefined procedures and functions are not permitted as parameters.

FUNCTION

3.3.2 Directives   Two additional directives, EXTERNAL and FORTRAN, are provided.

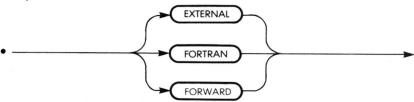

They are used to include procedures written in other languages in a Pascal program.

3.4 Pascal/Z

3.4.1 Procedural Parameters   Functions and procedures cannot be passed as parameters to a function. The syntax of the parameter list reflects this limitation.

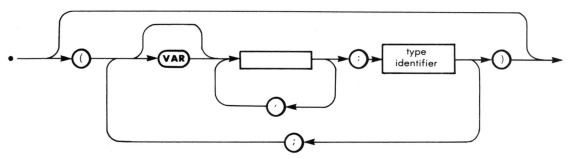

3.4.2 Directives   An additional directive, EXTERNAL, is provided. It is similar to the directive described in paragraph 3.1.1 of this heading.

3.5 UCSD

3.5.1 Procedural Parameters   Functions and procedures cannot be passed as parameters to a function. See paragraph 3.4.1 of this heading for the syntax of the formal parameter list.

3.5.2 String Parameters   The predefined type identifier STRING may not be used in the formal parameter list. If such parameters are necessary, a particular string type should be defined by a type declaration, and that type should be used for actual as well as formal parameters.

FUNCTION

3.5.3 Directives An additional directive, EXTERNAL, is provided. It is similar to the directive described in paragraph 3.1.1 of this heading.

3.5.4 Functions of Type String Although several predeclared functions return values of type STRING, it is not possible to define such functions.

4
EXAMPLES

4.1 Program Illustrating the Use of Functions

```
      PROGRAM POWERN(INPUT,OUTPUT);
          VAR N : 0..MAXINT;
              X : REAL;
          FUNCTION XTON(X : REAL; N : 0..MAXINT) : REAL;
          (* COMPUTES THE VALUE OF X TO THE POWER N *)
              VAR Z : REAL;
              BEGIN
                  Z := 1;
                  WHILE N > 0 DO
                  BEGIN
                      WHILE NOT ODD(N) DO
                          BEGIN
                              N := N DIV 2;
                              X := SQR(X)
                          END;
                      N := N - 1;
                      Z := Z * X
                  END;
                  XTON := Z
              END;
```

FUNCTION

BEGIN
    WRITELN('TO COMPUTE X TO THE NTH POWER, GIVE X AND N');
    READLN (X,N);
    WRITELN('X TO THE NTH POWER = ',XTON(X,N))
END.

4.2 Program Illustrating the Difference Between Value and Variable Parameters See program VALVAR under the PROCEDURE heading.

4.3 Program Illustrating the Use of the Function Parameter

PROGRAM HYPTAB;
(* PROGRAM TO TABULATE HYPERBOLIC FUNCTION, AND TO ILLUSTRATE THE FUNCTION PARAMETERS *)
FUNCTION CH(X : REAL) : REAL; (* HYPERBOLIC COSINE*)
    BEGIN
        CH := (EXP(X) + EXP(−X))/2.0
    END;
FUNCTION SH(X : REAL): REAL; (* HYPERBOLIC SINE*)
    BEGIN
        SH := (EXP(X) − EXP(−X))/2.0
    END;
PROCEDURE TABUL(FIRST,LAST : REAL; NUMBER : INTEGER;
                  FUNCTION F(X : REAL) : REAL);
    VAR STEP : REAL;
        I : INTEGER;
    BEGIN
        STEP := (LAST − FIRST)/(NUMBER − 1);
        FOR I := 1 **TO** NUMBER **DO**
            BEGIN
                X := FIRST + STEP * (I − 1);
                WRITELN('X = ',X,' F(X) = ',F(X))
            END
    END;

FUNCTION

BEGIN

    WRITELN('HYPERBOLIC SINE FUNCTION');
    WRITELN;
    TABUL(−1.0,+1.0,21,SH);
    WRITELN;
    WRITELN('HYPERBOLIC COSINE FUNCTION');
    WRITELN;
    TABUL(−1.0,+1.0,21,CH)
END.

4.4 Program Illustrating the Recursive Use of Functions   See example under the recursion heading.

4.5 Program Illustrating Side Effects   See example under the side effects heading.

GET is a standard procedure that transfers one record of a file to the associated buffer variable.

☐ SYMBOL   ■ STANDARD   ■ J & W/CDC   ☐ PASCAL/Z
■ IDENTIFIER   ■ HP 1000   ■ OMSI   ■ UCSD
☐ CONCEPT

1
SYNTAX

GET statement:

2
DESCRIPTION

The effect of the statement GET(F) can be described as follows (provided that, prior to its execution, the function EOF(F) had the value FALSE):

— The file window is advanced one position.

— **IF** a component is available under the window

     THEN   The value of that component is assigned to the buffer variable F↑ ; the function EOF(F) remains FALSE.

     ELSE   The buffer variable F↑ is undefined. The function EOF(F) becomes TRUE.

GET

The effect of executing the statement GET(F) while EOF(F) is TRUE is an error, and generally results in the abnormal termination of the program.

Before the first GET(F) statement is executed, the file must have been opened by a RESET(F) statement. No REWRITE(F), PUT(F), WRITE(F) or WRITELN(F) statements may be executed between the RESET(F) statement and any GET(F) statement.

3
IMPLEMENTATION-DEPENDENT FEATURES

3.1 HP 1000 Before the first GET(F) statement is executed, the file F must have been opened by RESET(F) or an OPEN(F) statement. If the file has been opened by the RESET statement, only GET operations are allowed, and the file is read sequentially. If the file was opened by the OPEN statement, then READ, WRITE, PUT and GET operations can be intermixed, and the file window can be arbitrarily moved by the SEEK procedure.

The behavior of the procedure GET is slightly different from that described in the standard: the actual transfer of data from the file to the buffer variable does not occur during execution of the GET procedure, but when an expression containing the buffer variable is evaluated. Due to this modification, data need not be available on a file before it is actually used in the program. This is convenient when a file is associated with an interactive I/O device, such as a CRT terminal.

3.2 J & W/CDC None known.

3.3 OMSI If adequate parameters have been used when the file was opened by the RESET or REWRITE procedures, PUT and GET operations on the same file can be intermixed, and the file window can be arbitrarily positioned by the SEEK procedure.

3.4 Pascal/Z The procedure GET is not available. READ and READLN should be used instead.

3.5 UCSD   The GET(F) statement is only valid if F is a typed file. (See the FILE heading for the particularities of UCSD files.) PUT and GET operations on the same file can be intermixed, and the file window can be arbitrarily positioned by the SEEK procedure.

4
EXAMPLE

See the program FILEMERGE under the FILE heading.

global

An identifier is global to a block if the identifier has been declared in a surrounding block, and has not been redeclared in the block itself.

☐ SYMBOL	■ STANDARD	■ J & W/CDC	■ PASCAL/Z
☐ IDENTIFIER	■ HP 1000	■ OMSI	■ UCSD
■ CONCEPT			

1
SYNTAX

Not applicable.

2
DESCRIPTION

Identifiers declared in a block are local to that block, and global with respect to all blocks declared inside that block.

It is a common but poor practice to declare type identifiers and constants that are often used in the outer block of a program. Such global variables should be used more carefully, as they can cause errors which are difficult to locate (such as those resulting from an unplanned side effect).

Some implementations access their non-local variables in a very inefficient way.

3
IMPLEMENTATION-DEPENDENT FEATURES

3.1 HP 1000 None known.

3.2 J&W/CDC The variables declared in the outermost block and the variables declared locally can be accessed through efficient hardware mechanisms, while global variables declared at intermediate levels require lengthy software table look-ups.

3.3 OMSI None known.

3.4 Pascal/Z None known.

3.5 UCSD The variables declared in the outermost block and the variables declared locally can be accessed through efficient hardware mechanisms, while global variables declared at intermediate levels require lengthy software table look-ups.

4
EXAMPLE

The following program tests the overhead associated with the access to global variables. It uses a function, CLOCK, which returns the amount of time that the program has already used the CPU. Another timing function can be substituted if CLOCK is not available.

```
PROGRAM GLOBALS(OUTPUT);
CONST
     MAX = 1000;
VAR
     LEVEL0 : INTEGER;
     PROCEDURE PLEVEL1;
     VAR
          LEVEL1 : INTEGER;
          PROCEDURE PLEVEL2;
          VAR
               LEVEL2 : INTEGER;
               CNT : INTEGER;
               START : INTEGER;
```

```
    BEGIN
        WRITELN(' PROGRAM TO TEST THE OVERHEAD ASSOCIATED WITH GLOBALS');
        WRITELN;
        WRITELN(' LEVEL 2 IS THE INNER LEVEL, AT WHICH THE TESTS ARE PERFORMED');
        WRITELN(' LEVEL 0 IS THE MOST GLOBAL LEVEL (MAIN PROGRAM)');
        WRITELN;
        LEVEL0 := 0;
        LEVEL1 := 0;
        LEVEL2 := 0;
        START := CLOCK;
        FOR CNT := 1 TO MAX DO
            LEVEL0 := LEVEL0 + 1;
        WRITELN(MAX:6,' OPERATIONS ON A LEVEL 0 VARIABLE
                TAKE ',CLOCK — START,' MS');
        START := CLOCK;
        FOR CNT := 1 TO MAX DO
            LEVEL1 := LEVEL1 + 1;
        WRITELN(MAX:6,' OPERATIONS ON A LEVEL 1 VARIABLE
                TAKE ',CLOCK — START,' MS');
        START := CLOCK;
        FOR CNT := 1 TO MAX DO
            LEVEL2 := LEVEL2 + 1;
        WRITELN(MAX:6,' OPERATIONS ON A LEVEL 2 VARIABLE
                TAKE ',CLOCK — START,' MS')
    END; (* PLEVEL2 *)
  BEGIN
        PLEVEL2
  END; (* PLEVEL1 *)
BEGIN
    PLEVEL1
END.
```

GOTO

The GOTO statement is used to indicate that processing should continue at another place in the program text.

- ■ SYMBOL
- □ IDENTIFIER
- □ CONCEPT

- ■ STANDARD
- ■ HP 1000

- ■ J & W/CDC
- ■ OMSI

- ■ PASCAL/Z
- ■ UCSD

1
SYNTAX

GOTO statement:

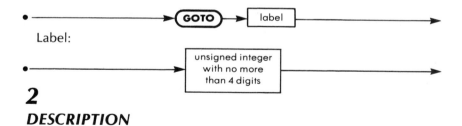

Label:

2
DESCRIPTION

A GOTO statement indicates that further processing should continue at the place referenced by the label. A GOTO statement located anywhere in a block may reference a labeled statement in the statement part of that block. This means that it is possible to jump out of a procedure defined within a block to a statement belonging to that block, but it is never possible to jump from outside a procedure into that procedure.

Jumps from outside into structured statements are prohibited, but are not always rejected by compilers. Their effect is unpredictable, and they should never be used.

Information on the usage and placement of labels is given in the STATEMENT and LABEL sections.

Note: GOTO statements should be avoided, as a general rule, since they obscure the structure of the program. They should only be used in exceptional situations, for example, to cause an orderly but abnormal termination of a program.

3
IMPLEMENTATION-DEPENDENT FEATURES

3.1 HP 1000   None known.

3.2 J & W/CDC   None known.

3.3 OMSI   None known.

3.4 Pascal/Z   None known.

3.5 UCSD   Jumps to labels outside of the block in which the GOTO statement appears are not allowed. A predefined procedure, EXIT, is provided for such a jump. Refer to the corresponding heading for more information.

   A special compiler option is provided to enable compilation of programs containing GOTO statements.

4
EXAMPLE

```
PROGRAM LOWUP2(INPUT,OUTPUT);
(* THIS PROGRAM CONVERTS THE FILE INPUT, WHICH SHOULD CONTAIN ONLY
UPPER AND LOWER CASE LETTERS AND BLANKS, INTO THE FILE OUTPUT, WHICH
WILL CONTAIN ONLY UPPER CASE LETTERS AND BLANKS. IF AN INVALID
CHARACTER IS FOUND IN INPUT, THEN THE PROGRAM STOPS *)
LABEL 1;
VAR LET : CHAR;
    OFFSET : INTEGER;
BEGIN
    OFFSET := ORD('A') — ORD('a');
    WHILE NOT EOF DO
```

```
        IF NOT EOLN
            THEN
                BEGIN
                    READ(LET);
                    IF LET IN['a'..'z'] THEN
                        LET := CHR(OFFSET + ORD(LET));
                    IF NOT (LET IN['A'..'Z',' ']) THEN
                        BEGIN
                            WRITELN;
                            WRITELN('*INPUT ERROR*');
                            GOTO 1;
                        END;
                    WRITE(LET)
                END
            ELSE
                BEGIN
                    READLN;
                    WRITELN
                END;
        WRITELN;
    1: END.
```

GOTOXY

GOTOXY is a non-standard predefined procedure that moves the cursor of the system terminal to a specified position.

☐ SYMBOL ☐ STANDARD ☐ J & W/CDC ☐ PASCAL/Z
■ IDENTIFIER ☐ HP 1000 ☐ OMSI ■ UCSD
☐ CONCEPT

1
SYNTAX

GOTOXY statement:

2
DESCRIPTION

GOTOXY has two integer parameters, the X and Y coordinates of the point on the screen to which the cursor has to be moved. In most implementations, the first parameter, X, must be in the range 0..79, and the second parameter, Y, in the range 0..23.

The upper left corner of the screen has coordinates 0,0.

3
IMPLEMENTATION-DEPENDENT FEATURES

GOTOXY is only implemented in UCSD Pascal. Its performance and the ranges of the parameters depend upon the terminal used.

GOTOXY

4
EXAMPLE

```
PROGRAM MOVCUR(OUTPUT);
(* MOVE CURSOR ALONG DIAGONAL *)
BEGIN
        GOTOXY(0,0);
        WRITE('THE');
        GOTOXY(1,1);
        WRITE('FOLLOWING');
        GOTOXY(2,2);
        WRITE('TEXT');
        GOTOXY(3,3);
        WRITE('WILL');
        GOTOXY(4,4);
        WRITE('APPEAR');
        GOTOXY(5,5);
        WRITE('ON');
        GOTOXY(6,6);
        WRITE('THE');
        GOTOXY(7,7);
        WRITE('DIAGONAL')
END.
```

HALT

HALT is a non-standard procedure that can be used to terminate the execution of a program.

☐ SYMBOL ☐ STANDARD ■ J & W/CDC ☐ PASCAL/Z
■ IDENTIFIER ■ HP 1000 ☐ OMSI ■ UCSD
☐ CONCEPT

1
SYNTAX

HALT statement:

●————————————▶(HALT)————————————▶

2
DESCRIPTION

The procedure HALT terminates the execution of a program. An error message is issued by the operating system. HALT is not intended to be used when a program terminates normally.

3
IMPLEMENTATION-DEPENDENT FEATURES

3.1 HP 1000 Implemented as described.

3.2 J & W/CDC Implemented as described.

3.3 UCSD Implemented as described.

heap

The heap is a part of the memory which is used to store dynamic variables during the execution of Pascal programs.

☐ SYMBOL ■ STANDARD ■ J & W/CDC ■ PASCAL/Z
☐ IDENTIFIER ■ HP 1000 ■ OMSI ■ UCSD
■ CONCEPT

1
SYNTAX

The heap cannot be explicitly referenced.

2
DESCRIPTION

The standard procedure NEW creates dynamically new variables, which are accessible through pointers. The part of memory where these variables are stored is usually called a heap.

A dynamic variable that does not have pointers pointing to it no longer exists, and should not take up memory space. Unfortunately, very few implementations allow this available space to be reused by the procedure NEW for the subsequent creation of variables.

Inconsiderate use of NEW can cause the heap to outgrow available memory. Such an incident is generally known as a "heap stack collision" in implementations where the heap and stack share memory.

The programmer can help the system to recover unused memory space by using the procedure DISPOSE to return unused dynamic variables.

Some implementations include additional heap management routines, such as MARK and RELEASE. These non-standard but frequently provided routines allow management of heap space like a stack.

identifier

Identifiers are symbolic names for programs, constants, types, variables, procedures, and functions.

☐ SYMBOL   ■ STANDARD   ■ J & W/CDC   ■ PASCAL/Z
☐ IDENTIFIER   ■ HP 1000   ■ OMSI   ■ UCSD
■ CONCEPT

1
SYNTAX

Identifier:

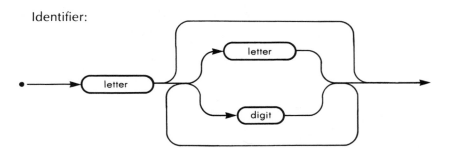

Note: No blanks may appear within an identifier.

The syntax of identifiers implicitly limits their length to one source line.

2
DESCRIPTION

2.1 Upper and Lower Case Letters No distinction is made between upper and lower case letters in identifiers and reserved words. Both are allowed, and are not distinguished.

Several implementations have restrictions on this particular point.

2.2 Number of Significant Characters Although the syntax allows identifiers of arbitrary length, only a limited number of characters are used by some compilers to distinguish between identifiers. Therefore it is important to identify distinct objects by identifiers that are different in their first eight characters, since this is the least number commonly used.

3

IMPLEMENTATION-DEPENDENT FEATURES

3.1 HP 1000 The underscore character (ASCII 95) is allowed in identifiers.

Identifier (HP 1000):

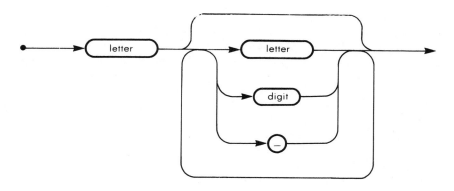

All characters are significant.

3.2 J & W/CDC Only the first ten characters are significant, and only upper case letters are allowed.

3.3 OMSI All characters are significant.

3.4 Pascal/Z The characters __ (ASCII 95), # (ASCII 35) and $ (ASCII 36) are allowed in identifiers.

identifier

Identifier (Pascal/Z):

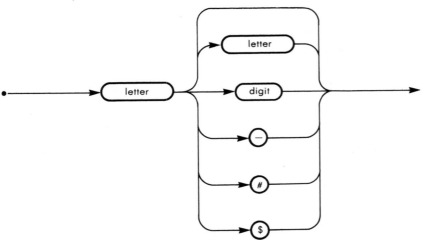

3.5 UCSD In some implementations of UCSD Pascal (Intel) the underscore __ (ASCII 95) may appear in identifiers, but is ignored. In Apple Pascal, the underscore is allowed and is significant. Only eight characters are significant in all UCSD Pascal implementations.

4
EXAMPLE

LEGAL IDENTIFIERS:	ILLEGAL IDENTIFIERS:
MYNAME	MY NAME
	▲
X123	123X
	▲
HASHTABLE	HASH__TABLE
	▲

HASH__TABLE is not allowed in standard Pascal, but allowed in HP 1000, Pascal/Z and some UCSD versions.

HASH__TABLE and HASHTABLE are equivalent in many implementations of UCSD Pascal.

The IF statement allows the conditional execution of statements.

■ SYMBOL   ■ STANDARD   ■ J & W/CDC   ■ PASCAL/Z
☐ IDENTIFIER   ■ HP 1000   ■ OMSI   ■ UCSD
☐ CONCEPT

1
SYNTAX

IF statement:

The expression must be a Boolean expression.

2
DESCRIPTION

The following flowcharts diagrammatically show the flow of control in an IF statement.

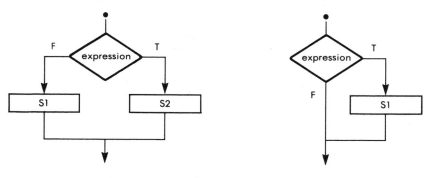

When the expression has the value TRUE, the statement S1 is executed; otherwise, if the expression is FALSE, and if the ELSE branch does exist, S2 is executed.

When the THEN statement in an IF is itself a two-branch IF:

IF B1 **THEN IF** B2 **THEN** S3 **ELSE** S4 **ELSE** S2

The ELSE relates to the nearest incomplete IF, i.e., the above statement is equivalent to:

```
IF B1 THEN
    BEGIN
        IF B2 THEN S3
            ELSE S4
    END
    ELSE S2
```

3
IMPLEMENTATION-DEPENDENT FEATURES

None known.

4
EXAMPLES

```
PROGRAM TESTIF1(OUTPUT);
VAR I : INTEGER;
BEGIN
    I := 1;
    IF I = 1
        THEN WRITELN('OK')
        ELSE WRITELN('STRANGE')
END.
```

```
PROGRAM TESTIF2(OUTPUT);
VAR I : INTEGER;
BEGIN
     FOR I := 1 TO 3 DO
     IF I > 1 THEN
          IF I = 2 THEN WRITELN('FIRST LINE TO BE PRINTED')
                    ELSE
                         IF I = 3   THEN WRITELN('THIS IS OK')
                                    ELSE WRITELN('THIS IS WRONG')
END.
```

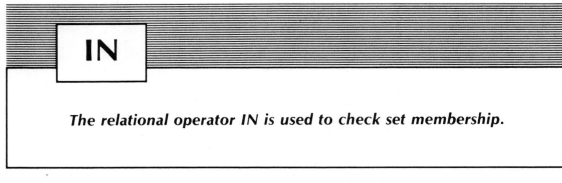

IN

The relational operator IN is used to check set membership.

■ SYMBOL   ■ STANDARD   ■ J & W/CDC   ■ PASCAL/Z
□ IDENTIFIER   ■ HP 1000   ■ OMSI   ■ UCSD
□ CONCEPT

1
SYNTAX

1.1 Relational Expression

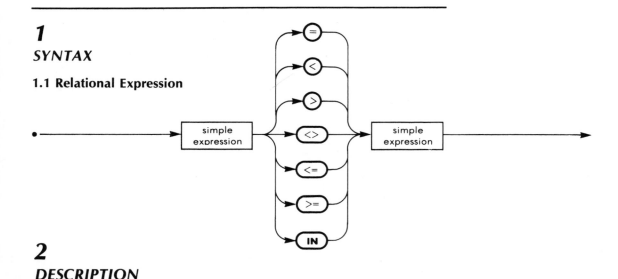

2
DESCRIPTION

The right operand must be a SET of objects, while the left operand must be an object of the same type of which the SET is made. The result of the operation is TRUE when the left operand is an element of the set on the right, otherwise it is FALSE.

3
IMPLEMENTATION-DEPENDENT FEATURES

None known.

4
EXAMPLE

```
PROGRAM WEEKDAYS(OUTPUT);
TYPE DAYS = (MO,TU,WE,TH,FR,SA,SU);
      WEEK = SET OF DAYS;
VAR WORKDAY,HOLIDAY,WEEKDAY : WEEK;
      D : DAYS;
PROCEDURE WRITEDAY(X : DAYS);
      BEGIN
          CASE X OF
              MO : WRITE('MONDAY ');
              TU : WRITE('TUESDAY ');
              WE : WRITE('WEDNESDAY ');
              TH : WRITE('THURSDAY ');
              FR : WRITE('FRIDAY ');
              SA : WRITE('SATURDAY ');
              SU : WRITE('SUNDAY ')
          END
      END;
BEGIN
      WORKDAY := [MO..FR];
      HOLIDAY := [SA..SU];
      WEEKDAY := WORKDAY + HOLIDAY;
      FOR D := MO TO SU DO
          IF D IN WEEKDAY THEN
              BEGIN
                  WRITEDAY(D);
                  WRITELN('IS A WEEKDAY')
              END
END.
```

INPUT

INPUT is a predeclared file of type TEXT. It is generally associated with an input device such as a keyboard or a card reader.

☐ SYMBOL	■ STANDARD	■ J & W/CDC	■ PASCAL/Z
■ IDENTIFIER	■ HP 1000	■ OMSI	■ UCSD
☐ CONCEPT			

1
SYNTAX

The text file INPUT does not need to be declared, but then must appear in the list of program parameters if any of the standard functions using INPUT appear in the program.

2
DESCRIPTION

2.1 Standard Procedures   The following standard procedures and functions can be applied to the file INPUT:

GET(INPUT): transfers one character from INPUT to the buffer variable INPUT ↑ .

READ(X): if X is of type CHAR, assigns the value of INPUT↑ to the variable X, and transfers one character from INPUT to INPUT↑. Otherwise, skips preceding blanks and/or ends-of-lines, reads the longest contiguous sequence of characters that make up the textual representation of a value of type X, assigns the value to X, and leaves the character that terminated the sequence in INPUT ↑ . An error condition is raised if the characters read do not form a textual representation of a value of type X.

READLN(X): similar to READ, but moves to the beginning of the next line after the READ has been completed.

EOLN: Boolean function yielding the value TRUE when an end of line is encountered on INPUT.

EOF: Boolean function yielding the value TRUE when an end-of-file is encountered on INPUT.

INPUT

2.2 Remarks

1. The filename can be omitted (as shown above) when the functions READ, READLN, EOLN, and EOF are used with the INPUT file.

2. A statement RESET(INPUT) is implicitly executed at the beginning of a program containing the filename INPUT in the program heading.

3. Alternate forms exist for the functions READ and READLN. Consult the corresponding sections.

4. The function REWRITE may not be applied to the file INPUT.

3

IMPLEMENTATION-DEPENDENT FEATURES

3.1 HP 1000   None known.

3.2 J & W/CDC   None known.

3.3 OMSI   None known.

3.4 Pascal/Z   The identifier INPUT is not predeclared. It is not possible to associate a file with the identifier INPUT and have it refer to the unnamed default input file.

3.5 UCSD   The predefined file INPUT is of the predefined type INTERACTIVE, and is normally associated with a keyboard. All characters entered on that keyboard are automatically echoed to the device associated with the predefined file OUTPUT.

If such an echo is not desirable, the predefined file KEYBOARD can be used instead of INPUT.

The effect of the procedures RESET, READ and READLN is slightly different on INTERACTIVE files than on TEXT files:

— RESET does not assign the buffer variable.

— READ and READLN perform a GET operation first, before assigning to the corresponding variable parameter.

4

EXAMPLE

An example of the use of the file INPUT can be found under the CHARacter heading (Program LOW).

INSERT

INSERT is a non-standard predefined procedure that inserts a string into another string, at a specified position.

☐ SYMBOL	☐ STANDARD	☐ J & W/CDC	☐ PASCAL/Z
■ IDENTIFIER	☐ HP 1000	☐ OMSI	■ UCSD
☐ CONCEPT			

1
SYNTAX

INSERT statement:

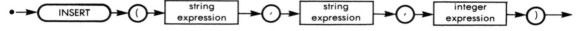

2
DESCRIPTION

The procedure INSERT has three parameters. The first, called Source, is of the UCSD STRING type, the second, which is a variable parameter, is also a string called Destination, and the third, called Index, is a positive integer:

INSERT(Source,Destination,Index);

The string Source is inserted in the string Destination starting at the Index'th position in the original Destination.

3
IMPLEMENTATION-DEPENDENT FEATURES

INSERT is only implemented as a predefined procedure in UCSD Pascal.

4
EXAMPLE

```
PROGRAM STRING5;
(* UCSD ONLY *)
VAR ST : STRING;
BEGIN
     ST := 'ONE,THREE';
     INSERT('TWO,',ST,POS('TH',ST));
     IF ST = 'ONE,TWO,THREE'
          THEN WRITELN('''',ST,''' OK !')
          ELSE WRITELN('''',ST,''' STRANGE !')
END.
```

INTEGER

The type INTEGER is a predefined type, and is used to represent integer numerical data.

☐ SYMBOL ■ STANDARD ■ J & W/CDC ■ PASCAL/Z
■ IDENTIFIER ■ HP 1000 ■ OMSI ■ UCSD
☐ CONCEPT

1
SYNTAX

1.1 Integer Type

1.2 Integer Subrange Type

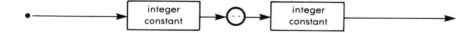

1.3 Integer Constant

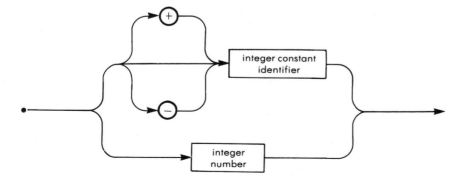

1.4 Integer Number

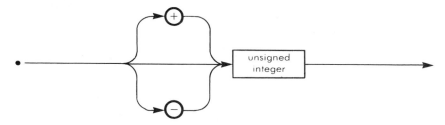

1.5 Unsigned Integer

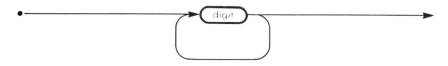

No blanks may appear within an unsigned integer.

2

DESCRIPTION

2.1 Range Variables of the type INTEGER can take an integer value. The minimal range is − MAXINT to + MAXINT, MAXINT being a predefined named constant whose value is implementation-dependent.

Variables of an INTEGER subrange type can take any integer value within the range defined by the two integer constants in the type declaration. The left constant must be less than or equal to the right.

2.2 Arithmetic Operators The arithmetic operations applicable to integer operands are:

+	addition	All of these operations are
−	subtraction	guaranteed to give exact
*	multiplication	results, as long as the range
DIV	integer quotient	− MAXINT to + MAXINT is
MOD	integer remainder	not exceeded.

When expressions are evaluated, the *, DIV, and MOD operations

INTEGER

are performed before the + and − operations, unless parentheses modify this rule of precedence.

2.3 Relational Operators   The relational operators applicable to integer operands are:

=	equal to
<>	not equal to
<	less than
>	greater than
<=	less than or equal to
>=	greater than or equal to

2.4 Standard Functions   The standard functions yielding integer values are:

ABS(x)	yielding the absolute value of the INTEGER expression x.
SQR(x)	yielding the square of the INTEGER expression x.
TRUNC(x)	yielding the whole part of the REAL expression x.
ROUND(x)	yielding the integer value closest to the value of the REAL expression x.
SUCC(x)	yielding the value of the INTEGER expression x + 1.
PRED(x)	yielding the value of the INTEGER expression x − 1.

3

IMPLEMENTATION-DEPENDENT FEATURES

Some implementations allow values outside the range − MAXINT to + MAXINT, and also allow arithmetic operations outside of this range.

3.1 HP 1000   The range of values for an integer N is

$$-2^{31} <= N < 2^{31}$$

Significant savings in memory space and execution time are obtained by declaring integer variables as subrange types with upper and lower

INTEGER

limits UL and LL satisfying the relation:

$$-2^{15} <= LL < UL < 2^{15}$$

whenever possible.

The value of MAXINT is

$$2^{31} - 1 = 2147483647$$

An additional predefined integer constant MININT exists. The value of MININT is

$$-2^{31} = -2147483648$$

The negation of the MININT value cannot be performed and is outside the MAXINT range.

3.2 J & W/CDC The range of values for an integer N is

$$-2^{59} <= N < 2^{59}$$

The value of MAXINT is

$$2^{48} - 1 = 281474976710655.$$

Larger integers, up to $2^{59} - 1$ in absolute value, can be manipulated in additions, subtractions, and relational expressions, but not in multiplications, divisions, or I/O operations. Such integer values should be avoided whenever possible.

3.3 OMSI The range of values for an integer N is

$$-2^{15} <= N < 2^{15}$$

The value of MAXINT is

$$2^{15} - 1 = 32767.$$

The negation of the value -2^{15} is not performed correctly and no error is indicated. -2^{15} is outside the range $-$ MAXINT to $+$ MAXINT.

Three additional operators are defined for INTEGER expressions:

AND	Boolean AND bit per bit on all 16 bits of the two operands.
OR	Boolean OR bit per bit on all 16 bits of the two operands.

INTEGER

NOT   Boolean complement of all 16 bits of the operand.

These operators are used to set, test, or mask individual bits in low-level control operations.

3.4 Pascal/Z   The range of values for an integer N is

$$-2^{15} <= N < 2^{15}$$

Significant savings in memory space are obtained by declaring integer variables as subrange types with upper and lower limits UL and LL satisfying the relation:

$$-2^7 <= LL < UL < 2^7$$

whenever possible. When range-checking is being done, assignments to such subrange integers can be slower than assignments to normal integers.

The value of MAXINT is

$$2^{15} - 1 = 32767.$$

The negation of the value -2^{15} is not performed correctly and no error is indicated. -2^{15} is outside the range $-$MAXINT to $+$MAXINT.

3.5 UCSD

3.5.1 Range   The range of values for an integer N is

$$-2^{15} <= N < 2^{15}$$

The value of MAXINT is

$$2^{15} - 1 = 32767.$$

The negation of the value -2^{15} is not performed correctly and no error is indicated. -2^{15} is outside the range $-$MAXINT to $+$MAXINT.

3.5.2 Long Integers   A special long integer type exists in some implementations. This type provides large integers with complete accuracy (up to 36 decimal digits). A long integer type is declared by indicating the required maximum number of digits after the integer declaration.

INTEGER

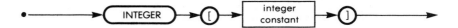

A constant defined by an integer number is considered as a long integer constant if the value of the number exceeds the range acceptable for integer constants.

The arithmetic operations defined for long integers are:

+	addition
–	subtraction
*	multiplication
DIV	division.

The same relational operators are applicable to integer and long integer expressions. Integer and long integer factors can be mixed in expressions. A long integer can be assigned an integer or real value; but reals or integers cannot be assigned long integer values.

The function TRUNC, when used with a long integer parameter, yields the integer value of the long integer parameter. The procedure STR converts an integer or long integer into a string, which can then be printed.

4
EXAMPLE

The programs DIVTEST under the DIV heading and MODTEST under the ORD heading illustrate the use of integers. The use of MAXINT is illustrated under the MAXINT heading.

The example section under the NUMBER heading shows many examples of integers.

INTERACTIVE

> **The type INTERACTIVE is a predefined non-standard file type, similar to TEXT. INTERACTIVE files are generally associated with interactive I/O devices, such as CRT terminals.**

☐ SYMBOL	☐ STANDARD	☐ J & W/CDC	☐ PASCAL/Z
■ IDENTIFIER	☐ HP 1000	☐ OMSI	■ UCSD
☐ CONCEPT			

1
SYNTAX

INTERACTIVE type:

2
DESCRIPTION

The standard definition of the RESET, READ and READLN procedures causes some problems when these procedures are used with files associated with interactive terminals. These procedures are organized in such a way that the buffer variable already contains the record that the program needs when a READ or READLN operation is performed. In an interactive environment, this could require an operator to answer a question before it is asked.

In UCSD Pascal, alternative versions of the RESET, READ and READLN procedures are provided to avoid this problem. They are automatically used with files of type INTERACTIVE.

— RESET does not assign to the buffer variable from the file.
— READ and READLN perform a GET operation first, before assigning to the corresponding variable parameter.

INTERACTIVE

Three files of type INTERACTIVE are predefined:

INPUT

KEYBOARD

OUTPUT.

The file KEYBOARD is analogous to the file INPUT, and is generally associated with the same input device; however, all characters read from the file INPUT are automatically echoed to the file OUTPUT, while those read on the file KEYBOARD are not echoed.

Except for the differences described, INTERACTIVE files are identical to TEXT files.

3
IMPLEMENTATION-DEPENDENT FEATURES

INTERACTIVE files are only implemented in UCSD Pascal.

4
EXAMPLE

See the KEYBOARD heading.

IORESULT

IORESULT is a non-standard predefined function that returns the result of I/O operations in an encoded form.

☐ SYMBOL   ☐ STANDARD   ☐ J & W/CDC   ☐ PASCAL/Z
■ IDENTIFIER   ☐ HP 1000   ☐ OMSI   ■ UCSD
☐ CONCEPT

1
SYNTAX

IORESULT function:

2
DESCRIPTION

The value of the integer function IORESULT is updated after every I/O operation. A zero value is returned by an error-free I/O operation. In order to have non-zero IORESULTs reported (rather than cause abnormal termination errors), automatic I/O error checking must have been inhibited by use of the compiler command (*$I— *). The meanings of the 15 other values are not described in this text. The mapping of actual I/O error onto IORESULT depends upon the particular system on which UCSD Pascal is installed.

3
IMPLEMENTATION-DEPENDENT FEATURES

IORESULT is only implemented in UCSD Pascal.

IORESULT

4
EXAMPLE

```
PROGRAM IORES(OUTPUT,FP);
(* EXAMPLE OF IORESULT—UCSD ONLY *)
VAR
     FP : TEXT
BEGIN
     RESET(FP);
(*$I— *)
     WRITELN(FP,'HELLO FILE');
     IF IORESULT < > 0
          THEN WRITELN('COULDN''T WRITE ON FILE')
          ELSE WRITELN('ABLE TO WRITE ON A FILE ONLY; ',
                       'OPEN FOR INPUT ONLY??')
     END.
```

KEYBOARD

KEYBOARD is a non-standard predefined file of type INTERACTIVE similar to INPUT except that characters from KEYBOARD are not echoed on OUTPUT, as characters from INPUT are.

☐ SYMBOL   ☐ STANDARD   ☐ J & W/CDC   ☐ PASCAL/Z
■ IDENTIFIER ☐ HP 1000   ☐ OMSI   ■ UCSD
☐ CONCEPT

1
SYNTAX

The file KEYBOARD does not need to be declared.

2
DESCRIPTION

Except for the echoing of characters, there is no difference between KEYBOARD and INPUT, as defined for the UCSD implementations.

3
IMPLEMENTATION-DEPENDENT FEATURES

KEYBOARD is only implemented in UCSD Pascal.

4
EXAMPLE

```
PROGRAM IO(KEYBOARD,OUTPUT);
(* GETS PROPER INPUT FROM A YES/NO QUESTION, AND PRINTS AN
APPROPRIATE RESPONSE. *)
FUNCTION YESNO : CHAR ;
     CONST
          BELL = 7;                   {IN ASCII, A BELL IS 7}
     BEGIN
          GET(KEYBOARD);             {NOTE, NOT ECHOED. THIS SETS KEYBOARD↑}
          WHILE NOT(KEYBOARD↑ IN['Y','N']) DO
          BEGIN
               WRITE(CHR(BELL));     {MAKE NOISE}
               GET(KEYBOARD)
          END;
          YESNO := KEYBOARD↑
     END;
BEGIN
     WRITE('DO YOU SPEAK PASCAL ? ');
     CASE YESNO OF
          'N' : WRITELN('PERHAPS THIS BOOK WILL HELP ');
          'Y' : WRITELN('THIS IS A GOOD LANGUAGE ')
     END
END.
```

LABEL

LABELS are used to identify statements so that they can be referenced in a GOTO statement.

- ■ SYMBOL
- □ IDENTIFIER
- □ CONCEPT

- ■ STANDARD
- ■ HP 1000

- ■ J & W/CDC
- ■ OMSI

- ■ PASCAL/Z
- ■ UCSD

1
SYNTAX

No blanks are permitted within a label.

1.1 Label Declaration

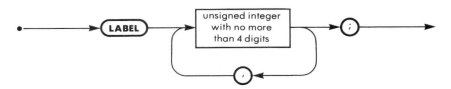

1.2 Labeled Statement

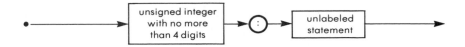

2
DESCRIPTION

A label is used to enable a GOTO statement to specify the statement that should be executed next. It is an integer number, not longer than 4 digits, followed by a colon and placed before a statement in a program.

3
IMPLEMENTATION-DEPENDENT FEATURES

None known.

4
EXAMPLE

```
PROGRAM LABELS(OUTPUT);
LABEL 1;
BEGIN
    GOTO 1;
    WRITELN('THIS LINE MAY NOT BE PRINTED');
1 : WRITELN('THIS LINE SHOULD BE PRINTED')
END.
```

LENGTH

LENGTH is a non-standard predefined function that returns the length of its string parameter.

□ SYMBOL   □ STANDARD   □ J & W/CDC   □ PASCAL/Z
■ IDENTIFIER   □ HP 1000   □ OMSI   ■ UCSD
□ CONCEPT

1
SYNTAX

Factor containing the LENGTH function:

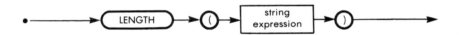

2
DESCRIPTION

The function LENGTH has one parameter, of type STRING. The returned value is of type INTEGER, and is equal to the number of characters in the string.

3
IMPLEMENTATION-DEPENDENT FEATURES

LENGTH is only implemented as a predefined function in UCSD Pascal.

LENGTH

4
EXAMPLE

```
PROGRAM STRING2;
(* UCSD ONLY *)
VAR ST : STRING[255];
BEGIN
     WRITELN('TYPE A STRING');
     READLN(ST);
     WRITELN('YOU TYPED',LENGTH(ST),' CHARACTERS')
 END.
```

LINELIMIT

LINELIMIT is a non-standard procedure that sets an upper limit to the number of lines which can be written on a textfile.

☐ SYMBOL   ☐ STANDARD   ■ J & W/CDC   ☐ PASCAL/Z
■ IDENTIFIER   ☐ HP 1000   ☐ OMSI   ☐ UCSD
☐ CONCEPT

1
SYNTAX

LINELIMIT statement:

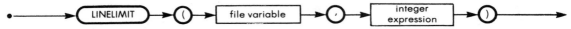

2
DESCRIPTION

The procedure LINELIMIT has two parameters. The first parameter, F, is the name of a textfile. The second parameter, X, is a positive INTEGER expression:

LINELIMIT(F,X)

The execution of the procedure LINELIMIT informs the operating system that no more than X lines will be written on the file F. If an attempt to write more than X lines is made, the operating system will cause an abnormal termination of the program.

3
IMPLEMENTATION-DEPENDENT FEATURES

LINELIMIT is only implemented in J & W/CDC Pascal.

LINEPOS

LINEPOS is a non-standard predefined function that counts the number of characters between the last end of line and the file window.

☐ SYMBOL   ☐ STANDARD   ☐ J & W/CDC   ☐ PASCAL/Z
■ IDENTIFIER   ■ HP 1000   ☐ OMSI   ☐ UCSD
☐ CONCEPT

1
SYNTAX

Factor containing the LINEPOS function:

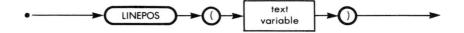

2
DESCRIPTION

The function LINEPOS has one argument of type TEXT. LINEPOS returns an integer value equal to the number of characters between the last end of line mark and the actual position of the file window.

3
IMPLEMENTATION-DEPENDENT FEATURES

LINEPOS is only implemented in HP 1000 Pascal.

4
EXAMPLE

```
PROGRAM CHECKFORMAT(INPUT,OUTPUT);
(* HP 1000 ONLY *)
(* A GIVEN TEXTFILE HAS IN EACH LINE A * IN COL 1 AND IN COL 60 *)
(* THIS PROGRAM CHECKS THE FORMAT AND PRINTS THE NUMBER OF
ERRONEOUS LINES. *)
VAR
      CH : CHAR;
      LINENUMBER : 0..9999;
BEGIN (* CHECKFORMAT *)
      LINENUMBER := 0;
      WHILE NOT EOF DO
          BEGIN
              LINENUMBER := LINENUMBER + 1;
              WHILE NOT EOLN DO
                  BEGIN
                      READ(CH);
                      IF ((LINEPOS(INPUT) = 1) AND (CH < > '*') OR
                          (LINEPOS(INPUT) = 60) AND (CH < > '*'))
                      THEN
                          WRITELN(' ERROR IN LINE ',LINENUMBER)
                  END;
              READLN
          END
END (* CHECKFORMAT *).
```

LN is a standard REAL function that returns the natural logarithm of its parameter.

☐ SYMBOL　　　■ STANDARD　　■ J & W/CDC　　■ PASCAL/Z
■ IDENTIFIER　■ HP 1000　　　■ OMSI　　　　■ UCSD
☐ CONCEPT

1
SYNTAX

Factor containing the LN function:

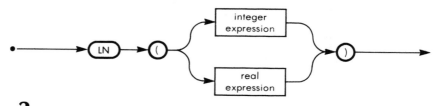

2
DESCRIPTION

The function LN(X) computes the value of the logarithm of X in the base e, the value of e being approximately 2.718281828. X may be INTEGER or REAL, but must be strictly positive. The value of LN(X) is always REAL. The logarithm function and the exponential function are inverse functions. (See the EXP heading.)

3
IMPLEMENTATION-DEPENDENT FEATURES

3.1 HP 1000　The parameters of LN can be of type LONGREAL. In this case, the returned value is also of type LONGREAL.

LN function (HP 1000):

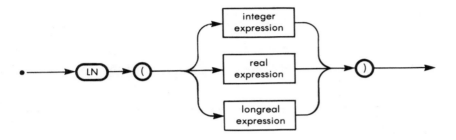

3.2 J & W/CDC   None known.

3.3 OMSI   None known.

3.4 Pascal/Z   None known.

3.5 UCSD   None known.

Note: in the APPLE implementation, LN is part of the TRANSCEND library.

4
EXAMPLE

```
PROGRAM LOGVAL(INPUT,OUTPUT);
VAR X,Y : REAL;
BEGIN
        WRITELN('TO OBTAIN THE LOGARITHM OF X IN BASE Y,');
        WRITELN('TYPE THE VALUES X AND Y SEPARATED BY A SPACE');
        READLN(X,Y);
        WRITELN('THE LOGARITHM OF ',X,' IN BASE ',Y,' IS : ',LN(X)/LN(Y))
END.
```

local

An identifier is local to the block in which it is declared.

☐ SYMBOL   ■ STANDARD   ■ J & W/CDC   ■ PASCAL/Z

☐ IDENTIFIER   ■ HP 1000   ■ OMSI   ■ UCSD

■ CONCEPT

1
SYNTAX

Not applicable.

2
DESCRIPTION

Identifiers declared in a block are local to that block and global with respect to all blocks declared inside that block. Formal parameters of procedures and functions passed by value are local to the block following the procedure or function heading.

Local variables provide good protection against undesirable interaction between different modules of a program. Whenever possible, objects should be declared locally.

3
IMPLEMENTATION-DEPENDENT FEATURES

In general, access to local variables is much faster than access to global variables.

4
EXAMPLE

Refer to the scope heading.

LOG

LOG is a non-standard predefined REAL function that returns the decimal logarithm of its parameter.

☐ SYMBOL   ☐ STANDARD   ☐ J & W/CDC   ☐ PASCAL/Z
■ IDENTIFIER ☐ HP 1000   ■ OMSI   ■ UCSD
☐ CONCEPT

1
SYNTAX

LOG function:

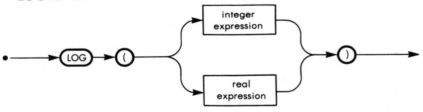

2
DESCRIPTION

The function LOG(X) computes the value of the logarithm of X to the base 10. X can be INTEGER or REAL, but must be strictly positive. The value of LOG(X) is always REAL.

LOG can be defined in standard Pascal, e.g. :

```
FUNCTION LOG (X : REAL) : REAL;
    BEGIN
        LOG = LN(X)/LN(10)
    END;
```

3

IMPLEMENTATION-DEPENDENT FEATURES

3.1 OMSI Implemented as described.

3.2 UCSD Implemented as described.

Note: in the Apple implementation, LOG is part of the TRANSCEND library.

4

EXAMPLE

```
PROGRAM LOGVAL;
(* OMSI UCSD *)
VAR X : REAL;
BEGIN
     WRITELN('TO OBTAIN THE LOGARITHM OF X, TYPE THE VALUE OF X');
     READLN (X);
     WRITELN('THE LOGARITHM OF ',X,'IS : ',LOG(X))
END.
```

LONGREAL

> **The type LONGREAL is a non-standard predefined type, representing fractional numerical data, with a better resolution than the REAL type.**

☐ SYMBOL   ☐ STANDARD   ☐ J & W/CDC   ☐ PASCAL/Z
■ IDENTIFIER   ■ HP 1000   ☐ OMSI   ☐ UCSD
☐ CONCEPT

1
SYNTAX

1.1 Longreal Type

1.2 Longreal Constant

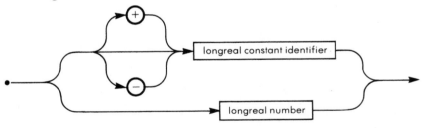

1.3 Longreal Number

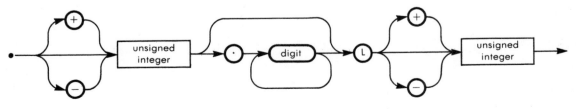

LONGREAL

2
DESCRIPTION

All features of REALS are applicable to LONGREALs. The predefined functions yielding REAL values, when used with LONGREAL parameters, will yield LONGREAL values.

Refer to the REAL heading for further explanation.

3
IMPLEMENTATION-DEPENDENT FEATURES

3.1 HP 1000

3.1.1 Range

either $X = 0$
or $10^{-38} <= |X| <= 10^{38}$

3.1.2 Resolution

16.5 digits

4
EXAMPLE

Longreal constant:

$E = 2.718281828459045L0$

MARK

MARK is a non-standard predefined procedure that allows the programmer to record the extent of the heap at the moment the procedure MARK is executed.

☐ SYMBOL   ☐ STANDARD   ☐ J & W/CDC   ■ PASCAL/Z
■ IDENTIFIER   ■ HP 1000   ☐ OMSI   ■ UCSD
☐ CONCEPT

1
SYNTAX

MARK statement:

2
DESCRIPTION

The procedure MARK has one parameter: a pointer variable. Execution of the statement MARK(P) causes the first free address in the heap to be assigned to P. Subsequent executions of the procedure NEW will build data structures, beginning at the address contained in P.

Execution of the statement RELEASE(P) will restore the heap to the size it was at the moment MARK(P) was executed, effectively destroying all of the data structures built in the meantime.

The value of P may not be changed between the execution of MARK(P) and RELEASE(P).

The type of the dynamic variable towards which P points is irrelevant, since P should only be used with the procedures MARK and RELEASE, and never with NEW.

3
IMPLEMENTATION-DEPENDENT FEATURES

3.1 HP 1000 None known.

3.2 Pascal/Z None known.

3.3 UCSD None known.

4
EXAMPLE

```
PROGRAM LIFOL(INPUT, OUTPUT);
(* REVERSES THE ORDER OF THE CHARACTERS IN A LINE *)
(* HP 1000, PASCAL/Z, UCSD *)
TYPE
      LINK = ↑ELEM;
      ELEM = RECORD
                    NEXT : LINK;
                    CARA : CHAR
             END;
VAR
      FIRST,P,Q : LINK;
BEGIN (* LIFOL *)
      WHILE NOT EOF DO
          BEGIN
              MARK(Q);
              FIRST := NIL;
              WHILE NOT EOLN DO
                  BEGIN
                      NEW(P);
                      READ(P↑.CARA);
                      P↑.NEXT := FIRST;
                      FIRST := P
                  END;
```

```
        READLN;
        P := FIRST;
        WHILE P < > NIL DO
            BEGIN
                WRITE(P↑.CARA);
                P := P↑.NEXT
            END;
        WRITELN;
        RELEASE(Q)
    END
END (* LIFOL *).
```

MAXINT

MAXINT is a predefined integer constant, which defines the range of correct integer arithmetic.

☐ SYMBOL
■ IDENTIFIER
☐ CONCEPT

■ STANDARD
■ HP 1000

■ J & W/CDC
■ OMSI

■ PASCAL/Z
■ UCSD

1
SYNTAX

MAXINT is an integer constant identifier.

2
DESCRIPTION

To ensure exact evaluation of integer expressions, all values to be used during the evaluation of an expression should remain within the interval bounded by $-$MAXINT and $+$MAXINT.

3
IMPLEMENTATION-DEPENDENT FEATURES

3.1 HP 1000 MAXINT $:= 2^{31} - 1 = 2147483647$

3.2 J & W/CDC MAXINT $:= 2^{48} - 1 = 281474976710655$

3.3 OMSI MAXINT $:= 2^{15} - 1 = 32767$

3.4 Pascal/Z MAXINT $:= 2^{15} - 1 = 32767$

3.5 UCSD MAXINT $:= 2^{15} - 1 = 32767$

MAXINT

4
EXAMPLE

```
PROGRAM MAXI(OUTPUT);
BEGIN
      WRITELN ('RANGE FOR CORRECT INTEGER MATH IS: ',MAXINT)
END.
```

MAXPOS

MAXPOS is a non-standard predefined integer function that returns the largest value that can ever be returned by the function POSITION.

☐ SYMBOL ☐ STANDARD ☐ J & W/CDC ☐ PASCAL/Z
■ IDENTIFIER ■ HP 1000 ☐ OMSI   ☐ UCSD
☐ CONCEPT

1
SYNTAX

Factor containing the MAXPOS function:

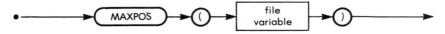

2
DESCRIPTION

The function MAXPOS has one parameter, of type FILE. MAXPOS returns an integer value, which is the value that the function POSITION returns when the file window has reached the physical end of the file. MAXPOS can only be used if the file has been opened by the OPEN statement. When POSITION(F) = MAXPOS(F), execution of any of the functions PUT(F), GET(F), READ(F) or WRITE(F) will result in an error.

3
IMPLEMENTATION-DEPENDENT FEATURES

MAXPOS is only implemented in HP 1000.

4
EXAMPLE

See the program UPDATE SALARY under the READDIR heading.

MEMAVAIL

MEMAVAIL is a non-standard predefined integer function that returns the amount of memory available between the stack and the heap.

1
SYNTAX

MEMAVAIL function:

```
●─────────────────────▶( MEMAVAIL )────────────────────▶
```

2
DESCRIPTION

Two data structures, the stack and the heap, have a variable size during program execution. The stack contains the local variables of all active procedures and functions, while the heap contains all of the dynamic variables created by the procedure NEW. Memory is organized in such a fashion that stack and heap grow towards each other, so that the part of memory between the top of the stack and the top of the heap is available for stack or heap expansions. The function MEMAVAIL returns the number of 16-bit words available between the top of the stack and the top of the heap.

3
IMPLEMENTATION-DEPENDENT FEATURES

MEMAVAIL is only implemented in UCSD Pascal.

MEMAVAIL

4
EXAMPLE

```
PROGRAM MEMUSE(OUTPUT);
(* THIS PROGRAM CHECKS HOW MANY COPIES OF A STRUCTURED VARIABLE CAN
BE MADE IN THE AVAILABLE MEMORY *)
(* UCSD ONLY *)
TYPE
      STRUCT = ARRAY[1..100] OF INTEGER;
VAR
      STRU : STRUCT;
      STRUPTR :  ↑STRUCT;
      NCOPY : INTEGER;
BEGIN
      NCOPY := 0;
      WHILE MEMAVAIL  >= SIZEOF(STRU) DO
         BEGIN
              NEW(STRUPTR);
              NCOPY := NCOPY + 1
         END;
      WRITELN(NCOPY,' COPIES OF STRUCT HELD IN MEMORY.')
END (* MEMUSE *).
```

MESSAGE

> **MESSAGE is a non-standard predefined procedure that causes a string to be written in the system's dayfile.**

☐ SYMBOL	☐ STANDARD	■ J & W/CDC	☐ PASCAL/Z
■ IDENTIFIER	☐ HP 1000	☐ OMSI	☐ UCSD
☐ CONCEPT			

1
SYNTAX

MESSAGE statement:

2
DESCRIPTION

The procedure MESSAGE has one parameter, a string of no more than 40 characters. When MESSAGE is executed, the string is written in the dayfile of the operating system.

3
IMPLEMENTATION-DEPENDENT FEATURES

MESSAGE is only implemented in J & W/CDC Pascal.

MININT

MININT is a non-standard predefined integer constant, equal to the most negative value an integer value can take; it is not related to MAXINT.

☐ SYMBOL   ☐ STANDARD   ☐ J & W/CDC   ☐ PASCAL/Z
■ IDENTIFIER   ■ HP 1000   ☐ OMSI   ☐ UCSD
☐ CONCEPT

1
SYNTAX

MININT is an integer constant identifier.

2
DESCRIPTION

To ensure exact evaluation of integer expressions all values to be used during the evaluation of the expression should remain within the interval bounded by −MAXINT and MAXINT. Integer expressions with values outside the interval may function correctly. MININT is the most negative value that may be used or held in an INTEGER variable.

3
IMPLEMENTATION-DEPENDENT FEATURES

3.1 HP 1000

$$MININT = -2^{31} = -2147483648$$

4
EXAMPLE

```
PROGRAM MINI(OUTPUT);
BEGIN
    WRITELN('MOST NEGATIVE INTEGER IS:',MININT)
END.
```

MOD

The operator MOD is used to compute the remainder of the division of two integer factors.

- ■ SYMBOL
- □ IDENTIFIER
- □ CONCEPT

- ■ STANDARD
- ■ HP 1000

- ■ J & W/CDC
- ■ OMSI

- ■ PASCAL/Z
- ■ UCSD

1
SYNTAX

Refer to the expression heading.

2
DESCRIPTION

When the MOD reserved word appears between integer (or subranges thereof) factors in a term, the values of these factors are first evaluated. Then, the remainder of the division of the left factor by the right factor is computed. This remainder is of type INTEGER. The right factor should be greater than zero in standard Pascal programs.

3
IMPLEMENTATION-DEPENDENT FEATURES

Negative right-hand factors (divisors) produce widely varying results across implementations.

3.1 HP 1000   None known.

3.2 J & W/CDC   None known.

3.3 OMSI   The MOD of a negative value by a value (divisor) which is a power of two produces different results depending on whether the divisor value is a constant or a variable.

3.4 Pascal/Z None known.

3.5 UCSD Long integer factors are not allowed with the MOD operator. There are differences between various UCSD Pascal implementations for negative divisors.

4
EXAMPLE

```
PROGRAM MODTEST(OUTPUT);
CONST I = 5; J = 2;
VAR K,L : INTEGER;
BEGIN
      K := I MOD J;
      L := I DIV J;
      IF I = L * J + K THEN WRITELN('MOD AND DIV WORK AS
                        EXPECTED')
                   ELSE WRITELN('WHAT HAPPENS?')
END.
```

MOVELEFT

MOVELEFT is a non-standard predefined procedure that moves a specified number of bytes, starting with the leftmost data, between specified parts of memory.

□ SYMBOL   □ STANDARD   □ J & W/CDC   □ PASCAL/Z
■ IDENTIFIER   □ HP 1000   □ OMSI   ■ UCSD
□ CONCEPT

1
SYNTAX

MOVELEFT statement:

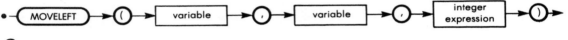

2
DESCRIPTION

MOVELEFT has three parameters. The first parameter, Source, and the second parameter, Destination, are the names of variables of any type, except FILE. The third parameter, Count, is an integer expression:

MOVELEFT(Source, Destination,Count);

MOVELEFT moves the data, one byte at a time, from the address of Source to the memory locations beginning at the address of Destination:

from @Source	to @Destination
from @Source + 1	to @Destination + 1
. . .	
from @Source + LENGTH − 2	to @Destination + LENGTH − 2
from @Source + LENGTH − 1	to @Destination + LENGTH − 1.

MOVELEFT

The notation @X denotes the address of the variable X (or of the first element if X is structured).

Great care is required if the blocks of data corresponding to the Source and Destination of a MOVELEFT overlap. In that case, MOVELEFT should only be used if the address of Destination is smaller than the address of Source.

The procedure MOVERIGHT is provided for the opposite case.

3
IMPLEMENTATION-DEPENDENT FEATURES

MOVELEFT is only implemented in UCSD Pascal.

4
EXAMPLE

```
PROGRAM MOVES(OUTPUT);
VAR
      STR : PACKED ARRAY[1..12] OF CHAR;
      STR := '   GIRLS,BYE';
      MOVELEFT(STR[4], STR[1], 9);
      WRITELN('MOVELEFT : ', STR);
      STR := '   GIRLS,BYE';
      MOVERIGHT(STR[4], STR[1], 9);
      WRITELN('MOVERIGHT : ', STR)
END (* MOVES *).
```

Execution of this program will give the following printout:

```
MOVELEFT : GIRLS,BYEBYE
MOVERIGHT : BYEBYEBYEBYE
```

MOVERIGHT

MOVERIGHT *is a non-standard predefined procedure that moves a specified number of bytes, starting with the rightmost data, between specified parts of memory.*

☐ **SYMBOL**   ☐ **STANDARD**   ☐ **J & W/CDC**   ☐ **PASCAL/Z**
■ **IDENTIFIER**   ☐ **HP 1000**   ☐ **OMSI**   ■ **UCSD**
☐ **CONCEPT**

1
SYNTAX

MOVERIGHT statement:

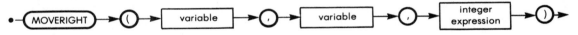

2
DESCRIPTION

MOVERIGHT has three parameters. The first parameter, Source, and the second parameter, Destination, are the names of variables of any type, except FILE, and the third parameter, Count, is an integer expression:

MOVERIGHT(Source,Destination,Count);

MOVERIGHT moves data, one byte at a time, from the address of Source, plus LENGTH, minus one, to the memory locations beginning at the address of Destination, plus LENGTH, minus one. Successive transfers use decreasing addresses:

from @Source + LENGTH − 1	to @Destination + LENGTH − 1
from @Source + LENGTH − 2	to @Destination + LENGTH − 2
. . .	
from @Source + 1	to @Destination + 1
from @Source	to @Destination.

MOVERIGHT

The notation @X denotes the address of the variable X (or of the first element if X is structured).

Great care is required if the parts of memory corresponding to the Source and Destination of a MOVERIGHT overlap. In that case, MOVERIGHT should only be used if the address of Destination is greater than the address of Source.

The procedure MOVELEFT is provided for the opposite case.

3
IMPLEMENTATION-DEPENDENT FEATURES

MOVERIGHT is only implemented in UCSD Pascal.

4
EXAMPLE

```
PROGRAM MOVES(OUTPUT);
VAR
        STR : PACKED ARRAY[1..15] OF CHAR;
BEGIN (* MOVES *)
        STR := 'HELLO,BOY      ';
        MOVERIGHT(STR[1], STR[7], 9);
        WRITELN('MOVERIGHT : ', STR);
        STR := 'HELLO,BOY      ';
        MOVELEFT(STR[1], STR[7], 9);
        WRITELN('MOVELEFT : ', STR)
END (* MOVES *).
```

Execution of this program will give following printout:

```
MOVERIGHT : HELLO,HELLO,BOY
MOVELEFT : HELLO,HELLO,HEL
```

NEW

NEW is a standard procedure that allocates space for a new dynamic variable.

☐ SYMBOL   ■ STANDARD   ■ J & W/CDC   ■ PASCAL/Z
■ IDENTIFIER   ■ HP 1000   ■ OMSI   ■ UCSD
☐ CONCEPT

1
SYNTAX

NEW statement:

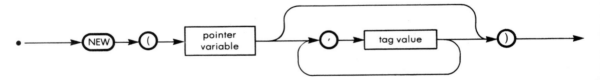

2
DESCRIPTION

The standard procedure NEW(p) allocates space for a new dynamic variable. After execution of NEW(p), the pointer variable p contains the address of the newly-created dynamic variable. If the type of the dynamic variable is a RECORD type with variants, then the values of the tag fields may be communicated to the procedure NEW. The tag values must be listed contiguously and in the order of their declaration. They then cannot be changed during execution.

3

IMPLEMENTATION-DEPENDENT FEATURES

3.1 HP 1000   None known.

3.2 J & W/CDC   None known.

3.3 OMSI   Tag values can be given when NEW is called, but they are ignored. Memory to accommodate the largest possible variant of a record is always reserved when NEW is called.

3.4 Pascal/Z   None known.

3.5 UCSD   None known.

NIL

NIL is a value of all pointer types, which is used when a pointer does not identify a dynamic variable.

■ SYMBOL   ■ STANDARD   ■ J & W/CDC   ■ PASCAL/Z
□ IDENTIFIER ■ HP 1000   ■ OMSI   ■ UCSD
□ CONCEPT

1
SYNTAX

Unsigned constant:

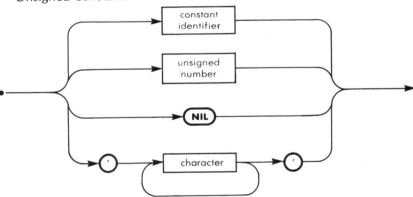

2
DESCRIPTION

When linked lists of dynamic variables are used, the pointer in the last element of the list must have a particular value which indicates that no more elements can be found. This particular value is usually the value NIL.

3
IMPLEMENTATION-DEPENDENT FEATURES

NIL is not a reserved word in UCSD Pascal.

4
EXAMPLE

Refer to the pointer heading.

NOT

The Boolean operator NOT is used to obtain the complement of a Boolean factor.

- ■ SYMBOL
- □ IDENTIFIER
- □ CONCEPT

- ■ STANDARD
- ■ HP 1000

- ■ J & W/CDC
- ■ OMSI

- ■ PASCAL/Z
- ■ UCSD

1
SYNTAX

Refer to the expression heading.

2
DESCRIPTION

The operator NOT followed by a Boolean factor is itself a Boolean factor, the value of which is the complement of the value of the factor following NOT.

When using Boolean expressions, it is important to remember the order of precedence of Boolean operators:

NOT, AND, OR, relational operators.

(For more details, see the expression heading).

3
IMPLEMENTATION-DEPENDENT FEATURES

3.1 HP 1000   None known.

3.2 J & W/CDC   None known.

3.3 OMSI   The operator NOT can be followed by an INTEGER factor. The resulting expression is of type INTEGER, and is the bitwise complement of the original operand.

3.4 Pascal/Z   None known.

3.5 UCSD   None known.

4
EXAMPLE

```
PROGRAM NOTEX(INPUT,OUTPUT);
VAR
      DIGIT : CHAR;
BEGIN
      WRITELN('TYPE A DIGIT PLEASE');
      READLN(DIGIT);
      IF NOT (DIGIT IN[0'..'9]) THEN
            WRITELN('SORRY, YOU DO NOT KNOW WHAT',
                  'A DIGIT IS! ')
END. (* NOTEX *)
```

number

Numbers are used to express constant numerical values.

□ SYMBOL   ■ STANDARD   ■ J & W/CDC   ■ PASCAL/Z
□ IDENTIFIER   ■ HP 1000   ■ OMSI   ■ UCSD
■ CONCEPT

1
SYNTAX

No blanks are permitted within a number.

1.1 Number

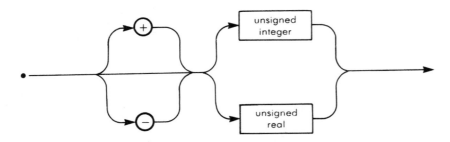

1.2 Unsigned Integer

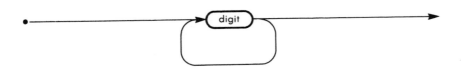

1.3 Unsigned Real

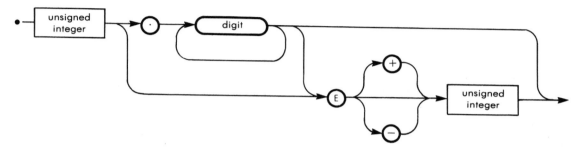

Note: A decimal point must be preceded and followed by at least one digit. Either a fractional part or an exponent must be present.

2
DESCRIPTION

The numeric representations are base ten.

The value of any number has to belong to the interval of possible values associated with its type. (See the headings INTEGER and TYPE.)

The exponent part of a real (which follows the "E") is the power of ten times which the base (the part to the left of the "E") is to be multiplied.

3
IMPLEMENTATION-DEPENDENT FEATURES

3.1 HP 1000 An additional predefined type, LONGREAL, exists.

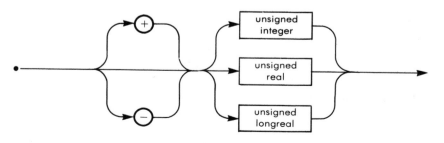

number

Unsigned LONGREAL (HP 1000):

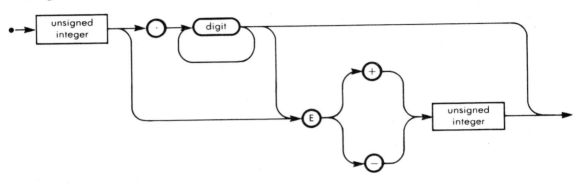

3.2 J & W/CDC   None known.

3.3 OMSI   Integer constants may be written in octal notation by appending the letter B to the number.

Unsigned Integer (OMSI):

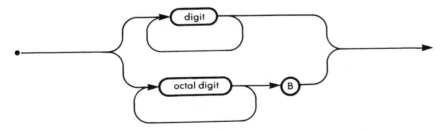

Note: the octal notation is not allowed when the unsigned integer is part of a real number.

3.4 Pascal/Z   None known.

3.5 UCSD   Some UCSD implementations have an additional type, long integer, which can be used to represent numbers with up to 36 digits. Nothing distinguishes the syntax of integer numbers and long integer numbers.

4
EXAMPLE

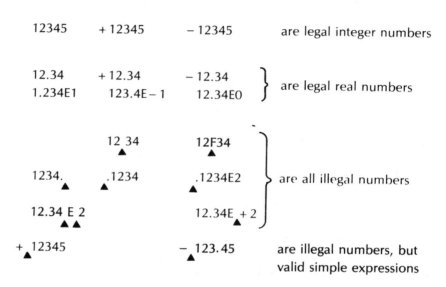

12345	+ 12345	− 12345	are legal integer numbers

12.34	+ 12.34	− 12.34	are legal real numbers
1.234E1	123.4E − 1	12.34E0	

12 34

12F34

1234.

.1234

.1234E2

12.34 E 2

12.34E + 2

are all illegal numbers

+ 12345

− 123.45

are illegal numbers, but valid simple expressions

ODD

ODD is a standard Boolean function that returns the value TRUE when its argument has an integer value which is odd.

☐ SYMBOL   ■ STANDARD   ■ J & W/CDC   ■ PASCAL/Z
■ IDENTIFIER   ■ HP 1000   ■ OMSI   ■ UCSD
☐ CONCEPT

1
SYNTAX

Factor containing the ODD function:

2
DESCRIPTION

The function ODD has one integer parameter. ODD takes the Boolean value TRUE when this parameter has an odd value, and the value FALSE when this parameter is even.

3
IMPLEMENTATION-DEPENDENT FEATURES

None known.

4
EXAMPLE

```
PROGRAM ODDTEST(INPUT,OUTPUT);
VAR N : INTEGER;
BEGIN
      WRITELN('TYPE AN INTEGER NUMBER');
      READLN(N);
      IF ODD(N)
          THEN WRITELN(N,' IS ODD')
          ELSE WRITELN(N,' IS EVEN')
END.
```

Another example can be found under the SQR heading.

OF

> *The reserved word OF is used in various declarations and in the CASE statement.*

■ SYMBOL   ■ STANDARD   ■ J & W/CDC   ■ PASCAL/Z
□ IDENTIFIER   ■ HP 1000   ■ OMSI   ■ UCSD
□ CONCEPT

1
SYNTAX

1.1 Array Type

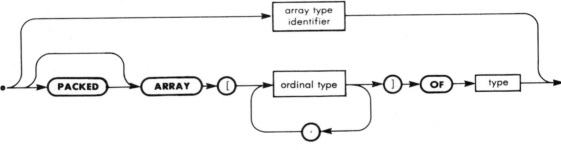

1.2 Set Type

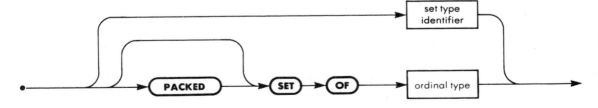

1.3 Field List

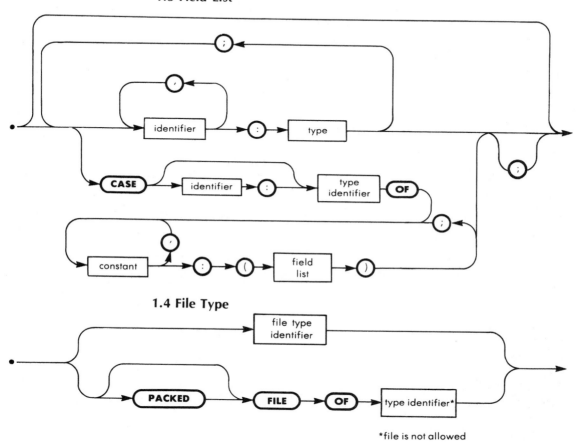

1.4 File Type

*file is not allowed

1.5 Case Statement

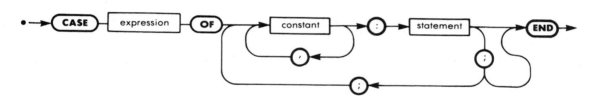

OF

2
DESCRIPTION

Use the words that appear in the syntax diagrams to refer to the relevant headings.

3
IMPLEMENTATION-DEPENDENT FEATURES

3.1 HP 1000 The reserved word OF is also used in the definition of constant arrays.

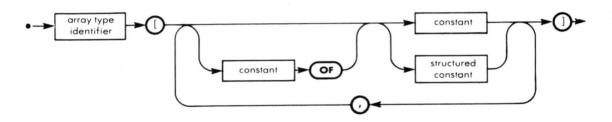

3.2 J & W/CDC None known.

3.3 OMSI None known.

3.4 Pascal/Z None known.

3.5 UCSD None known.

OPEN is a non-standard predefined procedure that opens a file for direct access operations.

□ SYMBOL   □ STANDARD   □ J & W/CDC   □ PASCAL/Z
■ IDENTIFIER   ■ HP 1000   □ OMSI   □ UCSD
□ CONCEPT

1
SYNTAX

OPEN statement (HP 1000):

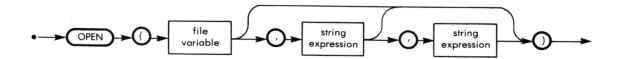

2
DESCRIPTION

The effect of the statement OPEN(F) can be described as follows:

— Subsequent PUT(F) and GET(F) operations are allowed.

— The procedure SEEK(F,L) can be executed.

— The functions MAXPOS(F) and POSITION(F) can be used.

These different procedures and functions allow the programmer to access files in a random rather than a sequential fashion. They cannot be used with text files.

OPEN

The first parameter of the OPEN procedure is the name of the file. The second parameter is a string containing the name of an external file, in the format required by the RTE operating system. The third parameter must be one of the following two strings:

'SHARED':   The external file can be open to several programs simultaneously.

'EXCLUS':   The external file cannot be open to several programs simultaneously.

The second and third parameters of the OPEN procedure provide an alternate method of associating Pascal files with external files. This method is more versatile than the method using program parameters.

3
IMPLEMENTATION-DEPENDENT FEATURES

OPEN is only implemented in HP 1000 Pascal.

4
EXAMPLE

See the program UPDATE SALARY under the READDIR heading.

OR

The Boolean operator OR is used to obtain the logical disjunction of two Boolean terms.

- ■ SYMBOL
- □ IDENTIFIER
- □ CONCEPT

- ■ STANDARD
- ■ HP 1000

- ■ J & W/CDC
- ■ OMSI

- ■ PASCAL/Z
- ■ UCSD

1
SYNTAX

Refer to the expression heading.

2
DESCRIPTION

When the OR operator appears between two Boolean terms, first their values are computed, and then the logical disjunction of their values is computed.

The value of the logical disjunction as a function of the value of its terms is given in the following table.

LEFT TERM \ RIGHT TERM	true	false
true	true	true
false	true	false

OR

When using Boolean expressions, it is important to remember the order of precedence of Boolean operators:

NOT, AND, OR, relational operators.

(For more details, see the expression heading.)

3
IMPLEMENTATION-DEPENDENT FEATURES

3.1 HP 1000 None known.

3.2 J & W/CDC None known.

3.3 OMSI The operator OR can be used with two INTEGER terms. The resulting expression is of type INTEGER, and is equal to the bitwise Boolean union of the operands.

3.4 Pascal/Z None known.

3.5 UCSD None known.

4
EXAMPLE

```
PROGRAM ORTEST(OUTPUT);
VAR I,J,K : INTEGER;
BEGIN
    I := 2; J := 3; K := 4;
    IF (J < I) OR (K < J)
        THEN WRITELN('J OUTSIDE [I,K]')
        ELSE WRITELN('J INSIDE [I,K]')
END.
```

ORD

ORD is a standard integer function that gives the ordinal number of the value of its parameter among all of the values this parameter can take.

1
SYNTAX

Factor containing the ORD function:

2
DESCRIPTION

The function ORD has one ordinal parameter. The returned value is integer, and is equal to the ordinal number of the value of the parameter in the set of values this parameter can take, according to its type.

When the ordinal expression is an integer expression, the value returned is the value of the expression.

3
IMPLEMENTATION-DEPENDENT FEATURES

3.1 HP 1000   None known.

ORD

3.2 J & W/CDC   None known.

3.3 OMSI   None known.

3.4 Pascal/Z   None known.

3.5 UCSD   The function ORD in the APPLE implementation of UCSD Pascal can be used to obtain an integer number equal to the address of a dynamic variable. To obtain this address, the parameter of ORD must be a pointer variable pointing to that dynamic variable.

4
EXAMPLE

```
PROGRAM ORDTEST(INPUT,OUTPUT);
VAR C : CHAR;
BEGIN
      WRITELN('TYPE A CHARACTER');
      READLN(C);
      WRITELN('THE ORDINAL NUMBER OF ',C:1,' IS ',ORD(C):2)
END.
```

Another example can be found under the CHAR heading.

An ordinal type is characterized by a set of values that can be mapped in a unique way on the set of natural numbers.

☐ SYMBOL	■ STANDARD	■ J & W/CDC	■ PASCAL/Z
☐ IDENTIFIER	■ HP 1000	■ OMSI	■ UCSD
■ CONCEPT			

1
SYNTAX

1.1 Ordinal Type

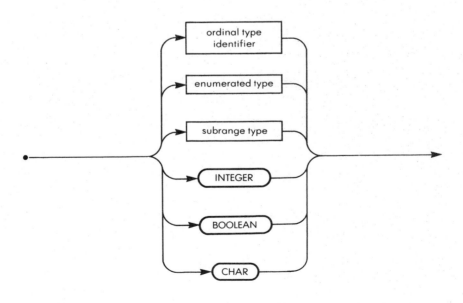

1.2 Enumerated Type

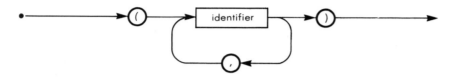

1.3 Subrange Type

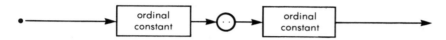

2
DESCRIPTION

2.1 Values   Ordinal types are declared by an enumeration of all of the values that variables and functions of that type can take, or by one of the predefined ordinal types (INTEGER, BOOLEAN and CHAR), or by a subrange specification of an enumerated or predefined ordinal type.

2.2 Operators   Relational operators are the only ones applicable to all ordinal types. The two operands of a relational operator must be of the same type, except for the IN operator, which requires a left operand of ordinal or subrange type, and a right operand of a set type of the same base type.

The relational operators applicable to ordinal operands are:

=	equal to
<>	not equal to
<	less than
>	greater than
<=	less than or equal to
>=	greater than or equal to
IN	member of

For ordinals defined by an enumeration of their values, the first enumerated value is considered the smallest, and the last, the largest.

2.3 Functions   Standard functions applicable to all ordinal types are:

SUCC(X)	which yields the next value in the ordered set of all values that the ordinal expression X can take. If the value of X is the largest possible, then SUCC(X) is undefined.
PRED(X)	which yields the preceding value in the ordered set of all values that the ordinal expression X can take. If the value of X is the smallest possible, then PRED(X) is undefined.
ORD(X)	which yields the ordinal number of the value of the ordinal expression X, in the ordered set of values that X can take. The ordinal number of the smallest possible value is 0, except that the ordinal number of an integer is that integer itself.

3
IMPLEMENTATION-DEPENDENT FEATURES

None known.

4
EXAMPLE

```
PROGRAM WEEKDAYS(OUTPUT);
TYPE DAYS = (MO,TU,WE,TH,FR,SA,SU);
     WEEK = SET OF DAYS;
VAR WORKDAY, HOLIDAY, WEEKDAY : WEEK;
    D : DAYS;
PROCEDURE WRDAY(X : DAYS);
```

```
BEGIN
    CASE X OF
        MO : WRITE('MONDAY ');
        TU : WRITE('TUESDAY ');
        WE : WRITE('WEDNESDAY');
        TH : WRITE('THURSDAY ');
        FR : WRITE('FRIDAY ');
        SA : WRITE('SATURDAY ');
        SU : WRITE('SUNDAY ')
    END
END;
BEGIN
    WORKDAY := [MO..FR];
    HOLIDAY := [SA,SUN];
    WEEKDAY := WORKDAY + HOLIDAY;
    FOR D := MO TO SU DO
        IF D IN WEEKDAY THEN
            BEGIN
                WRDAY(D);
                WRITELN('IS A WEEKDAY')
            END
END.
```

OTHERWISE

The non-standard reserved word OTHERWISE is a part of the CASE statement.

■ SYMBOL   □ STANDARD   □ J & W/CDC   □ PASCAL/Z
□ IDENTIFIER   ■ HP 1000   □ OMSI   □ UCSD
□ CONCEPT

1
SYNTAX

CASE statement (HP 1000):

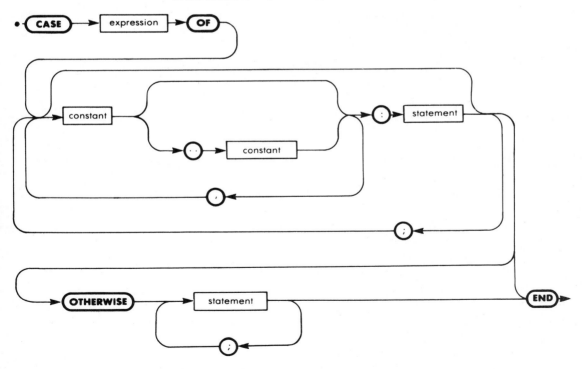

OTHERWISE

2
DESCRIPTION

See the CASE heading.

3
IMPLEMENTATION-DEPENDENT FEATURES

OTHERWISE is only used in HP 1000 Pascal.

OUTPUT

OUTPUT is a predeclared file of type TEXT. It is generally associated with an output device such as a CRT or a printer.

☐ SYMBOL   ■ STANDARD   ■ J & W/CDC   ■ PASCAL/Z
■ IDENTIFIER ■ HP 1000   ■ OMSI   ■ UCSD
☐ CONCEPT

1
SYNTAX

The TEXT file OUTPUT does not need to be declared, but may appear in the list of program parameters.

PAGE(OUTPUT):   causes subsequent text written to OUTPUT to be on a new page (assuming a suitable output device).

2
DESCRIPTION

2.1 Standard Procedures   The following standard procedures can be applied to the file OUTPUT:

PUT(OUTPUT):   transfers the value of the buffer variable OUTPUT↑ to the file OUTPUT.

WRITE(OUTPUT,X):   assigns successive characters of the textual representation of the value of the variable X to OUTPUT↑ and appends the value of OUTPUT↑ to the file OUTPUT.

WRITELN(OUTPUT):   appends an end of line to the file OUTPUT.

OUTPUT

2.2 Remarks

1. The file name can be omitted when using the procedures PAGE, WRITE, and WRITELN with the file OUTPUT.

2. A statement REWRITE(OUTPUT) is implicitly executed at the beginning of a program containing the file name OUTPUT in the program heading.

3. Alternate forms exist for the procedures WRITE and WRITELN; consult the appropriate headings.

4. The procedure RESET may not be applied to the file OUTPUT.

3
IMPLEMENTATION-DEPENDENT FEATURES

Some implementations require OUTPUT in the program parameters to allow run time error reporting.

3.1 HP 1000   None known.

3.2 J & W/CDC   The first character of a line is never printed by a line printer, but is used to control the movement of paper. The meaning of the first character in such systems is generally as follows:

+	no line feed before printing
blank	feed one line space before printing
0	feed two line spaces before printing
1	skip to the top of the next page before printing

It is the responsibility of Pascal programmers to generate OUTPUT files that are compatible with these conventions.

3.3 OMSI   The default file is always present, and is un-named (i.e., not called OUTPUT).

3.4 Pascal/Z   None known.

3.5 UCSD   OUTPUT is of the type INTERACTIVE rather than TEXT. The default file is always present, regardless of program heading.

OUTPUT

4
EXAMPLE

```
PROGRAM DEMO(OUTPUT);
(* OUTPUT DEMO *)
BEGIN
      WRITELN(OUTPUT,'THIS LINE GOES TO THE FILE "OUTPUT"');
      WRITELN('SO DOES THIS LINE')
END.
```

OVERPRINT

OVERPRINT is a non-standard predefined procedure that terminates a line on an output device without causing a line feed.

☐ SYMBOL   ☐ STANDARD   ☐ J & W/CDC   ☐ PASCAL/Z
■ IDENTIFIER   ■ HP 1000   ☐ OMSI   ☐ UCSD
☐ CONCEPT

1
SYNTAX

The syntax of the OVERPRINT procedure is identical to that used for the WRITELN statement (HP 1000).

2
DESCRIPTION

The statement OVERPRINT(F) is equivalent to the HP 1000 implementation of the statement WRITELN(F), except that no line feed is sent to the device associated with the file F. OVERPRINT is used to underline text, and to create special graphic effects on listings.

3
IMPLEMENTATION-DEPENDENT FEATURES

OVERPRINT is only implemented in HP 1000 Pascal.

OVERPRINT

4
EXAMPLE

```
PROGRAM UNDERLINE(OUTPUT);
(* HP 1000 *)
BEGIN
    OVERPRINT('KEY WORDS ARE UNDERLINED');
    WRITELN('                        _____);
END.
```

PACK

PACK is a standard procedure that transfers data from an ordinary array to a packed array.

☐ **SYMBOL**   ■ **STANDARD**   ■ **J & W/CDC**   ☐ **PASCAL/Z**
■ **IDENTIFIER**   ■ **HP 1000**   ☐ **OMSI**   ☐ **UCSD**
☐ **CONCEPT**

1
SYNTAX

PACK statement:

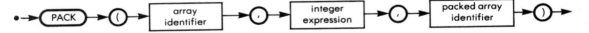

2
DESCRIPTION

If the arrays A and B are declared as follows:

A : **ARRAY**[M..N] **OF** T
B : **PACKED ARRAY**[U..V] **OF** T

with $N - M >= V - U$, then the statement

PACK(A,K,B)

is equivalent to:

FOR I := U **TO** V **DO** B[I] := A[I − U + K]

The integer expression K gives the value of the index of the first element in A to be packed.

3
IMPLEMENTATION-DEPENDENT FEATURES

3.1 HP 1000   None known.

3.2 J & W/CDC   None known.

3.3 OMSI   Not implemented.

3.4 Pascal/Z   Not implemented.

3.5 UCSD   Not implemented.

PACKED

The word PACKED is used in the definition of structured types, to tell the compiler that it should use a compact representation for the data.

- ■ SYMBOL
- □ IDENTIFIER
- □ CONCEPT

- ■ STANDARD
- ■ HP 1000

- ■ J & W/CDC
- ■ OMSI

- ■ PASCAL/Z
- ■ UCSD

1
SYNTAX

See the headings corresponding to the different structured types. (ARRAY, RECORD, SET, and FILE).

2
DESCRIPTION

Ordinarily, the compiler will put each item of a structured type in a different word of the computer's memory. This allows fast access to all data, but can be a waste of central memory space. (A Boolean stored in a 60-bit word is an extreme example.)

The use of the PACKED designation in the definition of a structured type requests the compiler to store data in a compact way. This may eventually result in significantly increased execution time.

When structured types contain other structured types, the word PACKED should be applied to all the structures to have the most effect.

3
IMPLEMENTATION-DEPENDENT FEATURES

3.1 HP 1000   None known.

3.2 J & W/CDC   Fields of a record are packed to a bit level.

PACKED

3.3 OMSI   The symbol PACKED may appear in declarations, but has no effect. Most objects use a compact representation anyway.

3.4 Pascal/Z   The symbol PACKED may appear in declarations, but has no effect.

3.5 UCSD   Each structured type is packed to a word boundary. Non-structured components of a record or array are packed to a bit level. The last element of a packed record will be byte-aligned if there is no additional space required.

4

EXAMPLE

```
TYPE ALLPAGE = PACKED ARRAY[1..80,1..24] OF CHAR;
     TBOOK = FILE OF ARRAY[1..80,1..24] OF CHAR;
     PBOOK = FILE OF PACKED ARRAY[1..80,1..24] OF CHAR;
     BOOK = FILE OF ALLPAGE;
```

The type ALLPAGE is packed. The elements of PBOOK and BOOK are packed. The elements of TBOOK are not packed.

PAGE

PAGE is a standard procedure that causes the print device associated with a text file to skip to the top of the next page, or a display device to be cleared with cursor moved to the home position.

☐ SYMBOL   ■ STANDARD   ■ J & W/CDC   ■ PASCAL/Z
■ IDENTIFIER ■ HP 1000   ■ OMSI   ■ UCSD
☐ CONCEPT

1
SYNTAX

PAGE statement:

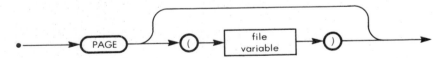

2
DESCRIPTION

The procedure PAGE(F) is used to position the printposition logically associated with the text file F at the top of the next page. If no end of line was written on F by a WRITELN procedure prior to the execution of PAGE, PAGE will write an end of line before performing the skip operation. When the file name is not specified, OUTPUT is implied.

3
IMPLEMENTATION-DEPENDENT FEATURES

None known.

parameter

Parameters are used to transfer information between procedures or functions and the block in which these procedures or functions are referenced.

☐ SYMBOL   ■ STANDARD   ■ J & W/CDC   ■ PASCAL/Z

☐ IDENTIFIER   ■ HP 1000   ■ OMSI   ■ UCSD

■ CONCEPT

1
SYNTAX

Refer to the PROCEDURE or FUNCTION headings.

2
DESCRIPTION

Refer to the PROCEDURE or FUNCTION headings.

pointer

A pointer is a variable used to access dynamic variables.

☐ SYMBOL   ■ STANDARD   ■ J & W/CDC   ■ PASCAL/Z
☐ IDENTIFIER   ■ HP 1000   ■ OMSI   ■ UCSD
■ CONCEPT

1
SYNTAX

1.1 Pointer Type

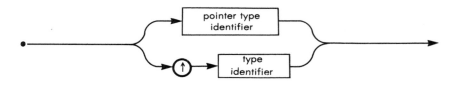

1.2 Variable Referenced Through a Pointer

The pointer identifier is a variable identifier or a field identifier of a pointer type.

2

DESCRIPTION

Pascal allows the use of dynamic variables that are created by the procedure NEW during program execution. These dynamic variables cannot be directly referenced through their identifier, since they do not have any; rather, they are referenced indirectly through a pointer variable. This pointer variable has a value that represents the address of the dynamic variable. A pointer variable can have one particular value, NIL, which means that the pointer does not represent any address.

The assignment of new values to a pointer, without saving the old values, can cause dynamic values to become inaccessible. Since most Pascal implementations do not have provisions for "garbage collection," the memory space used by inaccessible variables is wasted. A standard procedure DISPOSE allows the programmer to inform the memory-management routines of dynamic variables that are no longer used.

Record structures containing pointers which point to the record type can be declared as dynamic variables. This allows construction of finite linked data structures, such as trees. These declarations may pose a syntactical problem, however, since either the pointer definition or the record definition must contain a type identifier not yet defined. This is allowed within a single type definition.

3

IMPLEMENTATION-DEPENDENT FEATURES

3.1 HP 1000   Two additional procedures, MARK and RELEASE, are provided for the management of memory used by dynamic variables (heap). Refer to the MARK and RELEASE headings for more information.

3.2 J & W/CDC   None known.

3.3 OMSI   None known.

3.4 Pascal/Z   The procedure DISPOSE does not exist, but the procedures MARK and RELEASE can be used to manage the memory used

pointer

by dynamic variables (heap). Refer to the MARK and RELEASE headings for more information.

3.5 UCSD   The procedure DISPOSE does not exist, but the procedures MARK and RELEASE can be used to manage the memory used by dynamic variables (heap). Refer to the MARK and RELEASE headings for more information.

4
EXAMPLES

4.1 Program Illustrating Use of Pointers to Reverse Lines in a File

```
PROGRAM LIFO(INPUT,OUTPUT);
(* REVERSES THE ORDER OF LINES OF A FILE *)
CONST
      MAX = 20;
TYPE
      STRINGT = ARRAY [1..MAX] OF CHAR;
      LINK = ↑ID;
      ID = RECORD
                  NEXT : LINK;
                  NAME : STRINGT
            END;
VAR
      FIRST, P : LINK;
      I : 1.. MAX;
PROCEDURE READSTR(VAR STRNG : STRINGT);
      VAR
            I : 1..MAX;
      BEGIN
            FOR I := 1 TO MAX DO
                  STRNG[I] := ' ';
            I := 1;
            WHILE NOT EOLN DO
```

```
            BEGIN
                    READ(STRNG[I]);
                    I := I + 1
            END;
        READLN
    END (* READSTR *);
BEGIN (* LIFO *)
    FIRST := NIL;
    WHILE NOT EOF DO
        BEGIN
            NEW(P);
            READSTR(P↑.NAME);
            P↑.NEXT := FIRST;
            FIRST := P
        END
    P := FIRST;
    WHILE P <> NIL DO
        BEGIN
            FOR I := 1 TO MAX DO
                WRITE(P↑.NAME[I]);
            WRITELN;
            P := P↑.NEXT
        END
END (* LIFO *).
```

4.2 Program Illustrating Use of Pointers to Delete Names in a File

```
PROGRAM DELNAME(INPUT,OUTPUT,NAMES);
(* READS A FILE CONTAINING NAMES, READS FROM INPUT ONE NAME,
SEARCHES FOR THE NAME AMONG THE NAMES FROM THE FILE, AND
DELETES THE NAME IF FOUND, AND REWRITES THE REMAINING NAMES ON
THE FILE *)
CONST
    MAX = 20;
```

pointer

```
TYPE
    STRINGT = ARRAY [1..MAX] OF CHAR;
    LINKT = ↑DATAT;
    DATAT = RECORD
                    PREC : LINKT;
                    NEXT : LINKT;
                    NAME : STRINGT
            END;
VAR
    XNAME : STRINGT;
    NAMES : TEXT;
    FIRST,LAST,P : LINKT;
    I : 1..MAX;

PROCEDURE READSTR(VAR F : TEXT; VAR STRING : STRINGT);
    VAR
        I : 1..MAX;
    BEGIN
        FOR I := 1 TO MAX DO
            STRING[I] := ' ';
        I := 1;
        WHILE NOT EOLN(F) AND (I < MAX) DO
            BEGIN
                READ(F,STRING[I]);
                I := I + 1
            END;
        READLN(F)
    END (* READSTR *);
PROCEDURE READFILE(VAR F : TEXT);
(* READS F AND STORES THE NAMES FROM IT AS A SINGLE-LINKED LIST *)
BEGIN
    RESET(F);
    LAST := NIL;
    WHILE NOT EOF(F) DO
```

```
            BEGIN
                READSTR(F, P↑.NAME);
                P↑.PREC := LAST;
                LAST := P
            END
END (* READFILE *);
PROCEDURE WRITEFILE(VAR F : TEXT);
(* REWRITES THE NAMES ON THE ORIGINAL FILE *)
BEGIN
    REWRITE(F);
    P := FIRST;
    WHILE P < > NIL DO
        BEGIN
            FOR I := 1 TO MAX DO
            WRITE(F, P↑.NAME[I]);
            WRITELN(F);
            P := P↑.NEXT
        END
END (* WRITEFILE *);


PROCEDURE BACKLINK;
(* ADDS BACKWARD LINKS IN THE LINKED LIST CREATED BY READFILE *)
BEGIN
    P := LAST;
    FIRST := NIL;
    WHILE P <> NIL DO
        BEGIN
            P .NEXT := FIRST;
            FIRST := P;
            P := P .PREC
        END
END (* BACKLINK *);
```

pointer

```
PROCEDURE DELETE(XNAME : STRINGT);
(* REMOVES THE RECORD CONTAINING XNAME FROM THE DOUBLE-LINKED LIST *)
VAR
    I : 1..MAX;
FUNCTION DIFF(A,B : STRINGT) : BOOLEAN;
    VAR
        I : 1..MAX;
    BEGIN
        DIFF := FALSE;
        FOR I := 1 TO MAX DO
            IF A[I] < > B[I] THEN
                DIFF := TRUE
    END (* DIFF *);

BEGIN (* DELETE *)
    P := FIRST;
    WHILE DIFF(P↑.NAME,XNAME) AND (P↑.NEXT < > NIL) DO
        P := P↑.NEXT;
    IF DIFF(P↑.NAME,XNAME)
    THEN
        BEGIN
            FOR I := 1 TO MAX DO
                WRITE(XNAME[I]);
            WRITELN(' NOT FOUND ')
        END
    ELSE
        BEGIN
            IF (P↑.PREC < > NIL) AND (P↑.NEXT < > NIL)
            THEN
                BEGIN
                    P↑.PREC↑.NEXT := P↑.NEXT;
                    P↑.NEXT↑.PREC := P↑.PREC
                END
```

```
            ELSE
                IF P↑.PREC = NIL
                THEN
                    BEGIN
                        FIRST := P↑.NEXT;
                        P↑.NEXT↑.PREC := NIL
                    END
                ELSE
                    BEGIN
                        LAST := P↑.PREC;
                        P↑.PREC↑.NEXT := NIL
                    END;
            DISPOSE(P)
        END
END (* DELETE *);
BEGIN (* DELNAME *)
    READFILE(NAMES);
    BACKLINK;
    READSTR(INPUT,XNAME);
    DELETE(XNAME);
    WRITEFILE(NAMES)
END (* DELNAME *).
```

POS

POS is a non-standard predefined function that returns the position of the first occurrence of a given string in another string.

☐ SYMBOL　　　　☐ STANDARD　　　☐ J & W/CDC　　　☐ PASCAL/Z
■ IDENTIFIER　　☐ HP 1000　　　　☐ OMSI　　　　　■ UCSD
☐ CONCEPT

1
SYNTAX

Factor containing the POS function:

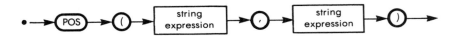

2
DESCRIPTION

The function POS has two parameters, both of type STRING. The first is called Pattern, and the second Source:

POS(Pattern,Source);

The string Source is usually much longer than the string Pattern. POS scans Source to find the first occurrence of Pattern in Source. The returned value is of type INTEGER, and is equal to the sequence number in Source of the first character of the matching pattern. If Pattern is not found, then the returned value is zero.

3
IMPLEMENTATION-DEPENDENT FEATURES

POS is only implemented as a predefined function in UCSD Pascal.

4
EXAMPLE

```
PROGRAM STRING3;
(* UCSD ONLY *)
VAR ST : STRING;
BEGIN
     ST := 'ONE,TWO,THREE';
     DELETE(ST,POS( 'TW',ST),4);
     IF ST =  'ONE,THREE'
          THEN WRITELN('''',ST,'''',OK !')
          ELSE WRITELN('''',ST,'''',STRANGE !')
END.
```

POSITION

POSITION is a non-standard predefined integer function that returns the actual position of a file window.

☐ SYMBOL   ☐ STANDARD   ☐ J & W/CDC   ☐ PASCAL/Z
■ IDENTIFIER   ■ HP 1000   ☐ OMSI   ☐ UCSD
☐ CONCEPT

1
SYNTAX

Factor containing the POSITION function (HP 1000):

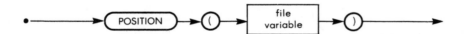

2
DESCRIPTION

The function POSITION has one parameter, of type FILE. POSITION returns an integer value, which is the number of the component that is currently under the file window. POSITION can only be used if the file has been opened by the OPEN statement. After execution of the SEEK(F,I) procedure, the value returned by the function POSITION(F) is equal to I.

3
IMPLEMENTATION-DEPENDENT FEATURES

POSITION is only implemented in HP 1000.

PRED

PRED *is a standard ordinal function that returns the value preceding a given value in the set of all values an ordinal type can take.*

☐ SYMBOL   ■ STANDARD   ■ J & W/CDC   ■ PASCAL/Z

■ IDENTIFIER   ■ HP 1000   ■ OMSI   ■ UCSD

☐ CONCEPT

1
SYNTAX

Factor containing the function PRED:

2
DESCRIPTION

The function PRED has one ordinal parameter. The returned value is of the same ordinal type, and is equal to the value preceding the value of the parameter in the set of values that ordinal type can take. The predecessor of the first defined value is undefined.

3
IMPLEMENTATION-DEPENDENT FEATURES

None known.

4
EXAMPLE

```
PROGRAM PREDTEST(INPUT,OUTPUT);
VAR C : CHAR;
BEGIN
     WRITELN('TYPE A CHARACTER');
     READLN(C);
     WRITELN('THE CHARACTER PRECEDING ',C:1,' IS ',PRED(C))
END.
```

A **PROCEDURE** *is a group of statements with a name that executes a specific task or algorithm. No value is associated with the procedure's name. A **PROCEDURE** is the part of a program defined by a **PROCEDURE** declaration.*

■ SYMBOL
□ IDENTIFIER
■ CONCEPT

■ STANDARD
■ HP 1000

■ J & W/CDC
■ OMSI

■ PASCAL/Z
■ UCSD

1
SYNTAX

1.1 Procedure Declaration

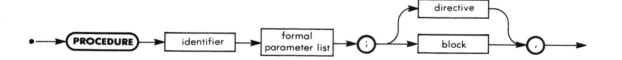

1.2 Formal Parameter List

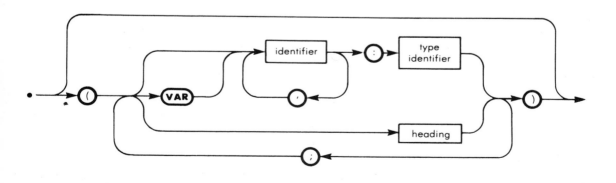

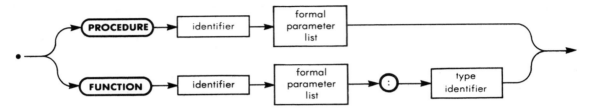

PROCEDURE

1.3 Heading

1.4 Directive

1.5 Procedure Statement

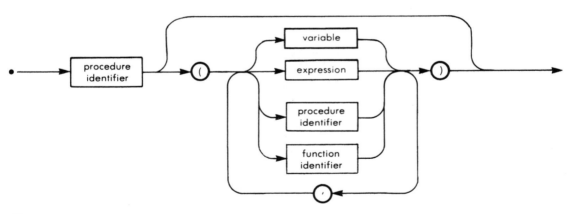

2
DESCRIPTION

Procedures are used to avoid repetition of identical pieces of code, and to enhance the clarity of a program by encouraging modularity.

2.1 Scope of Identifiers   The identifiers declared in the parameter list and in the declaration part of the block following the procedure heading are valid only inside that block. These identifiers are local to the procedure.

A procedure declaration is itself part of a block. Identifiers defined in this outer block are also meaningful inside the procedure. These identifiers are global to the procedure.

If a local identifier is identical to a global identifier, then the local declaration prevails, in accordance with the Pascal rules of scope.

2.2 Procedure Activation   A procedure is activated (its statements are executed) by a procedure statement. When the procedure has completed execution, the statement following the procedure activation (call) is executed.

In many implementations, memory for local variables is made available upon activation and released upon completion of activation.

2.3 Parameters   Data can be exchanged between a procedure and the block in which that procedure is activated by means of global variables or parameters to the procedure.

A list of formal parameters which are local to the procedure can be declared in the procedure heading. A list of corresponding actual parameters must be supplied in the procedure statement if formal parameters were supplied. The actual parameters are to be substituted for the formal parameter when the procedure is activated. The correspondence between actual and formal parameters is established by the positioning of the parameter in both lists.

Four different kinds of parameters exist: value, variable, function and procedure.

2.3.1 Value Parameters   Formal value parameters are variables local to the procedure. When the procedure is activated, the values of the actual parameters are evaluated and assigned to the corresponding parameters. *Note:* the value of actual parameters cannot be affected by any assignment made to the formal parameters.

Although value parameters minimize interaction between different modules of a program, and are most efficiently accessed in a procedure,

PROCEDURE

structured value parameters may waste memory space (actual and formal parameters occupy distinct places in memory) and processor time (each time that a procedure is activated, all of the value parameters have to be assigned, i.e., copied to the formal parameters) in some implementations.

Variables of type FILE cannot be passed as value parameters.

2.3.2 Variable Parameters Each list of formal variable parameters in the procedure heading is preceded by the word VAR.

The substitution mechanism used for variable parameters is such that any reference to a formal parameter is replaced by a reference to the actual parameter. Therefore, all actual parameters must be variables (constants and expressions are not allowed as actual parameters).

The value of actual parameters is affected by assignments made to the formal parameters.

Components of packed structures cannot be used as actual variable parameters.

2.3.3 Function and Procedure Parameters Formal function and procedure parameters have the same syntax as function and procedure headings. The variable identifiers that appear inside formal function and procedure parameters are meaningless, and their scope is limited to the heading in which they are used. Whenever a formal function or procedure parameter is referenced, the corresponding actual parameter is activated. Procedures and functions that are used as parameters to other procedures or functions can only have value parameters, and must have been declared in the program block.

2.4 Recursion Inside a procedure, a procedure statement can be used to reference that same procedure. This is called a recursive activation of a procedure, and is allowed in Pascal.

Another form of recursive activation occurs when procedure A contains a reference to a function or procedure B, which itself contains a reference to the procedure A. This form of a recursion is also allowed, but causes a syntactic problem: a procedure or function will be referenced before it is declared. This difficulty is solved by using the FORWARD declaration, which allows the programmer to announce in advance that a procedure or function will be declared.

2.5 Conformant Array   The concept of conformant array has been proposed in the draft of the ISO standard. Since this extension has not been approved, and is implemented in none of the described versions, a description of conformant arrays has not been included in this handbook.

3

IMPLEMENTATION-DEPENDENT FEATURES

3.1 HP 1000   An additional directive, EXTERNAL, is provided.

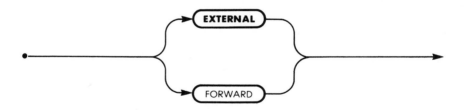

The EXTERNAL directive is used to include procedures written in other languages in a Pascal program. Refer to the EXTERNAL heading for more information.

Only the first five characters of a procedure or function identifier are significant due to limitations in the present versions of the RTE operating system and the relocating loader.

3.2 J & W/CDC

3.2.1 Syntax   The syntax of the parameter list is different in the declaration of procedure and function parameters.

PROCEDURE

Procedure and Function declaration (J & W/CDC):

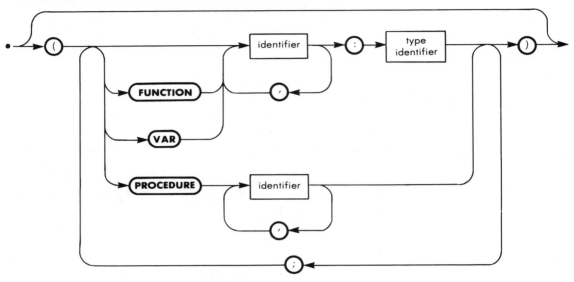

Predefined procedures and functions are not permitted as parameters.

3.2.2 Directives Two additional directives, EXTERN and FORTRAN, are provided.

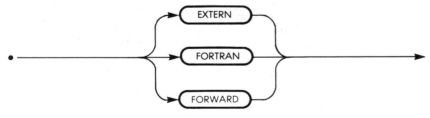

The EXTERN and FORTRAN directives are used to include procedures written in other languages in a Pascal program.

3.3 OMSI

3.3.1 Syntax The syntax of the formal parameter list is as described in paragraph 3.2.1 in this section.

Predefined procedures and functions are not permitted as parameters.

3.3.2 Directives Two additional directives, EXTERNAL and FORTRAN, are provided.

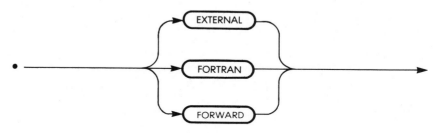

They are used to include procedures written in other languages in a Pascal program.

3.4 Pascal/Z

3.4.1 Procedural Parameters Functions and procedures cannot be passed as parameters to a procedure. The syntax of the formal parameter list reflects this limitation.

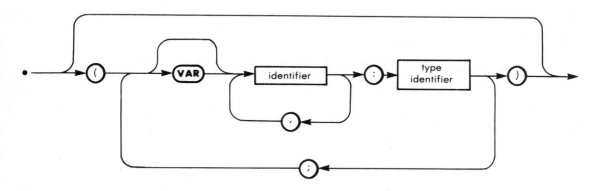

3.4.2 Directives An additional directive, EXTERNAL, is provided. It is similar to the directive described in paragraph 3.1 of this heading.

PROCEDURE

3.5 UCSD

3.5.1 Procedural Parameters Functions and procedures cannot be passed as parameters to a procedure. See paragraph 3.4.1 of this heading for the syntax of the formal parameter list.

3.5.2 String Parameters The predefined identifier STRING may not be used in the formal parameter list. If such parameters are necessary, a particular string type should be defined at an outer level, and that type should be used for actual as well as formal parameters.

3.5.3 Directives An additional directive, EXTERNAL, is provided. It is similar to the directive described in paragraph 3.1 of this heading.

4
EXAMPLES

4.1 Program Illustrating the Difference Between Value and Variable Parameters

```
PROGRAM VALVAR(OUTPUT);
(* PROGRAM TO ILLUSTRATE THE DIFFERENCE BETWEEN A VALUE
PARAMETER AND A VARIABLE PARAMETER. *)
VAR X,Y : INTEGER;
PROCEDURE ZERO(VALUE : INTEGER; VAR VARIABLE : INTEGER);
    BEGIN
        VALUE := 0;
        VARIABLE := 0
    END;
PROCEDURE PRINT(A,B : INTEGER);
    BEGIN
        WRITELN('THE VAL PARAMETER = ',A:10);
        WRITELN('THE VAR PARAMETER = ',B:10)
    END;
```

BEGIN

    X := 1;

    Y := 1;

    PRINT(X,Y);

    ZERO(X,Y);

    WRITELN('ZERO HAS BEEN EXECUTED');

    PRINT(X,Y)

END.

4.2 Program Illustrating the Function and Procedure Parameters See program HYPTAB under the FUNCTION heading.

4.3 Program Illustrating Recursion See the recursion heading.

4.4 Program Illustrating the Use of the Forward Declaration See the FORWARD heading.

PROGRAM

A PROGRAM is a self-contained description of the steps to be performed by a computer to accomplish a specific task.

- ■ SYMBOL
- □ IDENTIFIER
- ■ CONCEPT
- ■ STANDARD
- ■ HP 1000
- ■ J & W/CDC
- ■ OMSI
- ■ PASCAL/Z
- ■ UCSD

1
SYNTAX

Program:

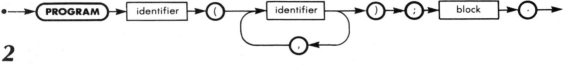

2
DESCRIPTION

The identifier following the reserved word PROGRAM is the name of the program. Although this identifier has no meaning inside the program, it may not be used as an identifier within the program. It can, however, be used by the operating system to identify the program. Some operating systems impose special restrictions on the identifiers they have to manipulate.

The identifiers following the program name are formal parameters that allow communication between the operating system and the program. The substitution of the formal parameters by the actual parameters is done at the moment that the program is started by the operating system. These actual parameters are usually external file names.

3

IMPLEMENTATION-DEPENDENT FEATURES

3.1 HP 1000 None known.

3.2 J & W/CDC When an actual parameter is omitted in the command used to start a program, the external file name is equal to the Pascal file name found in the program heading as a formal parameter.

3.3 OMSI Program parameters are allowed, but are meaningless and ignored by the compiler.

PROGRAM

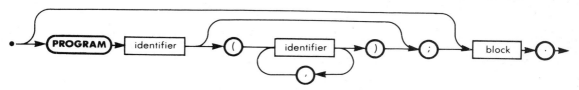

3.4 Pascal/Z   None known.

3.5 UCSD   Although program parameters are allowed in the program heading, they are meaningless and are ignored by the compiler.

Units may be included in line. Refer to the UNIT and USES headings for their syntax and description. If an identifier in a subsequent uses clause is the same as the identifier following UNIT in an in-line unit, the information from the in-line interface section will be used instead of the interface section from the library. The code from the compilation of the implementation section of the unit will accompany the compiled code from the block of the program in the object module produced, and will be used when linking is performed instead of the code from a similarly named unit in the library. Thus, corrections to a UNIT's interface or implementation sections can be made and tested without changing the library version of the unit.

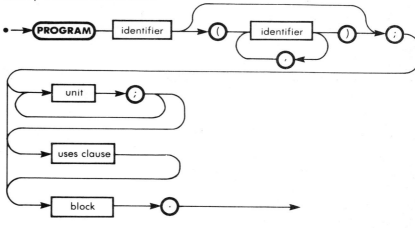

4
EXAMPLE

Examples can be found under almost all headings.

PROMPT

PROMPT is a non-standard predefined procedure similar to WRITELN that terminates a line on an output device without causing a carriage return or a line feed.

☐ SYMBOL   ☐ STANDARD   ☐ J & W/CDC   ☐ PASCAL/Z
■ IDENTIFIER   ■ HP 1000   ☐ OMSI   ☐ UCSD
☐ CONCEPT

1
SYNTAX

The syntax of the PROMPT procedure is identical to that used for the WRITELN statement (HP 1000).

2
DESCRIPTION

The statement PROMPT(F) is equivalent to the HP 1000 implementation of the statement WRITELN(F), except that no carriage returns or line feeds are sent to the device associated with the file F. PROMPT is used rather than WRITELN when a dialogue between an operator and a program is implemented.

3
IMPLEMENTATION-DEPENDENT FEATURES

PROMPT is only implemented in HP 1000 Pascal.

4
EXAMPLE

```
PROGRAM HPSQRVAL(INPUT,OUTPUT);
(* HP 1000 *)
VAR X : INTEGER;
BEGIN
      PROMPT('TYPE AN INTEGER NUMBER :');
      READLN(X);
      WRITELN('THE SQUARE OF ',X,' IS ',SQR(X))
END.
```

PUT

PUT is a standard procedure that appends the contents of a buffer variable to its file.

☐ SYMBOL   ■ STANDARD   ■ J & W/CDC   ☐ PASCAL/Z

■ IDENTIFIER   ■ HP 1000   ■ OMSI   ■ UCSD

☐ CONCEPT

1
SYNTAX

PUT statement:

2
DESCRIPTION

The effect of the statement PUT(F) can be described as follows (provided that, prior to its execution, the function EOF(F) was TRUE):

— The value of the buffer variable F↑ is appended to the file F.

— The value of the buffer variable becomes undefined.

— The value of the function EOF(F) remains TRUE.

Before the first PUT(F) statement is executed, the file must have been opened by a REWRITE(F) statement. No RESET(F), GET(F), READ(F) statements may be executed between the execution of the REWRITE(F) and PUT(F) operations.

3

IMPLEMENTATION-DEPENDENT FEATURES

3.1 HP 1000   Before the first PUT(F) statement can be executed, the file F must have been opened by one of the following statements:

> REWRITE(F)
>
> APPEND(F)
>
> OPEN(F)

If the file was opened by REWRITE or APPEND, the PUT procedure behaves as described in the standard. If the file was opened by OPEN, it is no longer required that EOF(F) should be TRUE before a PUT(F) operation is performed. PUT simply overwrites single components of F.

   Under these conditions, READ, WRITE, PUT and GET operations on the same file can be intermixed, and the file window can be arbitrarily moved by the SEEK procedure.

3.2 J & W/CDC   None known.

3.3 OMSI   If adequate parameters have been used when the file was opened by the RESET and REWRITE procedures, then PUT and GET operations on the same file can be intermixed, and the file window can be positioned arbitrarily by the SEEK procedure. It is not required that EOF(F) should be TRUE before a PUT(F) operation is performed. PUT simply overwrites single components on F.

3.4 Pascal/Z   The procedure PUT is not available. WRITE and WRITELN should be used instead.

3.5 UCSD   The PUT(F) statement is valid only if F is a typed file. (See the FILE heading for the particularities of UCSD files.) PUT and GET operations on the same file can be intermixed, and the file window can be positioned arbitrarily by the SEEK procedure. It is not required that EOF(F) should be TRUE before a PUT(F) operation is performed. PUT simply overwrites single components on F.

PUT

4
EXAMPLE

See the program MERGEAB under the FILE heading.

PWROFTEN

PWROFTEN is a non-standard predefined REAL function that returns the value of integer powers of ten.

☐ SYMBOL   ☐ STANDARD   ☐ J & W/CDC   ☐ PASCAL/Z
■ IDENTIFIER   ☐ HP 1000   ☐ OMSI   ■ UCSD
☐ CONCEPT

1
SYNTAX

PWROFTEN function:

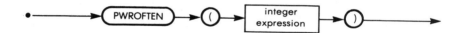

2
DESCRIPTION

The function PWROFTEN has one integer argument, N, in the range 0..37. It returns a real value equal to 10^N.

3
IMPLEMENTATION-DEPENDENT FEATURES

PWROFTEN is only implemented in UCSD Pascal.

READ

READ is a standard procedure that assigns the value of components of a file to variables, possibly with conversion if the file is a text file.

☐ SYMBOL   ■ STANDARD   ■ J & W/CDC   ■ PASCAL/Z
■ IDENTIFIER   ■ HP 1000   ■ OMSI   ■ UCSD
☐ CONCEPT

1
SYNTAX

READ statement:

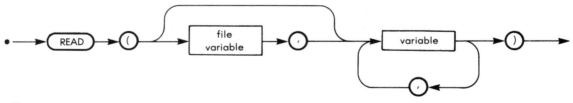

2
DESCRIPTION

2.1 Read(F,X) The exact meaning of READ(F,X) depends upon the types of F and X.

2.1.1 The components of F are of the same type as X. READ(F,X) is equivalent to:

BEGIN X := F↑; GET(F) **END**

2.1.2 The file F is of type TEXT. X is of type REAL, INTEGER, or a sub-range of INTEGER. Leading blanks and/or end of line marks are skipped and a string of characters representing a real or integer number according to the Pascal syntax is read, and the corresponding value is assigned to X.

READ

Note: consecutive numbers are separated by blanks or end of line marks; a number is terminated by any character not satisfying the syntactic definition of INTEGER or REAL.

X is of type CHAR, or subrange of CHAR. The next character is accessed and assigned to X (as in 2.1.1).

2.1.3 Other combinations   All other combinations of types are illegal.

2.2 Read(F,X1,X2,X3...)   The statement READ(F,X1,X2,X3) is equivalent to:

> **BEGIN** READ(F,X1); READ(F,X2); READ(F,X3) **END**

2.3 Read(X); Read(X1,X2,X3...)   When the file name is not specified, INPUT is implied.

2.4 Relationship Between Read and Eof   The function EOF(F) must be FALSE prior to execution of READ(F,X).

If the GET operations do not find any more data on the file, then EOF becomes TRUE, and F ↑ is left undefined.

2.5 Relationship Between Read and Eoln   On text files, consecutive READ operations automatically skip end of line marks when X is not a CHAR or subrange of CHAR. When X is a CHAR or subrange of CHAR, the end of line mark is input as a blank.

2.6 Relationship Between Read(F) and Reset(F)   Before the first READ(F) statement is executed, the file F must have been opened by a RESET(F) statement. No REWRITE(F), PUT(F), WRITE(F) or WRITELN(F) statements may be executed between the RESET(F) statement and any READ(F) statement.

2.7 Implicit Reset(Input)   An implicit RESET(INPUT) statement is executed at the beginning of a program if the file INPUT appears in the program heading.

2.8 Errors on Read   The execution of READ while EOF is TRUE is undefined, but generally results in an abnormal termination of the program.

Since the value of X is assigned before a GET is performed in form 2.1.1, the READ(F,X) statement will always yield defined results, as long as EOF was FALSE prior to its execution. This is not necessarily true for the READ(F,X1,X2,X3) format, since it causes multiple READ operations.

Thus, an equivalent READ(F,X) other than the first (as in 2.2) can result in an abnormal termination.

When F is a TEXT file, and X is of type INTEGER, or REAL, an error occurs if a character that does not satisfy the appropriate Pascal syntax is read before a string of characters that does satisfy the syntax is read.

3
IMPLEMENTATION-DEPENDENT FEATURES

3.1 HP 1000

3.1.1 Strings When the file F is of type TEXT, the parameter X in the statement READ(F,X) can also be a string variable, i.e., a normal or a packed array of CHAR.

Reading begins at the current file position and continues until either the array is filled, or EOLN(F) becomes TRUE, in which case the array is filled with trailing blanks.

3.1.2 Longreals Variables of type LONGREAL can be read.

3.1.3 Prerequisites Before a READ(F,..) statement can be executed, the file F must have been opened by a RESET or an OPEN statement. If the file was opened by RESET, the procedure READ behaves as described in the standard. (Refer to the GET heading for information about differences in the behavior of GET.) If the file was opened by the OPEN statement, then READ, WRITE, PUT and GET operations can be intermixed, and the file window can be moved arbitrarily by the SEEK procedure.

3.2 J & W/CDC None known.

3.3 OMSI

3.3.1 Limitations on the Type of Files Only files of type TEXT can be read by READ.

3.3.2 Strings Standard string variables (i.e., packed arrays of CHAR), can be read as described in paragraph 3.1.1 of this heading.

READ

3.4 Pascal/Z Two important extensions have been made to the capabilities of the READ procedure: non-sequential access is possible with all files except text files, and enumerated types can be read from text files.

3.4.1 Syntax

READ statement:

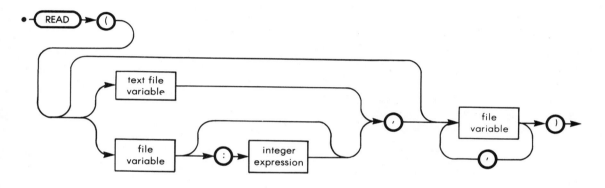

3.4.2 Direct Access By specifying a record number after the file identifier in the READ statement, it is possible to directly access any record in the file. The records are numbered from 1. Specifying record number 0 or giving no record number causes the next sequential record to be read.

3.4.3 Enumerated Types Variables of any enumerated type can be read from a textfile. Their value is represented by the identifiers used in their declaration.

3.4.4 Strings The READLN statement should be used to read (variable length) STRINGs rather than the READ statement.

If READ is used to read a variable of type STRING, consecutive characters will be read and assigned to the variable until the end of line mark is encountered. Any subsequent READ statements will return a zero length variable (an empty string), since only the READLN statement can skip an end of line.

READ

3.5 UCSD

3.5.1 Limitations on the Type of Files Only files of type TEXT or INTERACTIVE can be read by READ. In interactive files, the statement READ(F,X) is equivalent to

BEGIN GET(F); X := F **END**

while in text files it is equivalent to

BEGIN X := F↑;GET(F) **END**

3.5.2 Strings It is recommended that a READLN statement be used to read variables of type STRING, rather than the READ statement. The end of line, which is normally skipped over by a READLN, is used to indicate the end of a STRING variable. Such ends of lines are consumed by the READ statement.

The variable in a READ may not be a (standard) string, i.e., a packed array of CHAR.

4
EXAMPLE

```
PROGRAM AVERAGE1(CARDS,OUTPUT);
(* THIS PROGRAM COMPUTES THE AVERAGE VALUE OF AN ARBITRARY
NUMBER OF REAL VALUES, PUNCHED ON CARDS ACCORDING TO THE
SYNTAX OF PASCAL REAL NUMBERS. CONSECUTIVE VALUES ARE
SEPARATED BY AT LEAST ONE BLANK. THE NUMBER OF VALUES PER CARD
IS ARBITRARY. *)
VAR CARDS : TEXT;
    SUM,VALUE : REAL;
    NUM : INTEGER;
BEGIN
    NUM := 0;
    SUM := 0;
    RESET(CARDS);
    WHILE NOT EOF(CARDS) DO
```

```
BEGIN
        READ(CARDS,VALUE);
        NUM := NUM + 1;
        SUM := SUM + VALUE;
        WRITELN('SAMPLE NUMBER: ',NUM:4,' HAS VALUE ',VALUE:20:5)
    END
WRITELN
WRITELN('TOTAL NUMBER OF SAMPLES = ',NUM:4);
WRITELN('AVERAGE VALUE = ',SUM/NUM:20:6)
END.
```

Note: this program should be compared with the AVERAGE2 program presented under the READLN heading.

READDIR

READDIR is a non-standard predefined procedure that first positions the window of a direct access file, and then performs a READ operation.

☐ SYMBOL   ☐ STANDARD   ☐ J & W/CDC   ☐ PASCAL/Z
■ IDENTIFIER   ■ HP 1000   ☐ OMSI   ☐ UCSD
☐ CONCEPT

1
SYNTAX

READDIR statement:

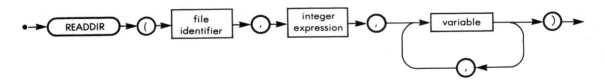

2
DESCRIPTION

The statement READDIR(F,K,V1,V2,V3) is equivalent to:

BEGIN
    SEEK(F,K);
    READ(F,V1,V2,V3)
END.

Refer to the SEEK and READ headings for additional information.
  Since the SEEK procedure can only be used with direct files, i.e., files opened with the OPEN statement, the same restriction applies to the READDIR procedure.

3

IMPLEMENTATION-DEPENDENT FEATURES

READDIR is only implemented in HP 1000 Pascal, but is similar to the Pascal/Z implementation of READ.

4

EXAMPLE

```
PROGRAM UPDATESALARY(INPUT,OUTPUT);
(* ON THE FILE SALFILE EACH COMPONENT CONTAINS THE NAME AND THE
SALARY OF A PERSON *)
(* THE NUMBER OF THE COMPONENT IS EQUAL TO THE ID OF THE PERSON *)
TYPE
     PERSONT = RECORD
                     NAME : PACKED ARRAY[1..20] OF CHAR;
                     SALARY : 0..10000
               END;
VAR
     PERSON : PERSONT;
     ID : INTEGER;
     SALFILE : FILE OF PERSONT;
     FILENAME : PACKED ARRAY[1..12] OF CHAR;
     YESNO : CHAR;
BEGIN
(* OPEN THE FILE *)
     PROMPT('NAME OF THE SALARY FILE = ?');
     READLN(FILENAME);
     OPEN(SALFILE,FILENAME,'EXCLUS');
```

READDIR

```
(* UPDATE SALARY *)
    REPEAT
        PROMPT('ID = ?');
        READLN(ID);
        IF ID <= MAXPOS(SALFILE)
            THEN
                BEGIN
                    READDIR(SALFILE,ID,PERSON);
                    WRITELN(PERSON.NAME,
                            'SALARY = ',PERSON.SALARY);
                    PROMPT('NEW SALARY = ? ');
                    READLN(PERSON.SALARY);
                    WRITEDIR(SALFILE,ID,PERSON)
                END
            ELSE
                WRITELN('WRONG ID');
        PROMPT('MORE (Y OR N) ? ');
        READLN(YESNO)
    UNTIL YESNO = 'N'
END.
```

READLN

READLN is a standard procedure similar to READ that skips to the beginning of the next line of a text file.

☐ SYMBOL ■ STANDARD ■ J & W/CDC ■ PASCAL/Z
■ IDENTIFIER ■ HP 1000 ■ OMSI ■ UCSD
☐ CONCEPT

1
SYNTAX

READLN statement:

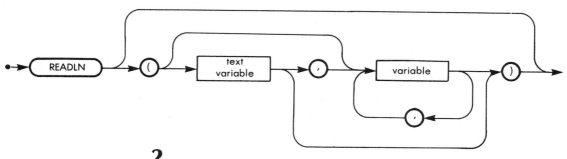

2
DESCRIPTION

2.1 Readln(F) F may only be a text file. The statement READLN(F) moves the file window past the next end of line mark on the file F. If this is not the end of file, it assigns the value of the first component of the new line to the buffer variable F↑.

2.2 Readln(F,X1,X2,X3...) The statement READLN(F,X1,X2,X3) is equivalent to:

BEGIN READ(F,X1,X2,X3); READLN(F) **END**

READLN

Note: Even if end of line marks are present between the components corresponding to the X1, X2, X3 variables, the window will be positioned on the first component, after the first end of line encountered after reading X1, X2, and X3.

Refer to the READ heading for additional information on the type of variables F, X1, X2.

2.3 Readln; Readln(X1,X2,X3...)   When the file name is not specified, INPUT is implied.

2.4 Relationship Between Readln and Eof   The function EOF(F) must be FALSE prior to the execution of READLN(F) or READLN(F,X1,X2,X3...).

Refer to section 2.4 of READ for an explanation of the relationship between EOF and READLN(F,X1,X2,X3 . . .).

2.5 Relationship Between Readln and Eoln   Whatever the value of EOLN is, the READLN function can be called, and will yield defined results. EOLN becomes FALSE after the execution of a READLN statement, except when the next line is empty.

2.6 Relationship Between Readln(F) and Reset(F)   Before the first READLN(F) statement is executed, the file F must have been opened by a RESET(F) statement. No REWRITE(F), PUT(F), WRITE(F) or WRITELN(F) statements may be executed between the RESET(F) statement and any READLN(F) statement.

3
IMPLEMENTATION-DEPENDENT FEATURES

3.1 HP 1000

3.1.1 Strings   When the file F is of type TEXT, the parameter X in the statement READLN(F,X) can also be a string variable, i.e., a normal or a packed array of CHAR.

READLN

Reading begins at the current file position, and continues until either the array is filled, or EOLN(F) becomes TRUE, in which case the array is filled with trailing blanks. In both cases, the first end of line mark after the read operation was completed is skipped.

3.1.2 Longreals Variables of type LONGREAL can be read.

3.2 J & W/CDC None known.

3.3 OMSI Standard string variables (i.e., packed arrays of CHAR) can be read as described in paragraph 3.1.1 of this heading.

3.4 Pascal/Z

3.4.1 Enumerated Types Variables of any enumerated type can be read from a textfile. Their value is represented by the string used in their declaration.

3.4.2 Strings The parameter X in the statement READLN(F,X) can be a variable of type STRING. In this case, consecutive characters will be read and assigned to X until the end of line is encountered. The end of line mark will be skipped, and the file window positioned on the first character of the next line.

3.5 UCSD

3.5.1 F may be a file of type TEXT or Interactive.

3.5.2 Variables of type STRING can be read as described above in paragraph 3.4.2 of this heading.

READLN

4
EXAMPLE

PROGRAM AVERAGE2(CARDS,OUTPUT);
(* THIS PROGRAM COMPUTES THE AVERAGE VALUE OF AN ARBITRARY
NUMBER OF REAL VALUES PUNCHED ON CARDS ACCORDING TO THE SYNTAX
OF PASCAL REAL NUMBERS. ALTHOUGH AN ARBITRARY NUMBER OF VALUES
SEPARATED BY AT LEAST ONE BLANK MAY BE PUNCHED ON THE CARDS,
ONLY THE FIRST VALUE OF EACH CARD IS CONSIDERED. *)
VAR CARDS : TEXT;
      SUM, VALUE : REAL;
      NUM : INTEGER;
BEGIN
      NUM := 0;
      SUM := 0;
      RESET(CARDS);
      WHILE NOT EOF (CARDS) **DO**
          BEGIN
              READLN(CARDS,VALUE);
              NUM := NUM + 1;
              SUM := SUM + VALUE;
              WRITELN('SAMPLE NUMBER: ',NUM:4,' HAS VALUE ',VALUE:20:5)
          END
      WRITELN;
      WRITELN('TOTAL NUMBER OF SAMPLES = ',NUM:4);
      WRITELN('AVERAGE VALUE = ',SUM/NUM :20:6)
END.

Note: this program should be compared with AVERAGE1, which is presented under the READ heading.

The type REAL is a predefined type, and is used to represent an implementation-defined subset of numerical data in the domain of real numbers.

☐ SYMBOL
■ IDENTIFIER
☐ CONCEPT

■ STANDARD
■ HP 1000

■ J & W/CDC
■ OMSI

■ PASCAL/Z
■ UCSD

1
SYNTAX

1.1 Real Type

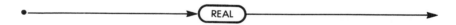

1.2 Real Constant

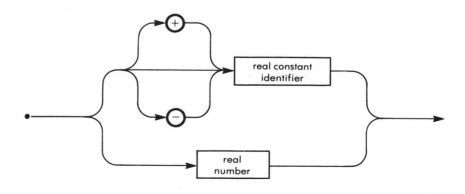

REAL

1.3 Real Number

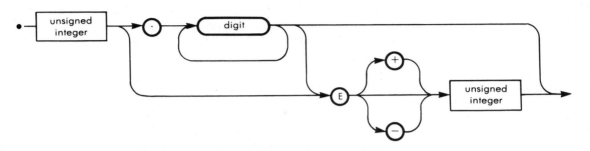

Note: No blanks are permitted within a real number.

2
DESCRIPTION

2.1 Range   Variables of type REAL are used to store numerical data in a format allowing a wide range of values, but a limited accuracy of representation.

Both the range and the accuracy are implementation-dependent.

2.2 Arithmetic Operators   The arithmetic operators applicable to real operands are:

+	addition	⎫
−	subtraction	All of these operations
*	multiplication	yield a real result.
/	division	⎭

When expressions are evaluated, the * and / operations are performed before the + and − operations, unless parentheses modify this rule of precedence.

2.3 Relational Operators   The relational operators applicable to real operands are:

=	equal to
<>	not equal to
<	less than
>	greater than
<=	less than or equal to
>=	greater than or equal to

Note: Due to the limited precision of real values, the = and <> operators should usually be avoided in relational expressions: A = B should be replaced by

$$ABS(A - B) < = EPSILON$$

where EPSILON is a positive constant chosen as a function of the values of A and B and the resolution allowed by the representation of real values.

2.4 Standard Functions   The standard functions yielding a REAL value are:

ABS(x)   yielding the absolute value of the expression x.

SQR(x)   yielding the square of the REAL expression x.

SIN(x)   yielding the sine of the REAL argument x, expressed in radians.

COS(x)   yielding the cosine of the REAL argument x, expressed in radians.

ARCTAN(x)   yielding the arctangent of the REAL argument x, in radians.

LN(x)   yielding the natural logarithm of the REAL argument x.

EXP(x)   yielding the natural exponential of the REAL argument x.

SQRT(x)   yielding the square root of the positive REAL expression x.

REAL

3
IMPLEMENTATION-DEPENDENT FEATURES

3.1 HP 1000

3.1.1 Range

either $X = 0$
or $10^{-38} <= |X| <= 10^{38}$

3.1.2 Significance

6.9 digits
A type, LONGREAL, exists, and gives better resolution (more significant digits).

3.2 J & W/CDC

3.2.1 Range

either $X = 0$
or $10^{-294} <= |X| <= 10^{322}$

3.2.2 Significance

14 digits

3.3 OMSI

3.3.1 Range

either $X = 0$
or $10^{-38} <= |X| <= 10^{38}$

3.3.2 Significance

6.9 digits with the single precision compiler option
15 digits with the double precision compiler option

3.4 Pascal/Z

3.4.1 Range

either $X = 0$
or $10^{-38} <= |X| <= 10^{38}$

3.4.2 Significance

6.9 digits

3.5 UCSD Range and resolution depend upon the processor used for the particular implementation.

Values similar to those described in paragraphs 3.1, 3.3 and 3.4 of this heading are typical for most microprocessor implementations.

4
EXAMPLE

The programs SALES under the + heading, ONE DOLLAR DISCOUNT under the − heading, and SALES TAX under the * heading illustrate the use of REALs.

The examples under the number heading illustrate real number constants.

RECORD

A RECORD is a structured type with a fixed number of elements, called fields, which can be of different types.

■ SYMBOL   ■ STANDARD   ■ J & W/CDC   ■ PASCAL/Z
□ IDENTIFIER   ■ HP 1000   ■ OMSI   ■ UCSD
□ CONCEPT

1
SYNTAX

1.1 Record Type

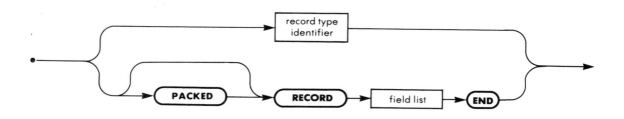

1.2 Field List

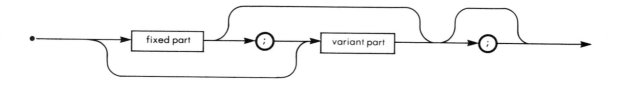

1.3 Fixed Part of Field List

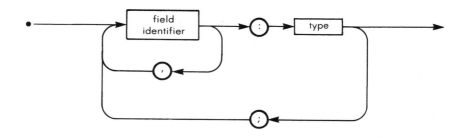

1.4 Variant Part of Field List

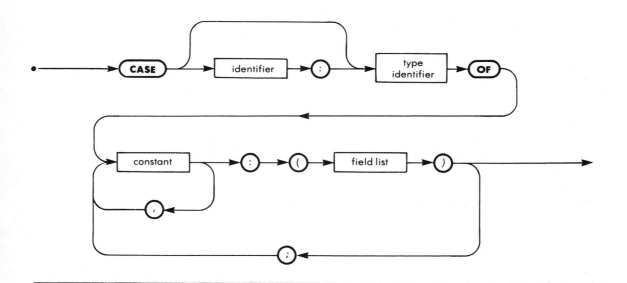

RECORD

1.5 Variable Referenced as a Part of a Record

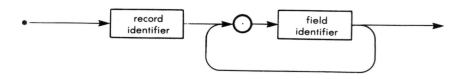

For statements involving the WITH statement, refer to the WITH heading.

2
DESCRIPTION

2.1 Fields Records are structured variables, composed of a fixed number of constituents, called fields. The different fields composing a RECORD do not have to be all of the same type. The number and the type of fields are defined by a record type definition. The scope of the field identifiers is limited to the record definition, i.e., fields in different records may have the same name, but within one record definition all identifiers must be distinct.

A particular field of a record variable is referenced by the name of the variable and the name of the field. Note how these two names differ: the first is the name of a variable, the second of a field. This improves readability, as similar fields in different variables are allowed to have the same field name.

2.2 With Statement References to record fields can be written in a more compact form by using the WITH statement. Refer to the corresponding heading for more information.

2.3 Variants It is possible to use a unique definition for records that differ in the type and/or number of fields. This declaration defines a record with a variant part. The definition of the variant part has a syntax somewhat similar to the CASE statement, but differs in that the variant selector rather than a variable is the type identifier used by the compiler to identify the different possible variants of the record. The variant selector must be an ordinal type. There may only be one variant in a record definition and it must be last. However, variants may be nested.

2.4 Tags It is often necessary to include a tag field in the record. The value of this field shows which variant is in effect. Its type is the same as the variant selector.

Although the tag field could be declared as any other fixed record field, a more compact form that combines the tag field and the variant selector in a single declaration is usually used:

CASE tag : variantselector OF

It is the responsibility of the programmer to use the correct variant of a record in each situation. A CASE statement, with the tag field as selector, is often used for this purpose.

3
IMPLEMENTATION-DEPENDENT FEATURES

3.1 HP 1000 None known.

3.2 J & W/CDC None known.

3.3 OMSI None known.

3.4 Pascal/Z None known.

3.5 UCSD No ; symbol is allowed at the end of a field list.

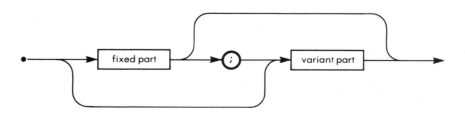

RECORD

4
EXAMPLES

```pascal
PROGRAM CMULT(INPUT,OUTPUT);
TYPE COMPLEX = RECORD
                      RE : REAL;
                      IM : REAL
              END;
VAR X,Y,Z : COMPLEX;
PROCEDURE CPROD(X,Y : COMPLEX; VAR P : COMPLEX);
    BEGIN
        P.RE := X.RE * Y.RE — X.IM * Y.IM;
        P.IM := X.RE * Y.IM + X.IM * Y.RE
    END;
BEGIN
    READLN(X.RE,X.IM,Y.RE,Y.IM);
    CPROD(X,Y,Z);
    WRITELN('THE COMPLEX PRODUCT OF');
    WRITELN('    ',X.RE:10:2,' + I',X.IM:10:2);
    WRITELN(' BY ',Y.RE:10:2,' + I',Y.IM:10:2);
    WRITELN(' IS: ',Z.RE:10:2,' + I',Z.IM:10:2)
END.
```

```pascal
PROGRAM VOLUME(INPUT,OUTPUT);
(* THIS PROGRAM COMPUTES THE VOLUME OF SPHERICAL OR
CYLINDRICAL CONTAINERS. TWO FORMATS OF INPUT DATA ARE
ACCEPTED:
            "SPHERE" RADIUS
            "CYLINDER" RADIUS HEIGHT
THE LAST TWO LETTERS OF THE WORD CYLINDER CAN BE OMITTED.
RADIUS AND HEIGHT ARE EXPRESSED IN METERS *)
```

RECORD

```
TYPE SHAPE = (SPHERE,CYLINDER);
    CONTAINER = RECORD
                        CASE TAG : SHAPE OF
                            SPHERE : (RADS : REAL);
                            CYLINDER : (RADC , HEIGHT : REAL)
                        END;
VAR CNTNR : CONTAINER;
PROCEDURE READSHAPE(VAR S : SHAPE);
    LABEL 1;
    VAR INP : PACKED ARRAY[1..6] OF CHAR;
        I : 1..6;
    BEGIN
        FOR I := 1 TO 6 DO READ(INP[I]);
        1 : READLN;
            IF INP = 'SPHERE'
                THEN S := SPHERE
                ELSE
                    IF INP = 'CYLIND'
                        THEN S := CYLINDER
                        ELSE
                            BEGIN
                                WRITELN('INPUT ERROR');
                                GOTO 1
                            END
    END;
FUNCTION VOL(C : CONTAINER) : REAL;
    CONST PI = 3.1416;
    BEGIN
        CASE C.TAG OF
            SPHERE : VOL := PI * SQR(C.RADS) * C.RADS * 4.0/3.0;
            CYLINDER : VOL := PI * SQR(C.RADC) * C.HEIGHT
        END
    END;
```

RECORD

```
BEGIN
    READSHAPE(CNTNR.TAG);
    CASE CNTNR.TAG OF
        SPHERE : READLN(CNTNR.RADS);
        CYLINDER : READLN(CNTNR.RADC,CNTNR.HEIGHT)
    END;
    WRITELN('THE VOLUME IS: ',VOL(CNTNR):10:3,' M3')
END.
```

recursion

Recursion is the execution of a procedure or a function while a previously initiated execution (of itself) has not completed.

☐ SYMBOL   ■ STANDARD   ■ J & W/CDC   ■ PASCAL/Z
☐ IDENTIFIER   ■ HP 1000   ■ OMSI   ■ UCSD
■ CONCEPT

1
SYNTAX

Recursions can cause infinite loops if some condition for termination is not included in at least one of the recursing procedures or functions.

2
DESCRIPTION

Recursion in Pascal is sometimes classified as self-recursion or mutual recursion.

A self-recursion occurs when a procedure or function contains a statement that references itself.

A mutual recursion occurs when a procedure or function A contains a statement that references a procedure or function B, and B contains a statement referencing A. A mutual recursion may involve more than two procedures or functions.

It is important to realize, when considering the use of recursive algorithms, that every activation of a procedure or function may cause new memory to be allocated. Some recursive algorithms can be replaced by simple iterations, which require less data memory, but are more complex.

Mutual recursion involves a syntactic problem: procedures or functions must be referenced before they can be defined. This problem is solved by the use of the FORWARD declaration, which allows the programmer to announce in advance that a procedure or a function will be declared.

recursion

3
IMPLEMENTATION-DEPENDENT FEATURES

None known.

4
EXAMPLES

4.1 Program Illustrating Self-Recursion

```
PROGRAM REVERSE(INPUT,OUTPUT);
(* PRINTS A STRING IN THE REVERSE ORDER FROM WHICH IT WAS ENTERED *)
PROCEDURE REV;
    VAR CH : CHAR;
    BEGIN
        READ(CH);
        IF NOT EOLN THEN REV;
        WRITE(CH)
    END;
BEGIN
    REV;
    WRITELN
END.
```

4.2 Program Illustrating Mutual Recursion:

```
PROGRAM MRECUR(OUTPUT);
    CONST MAXLEVEL = 5;
VAR LEVEL : INTEGER;
PROCEDURE B(VAR K : INTEGER); FORWARD;
PROCEDURE A(VAR K : INTEGER);
```

```
    BEGIN
        WRITELN('ENTER A ');
        B(K);
        WRITELN('QUIT A ')
    END;
PROCEDURE B;
    BEGIN
        WRITELN('ENTER B ');
        K := K + 1;
        IF K < = MAXLEVEL THEN A(K);
        WRITELN('QUIT B ')
    END;
BEGIN
    LEVEL := 0;
    A(LEVEL)
END.
```

4.3 Program Comparing an Iterative and a Recursive Algorithm:

```
PROGRAM FACTOR(INPUT,OUTPUT);
(* THIS PROGRAM ALLOWS A SIMPLE PERFORMANCE COMPARISON BETWEEN
A RECURSIVE AND AN ITERATIVE ALGORITHM TO COMPUTE THE FACTORIAL
FUNCTION *)
TYPE POSINT = 0..MAXINT;
VAR METHOD : CHAR;
    NUMBER : POSINT;
FUNCTION RFAC(N : POSINT) : INTEGER;
(* RECURSIVE ALGORITHM *)
    VAR F : POSINT;
    BEGIN
        IF N > = 1 THEN F := N * RFAC(N − 1)
                    ELSE F := 1;
        RFAC := F
    END;
```

recursion

```
FUNCTION IFAC(N : POSINT) : INTEGER;
(* ITERATIVE ALGORITHM *)
    VAR I,F : POSINT;
    BEGIN
        F := 1;
        FOR I := 2 TO N DO F := F * I;
        IFAC := F
    END;
BEGIN
    WRITELN('GIVE METHOD (I OR R) AND NUMBER');
    READLN(METHOD,NUMBER);
    IF METHOD = 'R'
        THEN WRITELN(NUMBER,'! = ',RFAC(NUMBER))
        ELSE WRITELN(NUMBER,'! = ',IFAC(NUMBER))
END.
```

RELEASE

RELEASE is a non-standard predefined procedure that restores the heap to its previous state (as recorded by the procedure MARK).

□ SYMBOL
■ IDENTIFIER
□ CONCEPT

□ STANDARD
■ HP 1000

□ J & W/CDC
□ OMSI

■ PASCAL/Z
■ UCSD

1
SYNTAX

RELEASE statement:

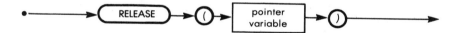

2
DESCRIPTION

The procedure RELEASE has one parameter: a pointer variable. Execution of the statement RELEASE(P) after the execution of a statement MARK(P) restores the heap to its state at the moment the statement MARK(P) was executed. All dynamic variables created after the MARK statement are effectively destroyed by RELEASE, and the memory space that they used is freed for new dynamic variables.

The value of P may not be changed between the execution of MARK(P) and RELEASE(P).

The type of the dynamic variable towards which P points is irrelevant, since P should only be used with the procedures MARK and RELEASE, and never with NEW.

Before executing a RELEASE statement, the programmer should be sure that no pointer variables are pointing to dynamic structures that RELEASE will destroy.

RELEASE

3
IMPLEMENTATION-DEPENDENT FEATURES

3.1 HP 1000   None known.

3.2 Pascal/Z   None known.

3.3 UCSD   None known.

4
EXAMPLE

See the program LIFOL under the MARK heading.

REPEAT

The REPEAT loop allows repeated execution of a group of statements. A Boolean expression, evaluated after each execution of the group of statements, determines if this execution will be repeated.

■ SYMBOL
□ IDENTIFIER
□ CONCEPT

■ STANDARD
■ HP 1000

■ J & W/CDC
■ OMSI

■ PASCAL/Z
■ UCSD

1
SYNTAX

REPEAT statement:

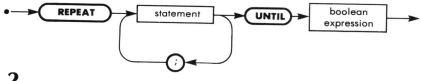

2
DESCRIPTION

The REPEAT UNTIL loop can be implemented by the following flowchart.

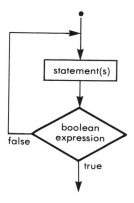

REPEAT

3
IMPLEMENTATION-DEPENDENT FEATURES

None known.

4
EXAMPLE

```
PROGRAM RLOOP(OUTPUT);
(* THIS PROGRAM USES A REPEAT LOOP TO EXECUTE A WRITELN
STATEMENT TEN TIMES. IT DOES SO TO ILLUSTRATE THE PROPERTIES
OF REPEAT LOOPS. NORMALLY A FOR LOOP SHOULD BE USED WHEN THE
NUMBER OF EXECUTIONS IS PREDETERMINED. *)
VAR I : INTEGER;
BEGIN
     I := 1;
     REPEAT
          WRITELN('LINE TO BE PRINTED 10 TIMES');
          I := I + 1;
     UNTIL I > 10
END.
```

A reserved word is a multi-character symbol used in Pascal programs that has a specific meaning, and cannot be redefined.

☐ SYMBOL   ■ STANDARD   ■ J & W/CDC   ■ PASCAL/Z
☐ IDENTIFIER   ■ HP 1000   ■ OMSI   ■ UCSD
■ CONCEPT

1
SYNTAX

The standard reserved words are:

AND	ARRAY	BEGIN	CASE	CONST
DIV	DO	DOWNTO	ELSE	END
FILE	FOR	FUNCTION	GOTO	IF
IN	LABEL	MOD	NIL	NOT
OF	OR	PACKED	PROCEDURE	PROGRAM
RECORD	REPEAT	SET	THEN	TO
TYPE	UNTIL	VAR	WHILE	WITH

2
DESCRIPTION

Since most character sets are insufficient to provide separate symbols for all Pascal commands, some symbols are formed by a concatenation of letters. These word-symbols are reserved, i.e., they cannot be used as identifiers.

Upper and lower case letters are equivalent in reserved words.

reserved word

3
IMPLEMENTATION-DEPENDENT FEATURES

Many Pascals add a very small number of additional reserved words. Some Pascals incorrectly make EXTERNAL and FORWARD reserved words.

3.1 HP 1000   One additional reserved word is provided:

OTHERWISE

3.2 J & W/CDC   One additional reserved word is provided:

SEGMENTED (Special FILE, mentioned but not described under heading segment in this handbook.)

Note: Only upper case letters can be recognized.

3.3 OMSI   Two additional reserved words are provided.

EXIT

ORIGIN

3.4 Pascal/Z   Three additional reserved words are provided.

EXTERNAL

FORWARD

STRING

reserved word

3.5 UCSD   Six additional reserved words are provided.

EXTERNAL

IMPLEMENTATION

INTERFACE

SEGMENT (Mentioned but not described in this handbook.)

UNIT

USES

RESET

RESET is a standard procedure that opens a file so that it can be read.

☐ SYMBOL   ■ STANDARD   ■ J & W/CDC   ■ PASCAL/Z
■ IDENTIFIER   ■ HP 1000   ■ OMSI   ■ UCSD
☐ CONCEPT

1
SYNTAX

RESET statement:

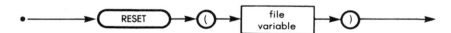

2
DESCRIPTION

The effect of the statement RESET(F) can be described as follows:

The file window is moved to the first component of the file;

IF the file is not empty

    THEN the value of the first component is assigned to the buffer variable F↑, the function EOF(F) becomes FALSE, and subsequent GET(F) operations are allowed.

    ELSE the buffer variable F↑ is undefined, and the function EOF(F) becomes TRUE.

When the filename is not specified, INPUT is implied. A statement RESET(INPUT) is implicitly executed at the beginning of a program if the filename INPUT appears in the program heading.

3
IMPLEMENTATION-DEPENDENT FEATURES

3.1 HP 1000

3.1.1 Access Mode   RESET opens an existing file in the sequential read-only mode. If the file was already open, it is closed and reopened.

3.1.2 External Files   An alternate form of the RESET procedure exists which allows the association of external files (managed by the operating system) with Pascal files, without using the program parameters. The syntax of the RESET statement is extended as follows:

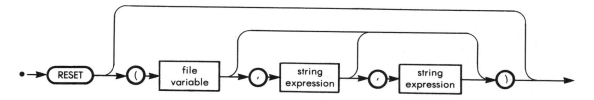

The first parameter is the name of the file. If omitted, the name INPUT is implied.

The second parameter is a string containing the name of an external file, in the format required by the RTE operating system.

The possible values of the third parameter are given by the following syntax diagram.

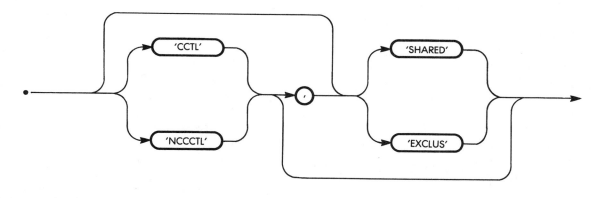

RESET

Note: only upper case letters are acceptable.

The meaning of the third parameter is as follows:

'CCTL': the external file has carriage control.

'NOCCTL': the external file has no carriage control.

'SHARED': the external file can be open to several programs simultaneously.

'EXCLUS': the external file cannot be open to several programs simultaneously.

The options CCTL and NOCCTL are only applicable to textfiles. They are ignored when used with other files.

A textfile with carriage control is a file associated with a printing device that uses the first character of each line to control the motion of the paper. (See paragraph 2.2 of the OUTPUT heading.)

3.1.3 Interactive Files   To simplify the communication with interactive terminals, the RESET procedure does not perform any assignment to the buffer variable. (Refer to the GET heading for more details.)

3.2 J & W/CDC   The RESET procedure is implemented as described in the standard. This causes a problem, however, when a file is associated with an interactive terminal, since the first data transfer should occur during the execution of the RESET procedure. The problem is usually circumvented by answering the first prompt character issued by the operating system with a carriage return.

3.3 OMSI

3.3.1 Access Mode   RESET is used to open existing files, for both READ and WRITE operations. If the file was already open, then it is closed, reopened, and the file window moved to the first component of the file.

3.3.2 External Files   An alternate form of the RESET procedure exists which allows the association of external files (managed by the operating system), with Pascal files.

The syntax of the RESET statement is extended as follows.

RESET

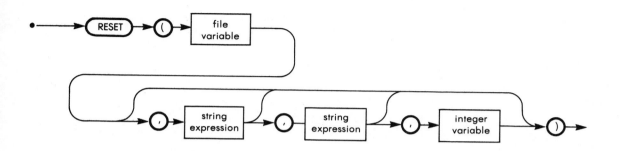

The first parameter is the name of the file. The second parameter is a string containing the name of an external file, in the format required by the operating system. The third parameter is similar to the second. All file options not mentioned in the second parameter are taken from the third.

The fourth parameter, which is a VAR parameter, contains (after execution of RESET), the length of the file, in blocks, as defined by the operating system. A length value of – 1 is returned when an I/O error occurred during the execution of RESET.

Note that the access mode of the file (READ, WRITE, or both) is part of the second parameter.

3.3.3 Interactive Files   When a file associated with an interactive terminal is RESET, the buffer variable is set to space, and EOLN is set to FALSE; however, no data transfer is performed.

3.4 Pascal/Z

3.4.1 Access Mode   RESET is used to open existing files for READ operations. If the file was already open, it is closed, reopened, and the file window is moved to the first component of the file.

3.4.2 External Files   The RESET procedure allows the association of existing external files (managed by the operating system) with Pascal files. The syntax of the RESET statement is extended as follows:

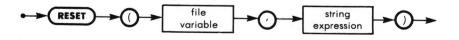

RESET

The first parameter is the name of the file. The second parameter is a string (variable of type STRING, ARRAY OF CHAR, or a normal string) containing the name of an external file, in the format required by the operating system.

3.4.3 Interactive Files   No special provisions have been made for files associated with interactive terminals, so that problems similar to those described in paragraph 3.2 of this heading can arise.

3.5 UCSD

3.5.1 Access Mode   RESET is used to open existing files for both READ and WRITE operations, and to move the file window to the first component of the file. Resetting an already open Pascal file with a new external file name generates an error. The file must be closed first (see the CLOSE heading).

3.5.2 External Files   The RESET procedure is used to associate existing external files (managed by the operating system) with Pascal files. The syntax of the RESET statement is extended as follows.

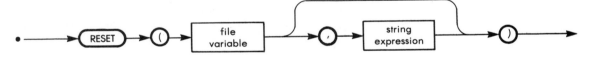

The first parameter is the name of the file. The second parameter is a string containing the title of an external file in the format required by the operating system. The second parameter must be omitted if the file is already open.

3.5.3 Interactive Files   When the first parameter of the RESET procedure is a file of type INTERACTIVE, the buffer variable is not assigned by RESET.

4
EXAMPLE

For an example of the RESET statement, refer to the program LOWUP1 under the TEXT heading.

REWRITE

REWRITE *is a standard procedure which opens a file so that it can be written on.*

☐ SYMBOL   ■ STANDARD   ■ J & W/CDC   ■ PASCAL/Z
■ IDENTIFIER   ■ HP 1000   ■ OMSI   ■ UCSD
☐ CONCEPT

1
SYNTAX

REWRITE statement:

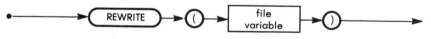

2
DESCRIPTION

The effect of the statement REWRITE(F) can be described as follows:

— The file F becomes an empty file (existing information is lost).

— The function EOF(F) becomes TRUE.

— Subsequent PUT operations are allowed.

A statement REWRITE(OUTPUT) is implicitly executed at the beginning of a program if the filename OUTPUT appears in the program heading. When the filename is not specified, OUTPUT is implied.

3
IMPLEMENTATION-DEPENDENT FEATURES

3.1 HP 1000

REWRITE

3.1.1 Access Mode REWRITE opens a file in the sequential write-only mode. After the execution of REWRITE, the contents of an existing file are lost.

3.1.2 External Files An alternate form of the REWRITE procedure exists which allows the association of external files (managed by the operating system) with Pascal files, without using the program parameters.

The syntax of the REWRITE statement is extended as follows.

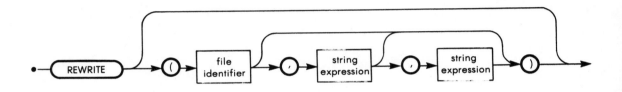

The first parameter is the name of the file. If omitted, the name OUTPUT is implied.

The second parameter is a string containing the name of an external file, in the format required by the RTE operating system.

The possible values of the third parameter are given by the following syntax diagram.

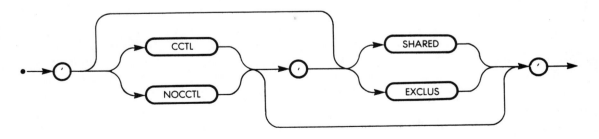

Note: only upper case letters are acceptable.

The meaning of the third parameter is as follows:

'CCTL': the external file has carriage control.

'NOCCTL': the external file has no carriage control.

'SHARED': the external file can be open to several programs simultaneously.

'EXCLUS': the external file cannot be open to several programs simultaneously.

The options CCTL and NOCCTL are only applicable to textfiles. They are ignored when used with other files.

A textfile with carriage control is a file associated with a printing device that uses the first character of each line to control the motion of the paper. (See paragraph 2.2 of the OUTPUT heading.)

3.2 J & W/CDC   None known.

3.3 OMSI

3.3.1 Access Mode   REWRITE is used to open new files, for both READ and WRITE operations.

3.3.2 External Files   An alternate form of the REWRITE procedure exists which allows the association of external files (managed by the operating system), with Pascal files.

The syntax of the REWRITE statement is extended as follows.

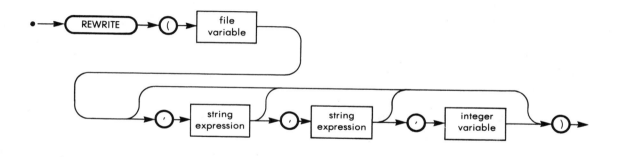

REWRITE

The first parameter is the name of the file. The second parameter is a string containing the name of an external file, in the format required by the operating system. The third parameter is similar to the second; all file options not mentioned in the second parameter are taken from the third. The fourth parameter, which is a VAR parameter, is used to specify the initial space in blocks to be allocated for the file. If an error occurs during the execution of REWRITE, the fourth parameter returns the value − 1.

Note that the access mode of the file (READ, WRITE, or both) is part of the second parameter.

3.4 Pascal/Z

3.4.1 Access Mode   REWRITE is used to open a file for WRITE operations. If the file already existed before the execution of REWRITE, then its contents are lost.

3.4.2 External Files   The REWRITE procedure allows the association of external files (managed by the operating system) with Pascal files.

The syntax of the REWRITE statement is extended as follows.

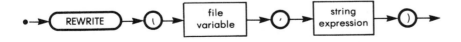

The first parameter is the name of the file. The second parameter is a string (variable of type STRING, ARRAY OF CHAR or normal string) containing the name of an external file, in the format required by the operating system.

3.5 UCSD

3.5.1 Access Mode   REWRITE is used to create new files for both READ and WRITE operations.

3.5.2 External Files   The REWRITE procedure allows the association of external files (managed by the operating system) with Pascal files.

The syntax of the REWRITE statement is extended as described in paragraph 3.4.2 of this heading.

4
EXAMPLE

For an example containing the REWRITE statement, see the program LOWUP1 under the TEXT heading.

ROUND

ROUND is a standard integer function that rounds a real value to the nearest integer value.

☐ SYMBOL   ■ STANDARD   ■ J & W/CDC   ■ PASCAL/Z

■ IDENTIFIER   ■ HP 1000   ■ OMSI   ■ UCSD

☐ CONCEPT

1
SYNTAX

Factor containing the ROUND function:

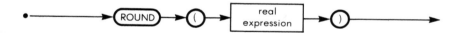

2
DESCRIPTION

The function ROUND has one real parameter. The returned value is integer, and is equal to the integer nearest to the value of the parameter. When the fractional part of the parameter is exactly .5, the rounding is up for positive values and down for negative values of the parameter. For example:

ROUND(3.9) = 4   ROUND(−3.9) = −4

ROUND(3.5) = 4   ROUND(−3.5) = −4

ROUND(3.4999) = 3   ROUND(−3.4999) = −3

A run time error occurs if the result of the rounding is not representable as an integer value, e.g., for very large values of the real parameter.

ROUND

3
IMPLEMENTATION-DEPENDENT FEATURES

3.1 HP 1000 ROUND can be used to round LONGREAL expressions.

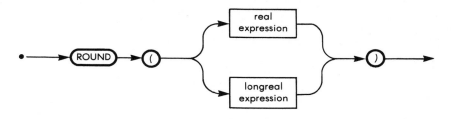

3.2 J & W/CDC   None known.

3.3 OMSI   None known.

3.4 Pascal/Z   None known.

3.5 UCSD   None known.

4
EXAMPLE

```
PROGRAM ROUNDTEST(INPUT,OUTPUT);
VAR R : REAL;
BEGIN
     WRITELN('TYPE A REAL NUMBER');
     READLN(R);
     WRITELN('THE ROUNDED VALUE OF ',R:10:3,' IS ',ROUND(R))
END.
```

SCAN

SCAN is a non-standard predefined function that scans a specified part of memory, in search of specified character values.

☐ SYMBOL   ☐ STANDARD   ☐ J & W/CDC   ☐ PASCAL/Z
■ IDENTIFIER   ☐ HP 1000   ☐ OMSI   ■ UCSD
☐ CONCEPT

1
SYNTAX

SCAN function:

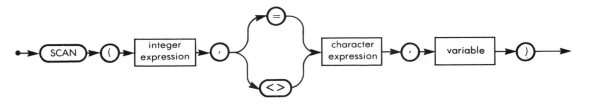

2
DESCRIPTION

The function SCAN has three parameters. The first, Limit, specifies the number of bytes that must be searched. A negative value for Limit corresponds to a backward search. The second parameter is a partial expression composed of one of the signs = or < > , followed by any expression yielding a character value. This character value is used to detect a match or a mismatch. The third parameter, Source, can be any variable except a file. The first byte of that variable will be the first byte to be searched for a match or a mismatch:

        SCAN(Limit,partial expression,Source);

The function SCAN terminates when a match or a mismatch has been found, or when Limit characters have been searched. The value of the function is the number of bytes that have been skipped during the search. If the first byte caused a match or a mismatch, the returned value will be 0. If no match or mismatch was found, the returned value will be equal to Limit. The sign of the returned value is the same as the sign of Limit.

3
IMPLEMENTATION-DEPENDENT FEATURES

SCAN is only implemented in UCSD Pascal.

4
EXAMPLE

```
PROGRAM DOSCAN(OUTPUT);
VAR
      LST  : STRING;
      CHR : CHAR;
BEGIN
      LST : = 'THIS IS A VERY LONG STRING';
      CHR : = 'Y';
      WRITELN('THE BYTE '' ',CHR,' '' OCCURS IN THE STRING');
      WRITELN(' '' ',LST,' '' AT POSITION ',SCAN(SIZEOF(LST),  = CHR,LST):4)
END (* DOSCAN *).
```

scope

The scope of an identifier is the part of the program in which this particular identifier is valid.

☐ SYMBOL   ■ STANDARD   ■ J & W/CDC   ■ PASCAL/Z
☐ IDENTIFIER   ■ HP 1000   ■ OMSI   ■ UCSD
■ CONCEPT

1
SYNTAX

Not applicable.

2
DESCRIPTION

Before identifiers can be used, they must be defined or declared. Every block begins with a declaration part in which labels, constants, types, fields, variables, procedures, and functions can be defined or declared. The scope of the identifiers declared as formal parameters in program, procedure, or function headings is the block of statements following this heading. An identifier is valid only in the block in which it was declared.

Nested blocks can appear inside a block or in procedure or function definitions. An identifier declared in a block is considered local to that block, and global within all nested blocks. Global identifiers can be redeclared or redefined in a nested block, in which case the local declaration prevails, and the global object represented by the identifier is inaccessible by name from the block in which the identifier has been redeclared or defined.

3
IMPLEMENTATION-DEPENDENT FEATURES

Almost all implementations have deviant scope checking systems which allow some errors to go undetected.

4
EXAMPLE

```
PROGRAM SCOPE(OUTPUT);
CONST STAR = '*';
VAR X : CHAR;
PROCEDURE WRITESTRING;
     CONST X = 'LOCAL AND GLOBAL IDENTIFIERS DO NOT INTERFERE';
     BEGIN
          WRITE(X)
     END;
BEGIN
     X := STAR;
     WRITE(X);
     WRITESTRING;
     WRITE(X)
END.
```

SEEK

SEEK is a non-standard predefined procedure that positions the file window in an arbitrary place.

☐ SYMBOL   ☐ STANDARD   ☐ J & W/CDC   ☐ PASCAL/Z
■ IDENTIFIER ■ HP 1000   ■ OMSI   ■ UCSD
☐ CONCEPT

1
SYNTAX

SEEK statement:

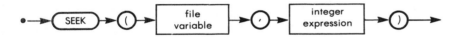

2
DESCRIPTION

The SEEK procedure is used on direct access files to position the file window before a PUT or GET operation is performed. SEEK has two parameters. The first parameter is the name of the file whose window is to be positioned. The desired position is given by the second parameter of the procedure, which must be a positive integer expression.

3
IMPLEMENTATION-DEPENDENT FEATURES

3.1 HP 1000   The procedure SEEK can only be used with files opened by the OPEN statement.

The components on a file are numbered sequentially, beginning with 1.

3.2 OMSI The procedure SEEK can only be used with files that have been opened by RESET or REWRITE procedures with adequate parameters (refer to the RESET or REWRITE headings).

The components on a file are numbered sequentially, beginning with 1.

3.3 PASCAL/Z SEEK is not implemented, but extensions to the READ and WRITE procedures provide similar capabilities.

3.4 UCSD The procedure SEEK can only be used with typed files (see the FILE heading).

The components on a file are numbered sequentially, beginning with 0.

4
EXAMPLE

```
PROGRAM EXAMINE(INPUT,OUTPUT,REC);
(* EXAMINES THE NTH COMPONENT OF A FILE *)
(* UCSD ONLY *)
CONST
      RECLEN = 20;
TYPE
      STR = STRING[RECLEN];
VAR
      REC : FILE OF STR;
      FILENAME : STR
      NUMBER : INTEGER;
BEGIN
      WRITE('WHICH FILE DO YOU WANT TO EXAMINE? ');
      READLN(FILENAME);
      RESET(REC, FILENAME);
      WRITE('WHICH RECORD DO YOU WANT TO EXAMINE? ');
      READLN(NUMBER);
      SEEK(REC,NUMBER);
      GET(REC);
      WRITELN('THAT RECORD CONTAINS : ',REC↑)
END.
```

SEGMENT

A SEGMENT is a portion of a program that is moved as a unit between central memory and secondary memory. The word SEGMENT is used with FILES, and PROCEDURES or FUNCTIONS. Both uses are nonstandard.

- ☐ SYMBOL
- ■ IDENTIFIER
- ■ CONCEPT

- ☐ STANDARD
- ■ HP 1000

- ■ J & W/CDC
- ☐ OMSI

- ☐ PASCAL/Z
- ■ UCSD

1
SYNTAX

Segmentation is not described in detail in this handbook.

2
DESCRIPTION

2.1 Segmented Files   In some implementations (J & W/CDC), sequential files can be subdivided into segments, thereby facilitating retrieval of random records. (This extension of Pascal is not described in this handbook.)

2.2 Segmented Programs   In several implementations (HP 1000, UCSD), it is possible to subdivide a program into several segments. Only the segments being executed are located in central memory; the other

SEGMENT

segments reside on secondary storage. This technique allows the execution of very large programs on machines with a relatively small memory.

Although segmentation commands can be intermixed with Pascal code in several implementations, they are basically compiler commands, and are not described in this handbook.

separator

A separator is any character or sequence of characters that is used to separate consecutive identifiers, numbers, or word symbols.

☐ SYMBOL   ■ STANDARD   ■ J & W/CDC   ■ PASCAL/Z
☐ IDENTIFIER   ■ HP 1000   ■ OMSI   ■ UCSD
■ CONCEPT

1
SYNTAX

Separator:

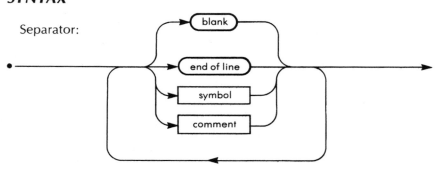

2
DESCRIPTION

Separators may not occur within an identifier, a number or a multiple-character symbol. They must appear between an identifier or word symbol (reserved word), and an identifier, word symbol, or number.

3
IMPLEMENTATION-DEPENDENT FEATURES

None known.

SET

Variables of type SET are used to manipulate objects corresponding to the mathematical definition of sets.

- ■ SYMBOL
- □ IDENTIFIER
- □ CONCEPT

- ■ STANDARD
- ■ HP 1000

- ■ J & W/CDC
- ■ OMSI

- ■ PASCAL/Z
- ■ UCSD

1
SYNTAX

1.1 Set Type

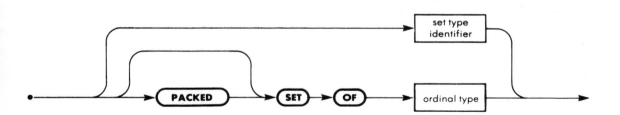

SET

1.2 Relational Expressions Involving Sets

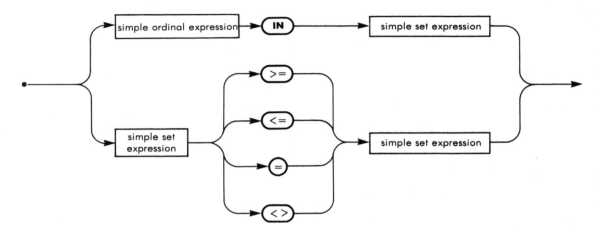

1.3 Simple Set Expression

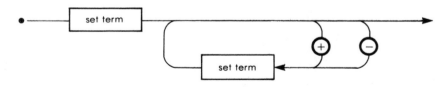

1.4 Set Term

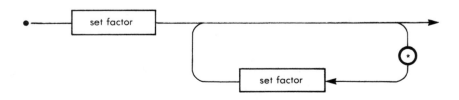

1.5 Set Factor

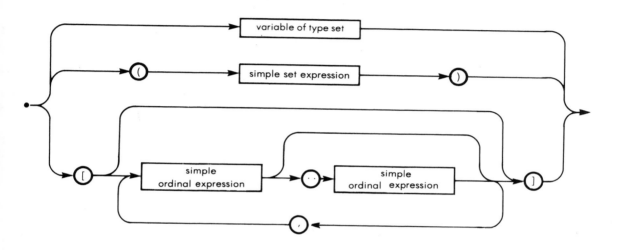

1.6 Variable of Type Set

2
DESCRIPTION

The possible values for a variable of type SET are all the subsets (including the empty set) of values that their base type can take. The base type of a set is mentioned in the set declaration, after the OF word. The base type of a set must be an ordinal type. The size and largest and smallest values of integer base types are implementation defined.

SET

The operations defined on set operands are:

+ set union	the resulting set contains all elements belonging either to the left or the right operand.
− set difference	the resulting set contains all elements belonging to the left operand and not to the right.
* set intersection	the resulting set contains all elements common to both operands.

The relational operators applicable to set operands are:

=	set equality	
<>	set inequality	
<=	set inclusion	TRUE if all elements of the left operand are also part of the right operand.
>=	set containment	TRUE if all elements of the right operand are also part of the left operand.
IN	set membership	TRUE when the left operand, which is of the base type of the right, is one of the elements of the right operand.

3
IMPLEMENTATION-DEPENDENT FEATURES

3.1 HP 1000   The maximum number of elements in a set is 32,768. If the size is not specified, then a default size of 256 is assumed.

The size of a constant set factor can be specified by giving the name of the set type before its contents.

Set factor (HP 1000):

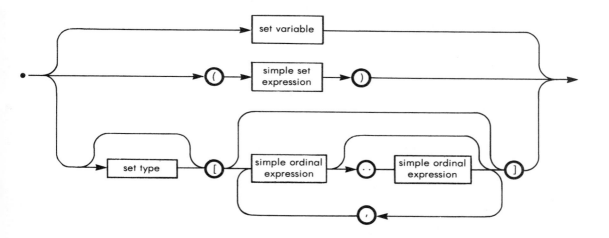

3.2 J & W/CDC   The maximum number of elements in a set is 58. The base type of a set must be either:

— an enumerated type with at most 58 elements.

— a subrange of integers, with all elements in the range 0..58.

— a subrange of the type CHAR with the last element less than or equal to the value of CHR(58).

3.3 OMSI   The maximum number of elements in a set is 64.

3.4 Pascal/Z   The maximum number of elements in a set is 256.

3.5 UCSD   The maximum number of elements in a set is 4,080.

Note: in the APPLE implementation, the maximum number of elements is 512 and no integer outside the range 0..511 can be part of a set.

SET

4
EXAMPLE

```
PROGRAM WEEKDAYS(OUTPUT);
TYPE DAYS = (MO,TU,WE,TH,FR,SA,SU);
     WEEK = SET OF DAYS;
VAR WORKDAY, HOLIDAY, WEEKDAY : WEEK;
     D : DAYS;
PROCEDURE WRDAY(X : DAYS);
     BEGIN
        CASE X OF
              MO : WRITE('MONDAY ');
              TU : WRITE('TUESDAY ');
              WE : WRITE('WEDNESDAY ');
              TH : WRITE('THURSDAY ');
              FR : WRITE('FRIDAY ');
              SA : WRITE('SATURDAY ');
              SU : WRITE('SUNDAY ')
        END
     END;
BEGIN
     WORKDAY := [MO..FR];
     HOLIDAY := [SA,SUN];
     WEEKDAY := WORKDAY + HOLIDAY;
     FOR D := MO TO SU DO
        IF D IN WEEKDAY THEN
           BEGIN
              WRDAY(D);
              WRITELN('IS A WEEKDAY')
           END
END.
```

SETPOINTER

SETPOINTER is a non-standard predefined procedure that sets a pointer variable to the address of a specified variable.

☐ SYMBOL
■ IDENTIFIER
☐ CONCEPT

☐ STANDARD
☐ HP 1000

☐ J & W/CDC
☐ OMSI

☐ PASCAL/Z
■ UCSD

1
SYNTAX

SETPOINTER statement:

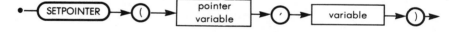

2
DESCRIPTION

SETPOINTER has two parameters. The first parameter, P, is a pointer variable, and the second parameter, V, is any variable. SETPOINTER assigns the value of the address of V to P. In the declaration of P, the type of variable towards which it points is of no importance:

SETPOINTER(P,V);

3
IMPLEMENTATION-DEPENDENT FEATURES

SETPOINTER is only implemented in the Intel version of UCSD Pascal. The operator @ implemented by OMSI has a similar function.

side effect

A side effect is the modification of the value of a global variable or a variable parameter by a function or procedure.

☐ SYMBOL   ■ STANDARD   ■ J & W/CDC   ■ PASCAL/Z
☐ IDENTIFIER   ■ HP 1000   ■ OMSI   ■ UCSD
■ CONCEPT

1
SYNTAX

Not applicable.

2
DESCRIPTION

A side effect occurs when the value of a global variable not declared as a variable parameter is changed by a function or procedure. Since the obvious task of a function is the assignment of a value to the function identifier, and not the alteration of other values, the use of side effects leads to an obscure programming style. Similarly, procedures with side effects can lead to programs that are difficult to understand and have unexpected results.

Another danger resulting from side effects occurs when a function and a variable modified by that function through a side effect appear in a single expression. The value of the expression then depends upon the order of evaluation of the parts of the expression. Since this order is implementation-dependent, serious problems may arise when programs with side effects are transported from one installation to another.

To avoid side effects, a function or procedure should never assign global variables, and, additionally, a function should not use variable parameters.

3
IMPLEMENTATION-DEPENDENT FEATURES

None known.

4
EXAMPLE

```
PROGRAM SIDEEFFECT(OUTPUT);
VAR A,B : INTEGER;
FUNCTION SMUL(VAR X,Y : INTEGER) : INTEGER;
(* COMPUTES PRODUCT OF X BY Y BY SUCCESSIVE ADDITIONS *)
        VAR Z : INTEGER;
        BEGIN
            Z := 0;  >
            WHILE Y   = 0 DO
                BEGIN
                    Z := Z + X;
                    Y := Y − 1
                END;
            SMUL := Z
        END;
BEGIN
        A := 2; B := 3;
        WRITELN('2 * 3 = ',SMUL(A,B):5);
        WRITELN('LET US TRY AGAIN');
        WRITELN('2 * 3 = ',SMUL(A,B):5)
END.
```

SIN

SIN is a standard REAL function that returns the sine of its parameter.

☐ SYMBOL ■ STANDARD ■ J & W/CDC ■ PASCAL/Z
■ IDENTIFIER ■ HP 1000 ■ OMSI ■ UCSD
☐ CONCEPT

1
SYNTAX

Factor containing the SIN function:

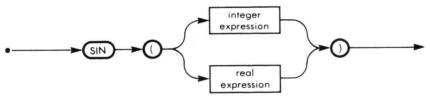

2
DESCRIPTION

The function SIN has one INTEGER or REAL parameter, which is an angle expressed in radians. (90° = $\pi/2$ radians). SIN returns the sine of that angle as a REAL value. In some implementations, the accuracy of the SIN function is degraded when the parameter has a value outside of the -2π, $+2\pi$ interval.

3
IMPLEMENTATION-DEPENDENT FEATURES

3.1 HP 1000 The parameter of the SIN function can also be of type LONGREAL, in which case the returned value is also of type LONGREAL.

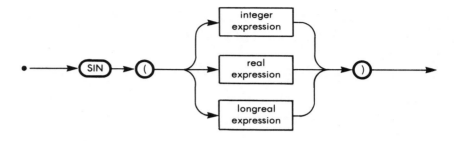

SIN

3.2 J & W/CDC   None known.

3.3 OMSI   None known.

3.4 Pascal/Z   None known.

3.5 UCSD   None known.

Note: in the APPLE implementation, SIN is part of the TRANSCEND library.

4
EXAMPLE

```
PROGRAM SINVAL(INPUT,OUTPUT);
CONST PI = 3.1415927;
VAR DEG,MIN,SEC : INTEGER;
    RAD : REAL;
BEGIN
    WRITELN('TYPE THE VALUE OF AN ANGLE IN DEGREES, MINUTES
            AND SECONDS');
    WRITELN('EACH SEPARATED BY AT LEAST ONE SPACE');
    READLN(DEG,MIN,SEC);
    RAD := PI * (DEG + MIN/60 + SEC/3600)/180;
    WRITELN('THE SINE OF ',DEG:2,' DEG. ',MIN:2,' MIN. ',
            SEC:2,' SEC. IS : ',SIN(RAD):10:5)
END.
```

SIZEOF

SIZEOF is a non-standard predefined integer function that returns the number of bytes a variable takes in memory.

☐ SYMBOL	☐ STANDARD	☐ J & W/CDC	☐ PASCAL/Z
■ IDENTIFIER	☐ HP 1000	☐ OMSI	■ UCSD
☐ CONCEPT			

1
SYNTAX

SIZEOF function:

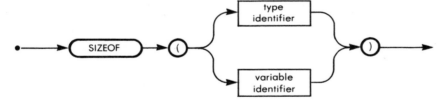

2
DESCRIPTION

The function SIZEOF has one parameter, which is the name of a type or a variable. SIZEOF returns an integer value equal to the number of bytes that variable, or any variable of the specified type occupies in memory.

3
IMPLEMENTATION-DEPENDENT FEATURES

SIZEOF is only implemented in UCSD Pascal.

4
EXAMPLE

See the program MEMUSE under the MEMAVAIL heading.

SQR

SQR is a standard function that returns the square of the value of its parameter.

☐ SYMBOL   ■ STANDARD   ■ J & W/CDC   ■ PASCAL/Z
■ IDENTIFIER   ■ HP 1000   ■ OMSI   ■ UCSD
☐ CONCEPT

1
SYNTAX

Factor containing the SQR function:

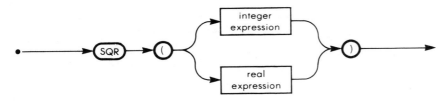

2
DESCRIPTION

The function SQR has one REAL or INTEGER parameter. The returned value is of the same type as the parameter, and is equal to the square of the value of the parameter.

3
IMPLEMENTATION-DEPENDENT FEATURES

3.1 HP 1000   The parameter of the SQR function can also be of type LONGREAL, in which case the returned value is also of type LONGREAL.

SQR function (HP 1000):

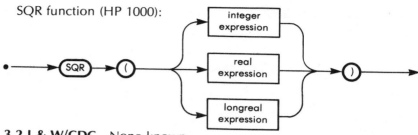

3.2 J & W/CDC   None known.

3.3 OMSI   None known.

3.4 Pascal/Z   None known.

3.5 UCSD   None known.

4
EXAMPLE

```
PROGRAM SQRVAL(INPUT,OUTPUT);
VAR T : CHAR;
    IVAL : INTEGER;
    RVAL : REAL;
BEGIN
    WRITELN('TYPE I FOLLOWED BY A SPACE AND AN INTEGER NUMBER,');
    WRITELN('OR R FOLLOWED BY A SPACE AND A REAL NUMBER');
    READ(T);
    IF T = 'I'
        THEN BEGIN
                READLN(IVAL);
                WRITELN('SQUARE OF ',IVAL:1,' IS : ',SQR(IVAL):1)
            END
        ELSE BEGIN
                READLN(RVAL);
                WRITELN('SQUARE OF ',RVAL:10:3,' IS : ',SQR(RVAL):10:3)
            END
END.
```

SQRT

SQRT is a standard REAL function that returns the square root of its parameter.

☐ SYMBOL   ■ STANDARD   ■ J & W/CDC   ■ PASCAL/Z
■ IDENTIFIER   ■ HP 1000   ■ OMSI   ■ UCSD
☐ CONCEPT

1
SYNTAX

Factor containing the SQRT function:

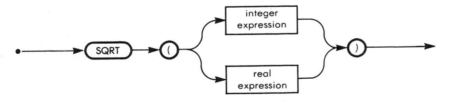

2
DESCRIPTION

The function SQRT(X) computes the square root of X. X may be REAL or INTEGER, but must be positive or zero. The value of SQRT(X) is always REAL.

3
IMPLEMENTATION-DEPENDENT FEATURES

3.1 HP 1000 The parameter of SQRT can be of type LONGREAL, in which case the returned value is also of type LONGREAL.

SQRT

SQRT function (HP 1000):

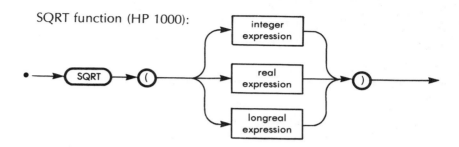

3.2 J & W/CDC None known.

3.3 OMSI None known.

3.4 Pascal/Z None known.

3.5 UCSD None known.

Note: in the APPLE implementation, SQRT is part of the TRANSCEND library.

4
EXAMPLE

```
PROGRAM SQUAREROOT(INPUT,OUTPUT);
VAR X : REAL;
BEGIN
      WRITELN('TO OBTAIN THE SQUARE ROOT OF A NUMBER, JUST TYPE IT');
      READLN(X);
      WRITELN('THE SQUARE ROOT OF ',X,' IS : ',SQRT(X))
END.
```

stack

A stack is a data structure organized in such a way that the data items inserted last are the first to be removed.

☐ SYMBOL   ■ STANDARD   ■ J & W/CDC   ■ PASCAL/Z
☐ IDENTIFIER   ■ HP 1000   ■ OMSI   ■ UCSD
■ CONCEPT

1
SYNTAX

No stacks are explicitly accessible in Pascal.

2
DESCRIPTION

In most implementations of Pascal, memory space is allocated for the static variables of a block when the block is activated. This memory space is organized as a stack, so that the data belonging to the most recently activated block are the easiest to access.

Although the stack contains only static data, its size is changed dynamically by the activation and deactivation of blocks. Since the memory space allocated to the stack is finite, it can become insufficient during program execution. This problem occurs when a procedure is activated recursively an unlimited number of times. It also occurs when too many dynamic variables are created. In most Pascal run time systems this error is reported as a "run time stack-overflow" or a "heap stack collision."

Standard procedures and standard functions are procedures or functions that are predefined in Standard Pascal.

☐ SYMBOL   ■ STANDARD   ■ J & W/CDC   ■ PASCAL/Z
☐ IDENTIFIER   ■ HP 1000   ■ OMSI   ■ UCSD
■ CONCEPT

1
SYNTAX

For the syntax of the specific procedures and functions listed below, refer to the corresponding headings.

2
DESCRIPTION

Standard procedures and standard functions can be used as if they had been declared with a scope surrounding the program. This means that they can be redefined in the program by using an identical identifier in a declaration.

Note: this kind of redefinition should be avoided.

The standard procedures are:

DISPOSE: returns space that is no longer required for dynamic variables.

GET: transfers one component of a file to the associated buffer variable.

NEW: allocates space for new dynamic variables.

standard procedures functions

PACK: transfers data from arrays to packed arrays.

PAGE: skips to the top of the next page on a printing device.

PUT: appends the contents of a buffer variable to its file.

READ: assigns the values of components of a file to variables.

READLN: skips to the beginning of the next line of a text file after performing a READ operation.

RESET: opens a file so that it can be read from.

REWRITE: opens a file so that it can be written on.

UNPACK: transfers data from packed arrays to non-packed arrays.

WRITE: appends values to a file.

WRITELN: appends 0, 1 or several characters and an end of line mark to a text file.

The standard functions are: :

ABS: computes the absolute value.

ARCTAN: computes the arc tangent.

CHR: returns the character with a given ordinal number.

COS: computes the cosine.

EOF: tests if an end of file is reached in a file.

EOLN: tests if an end of line is reached in a text file.

EXP: computes the exponential function.

LN: computes the natural logarithm.

ODD: tests if a number is odd.

ORD: gives the ordinal number of an ordinal value.

PRED:	gives the predecessor of an ordinal value.
ROUND:	rounds a real to the nearest integer.
SIN:	computes the sine.
SQR:	computes the square.
SQRT:	computes the square root.
SUCC:	gives the successor of an ordinal value.
TRUNC:	truncates a real value to its integer part.

3

IMPLEMENTATION-DEPENDENT FEATURES

3.1 HP 1000   All standard functions and procedures are available.

3.2 J & W/CDC   All standard functions and procedures are available.

3.3 OMSI   The procedures PACK, UNPACK and DISPOSE are not implemented.

3.4 Pascal/Z   The procedures PACK, UNPACK and DISPOSE are not implemented.

3.5 UCSD   The procedures PACK, UNPACK, and DISPOSE are not implemented. The procedures READ and WRITE can only be used with text or interactive files. The function ARCTAN is implemented only under the name ATAN. The TRANSCEND library of the Apple implementation contains ATAN, COS, EXP, LN, SQRT.

statement

Statements describe the actions performed by a computer.

□ SYMBOL ■ STANDARD ■ J & W/CDC ■ PASCAL/Z
□ IDENTIFIER ■ HP 1000 ■ OMSI ■ UCSD
■ CONCEPT

•

1
SYNTAX

1.1 Statement

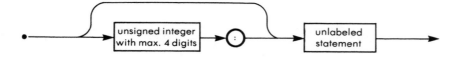

statement

1.2 Unlabeled Statement

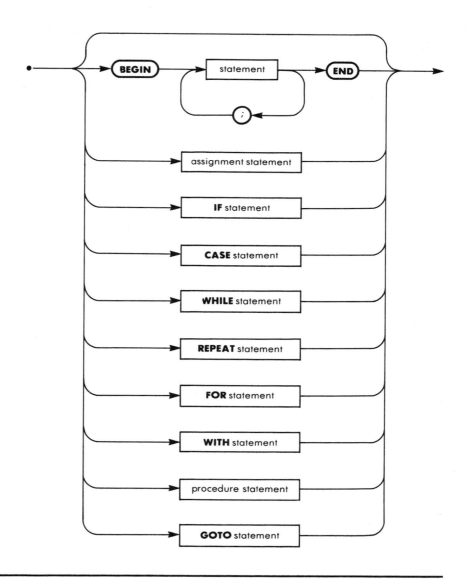

statement

2
DESCRIPTION

The assignment statement is used to give a value to a variable or a function. The IF statement allows selection for execution of one of two statements as a function of the value of a Boolean expression. The CASE statement allows selection for execution of one among several statements as a function of the value of an ordinal expression. The WHILE, REPEAT and FOR statements are used when a group of statements has to be executed repeatedly. The WITH statement is used to allow shorter notation when record fields are referenced. The procedure statement is used to start the execution of a procedure. The GOTO statement is used to modify the order of execution of the statements in a program.

3
IMPLEMENTATION-DEPENDENT FEATURES

See individual headings.

4
EXAMPLE

Examples of statements can be found under almost all headings.

STR is a non-standard predefined procedure that converts an integer or long integer into a STRING.

☐ SYMBOL   ☐ STANDARD   ☐ J & W/CDC   ☐ PASCAL/Z

■ IDENTIFIER   ☐ HP 1000   ☐ OMSI   ■ UCSD

☐ CONCEPT

1
SYNTAX

STR statement:

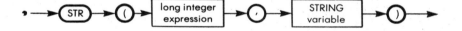

2
DESCRIPTION

The procedure STR has two parameters: the first is a long integer expression, and the second, which is a variable parameter, is a STRING. The long integer is converted into a STRING, so that it can be printed, or manipulated by the STRING functions and procedures.

3
IMPLEMENTATION-DEPENDENT FEATURES

STR is only implemented in UCSD Pascal.

4
EXAMPLE

```
PROGRAM STRDEMO(OUTPUT);
(* UCSD ONLY *)
VAR
      STRN : STRING;
      I : INTEGER[30];
BEGIN
      I := 1053961;
      STR(I,STRN);
      WRITELN('I = ',STRN)
END.
```

string

A standard character string constant is a non-empty sequence of characters enclosed by single quote marks. A standard string-type is a packed array of CHAR whose lower bound is one; a character string constant with more than one element is a string-type.

☐ SYMBOL   ■ STANDARD   ■ J & W/CDC   ■ PASCAL/Z

☐ IDENTIFIER   ■ HP 1000   ■ OMSI   ■ UCSD

■ CONCEPT

1
SYNTAX

String:

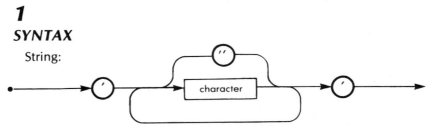

Note: a single quote in a string is denoted by two single quotes.

2
DESCRIPTION

A character string with a single element is a value of type CHAR. Character string constants with more than one element are packed arrays of characters. As such, they are the only structured constants in Pascal.

String constants with more than one element can be used as constants in the following statements:

1. In an assignment when the variable to be assigned to is of string-type (a packed array of characters), with the same number of elements as characters in the string.

2. As an operand for the relational operators =, <=, >=, <, > and <>, if the other operand is of string-type (a packed array of characters), with the same number of elements as characters in the string. To order unequal strings, the ordinal numbers of the characters of both strings are compared consecutively, as they appear in the strings. The first pair of different characters determines the ordering of the strings. *Note:* two string-type variables are also compared in this manner.

3. As an actual parameter of the functions WRITE and WRITELN. *Note:* string-types may also be used as actual parameters of WRITE and WRITELN.

4. As actual parameters corresponding to formal parameters declared to be string-types.

3

IMPLEMENTATION-DEPENDENT FEATURES

3.1 HP 1000

3.1.1 Syntax   The syntax of strings is extended.

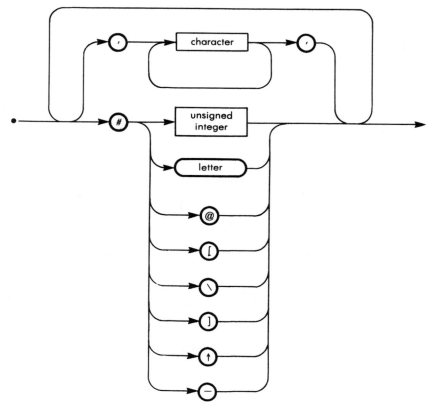

In strings the character # (ASCII 35) can play three different roles:

— In a string delimited by quotes, # represents itself.

— Followed by an unsigned integer, # represents the ASCII character of which the ordinal number is equal to the unsigned integer.

— Followed by a letter, or any of the characters @ [\ ] ↑ __, # corresponds to the character generated by an ASCII keyboard when the control key and a letter or a special character key are struck.

3.1.2 String Expressions In the syntax of HP 1000, string expressions are not limited to string constants and string-types (packed arrays of CHAR). Normal arrays of CHAR are also acceptable.

String-type:

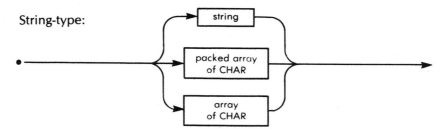

String-types may be copied by assignment statements, and compared in relational expressions. Two strings are equal when their contents are equal, after the shorter is extended by trailing blanks to match the length of the longer.

The three varieties of string-types may be mixed in assignments and relational operators.

When a shorter string is assigned to a longer string, the shorter is extended by trailing blanks. It is illegal to assign a string to a variable which is not long enough to hold it.

Packed or unpacked strings and string constants may be passed as value parameters to procedures or functions when these procedures or functions expect packed or unpacked strings with a length not less than the length of the actual parameters.

The three varieties of strings can be used as actual parameters for the READ and WRITE procedures.

string

3.2 J & W/CDC Strings can be used in relational expressions with the operators = or <> if, and only if, the strings have less than ten characters, or an exact multiple of ten characters.

3.3 OMSI None known.

3.4 Pascal/Z Strings as described in the standard are available, but a predefined type STRING also exists. Refer to the predefined type STRING heading.

Character string constants with more than one element may not appear on the left of a relational operator.

3.5 UCSD Strings as described in the standard are available, but a predefined type STRING also exists. Refer to the predefined type STRING heading.

When character string constants are compared with STRING types, the comparison is strictly lexicographic. The two operands do not have to be of the same length.

4
EXAMPLE

```
PROGRAM BLACKWHITE(INPUT,OUTPUT);
VAR DATA,ANSWER : PACKED ARRAY[1..5] OF CHAR;
     I : 1..5;
BEGIN
     WRITELN('TYPE BLACK OR WHITE');
     FOR I := 1 TO 5 DO READ(DATA[I]);
     WRITELN;
     IF DATA = 'BLACK'
          THEN ANSWER := 'WHITE'
          ELSE
               IF DATA = 'WHITE'
                    THEN ANSWER := 'BLACK'
                    ELSE ANSWER := 'SORRY';
     WRITELN('I LIKE CONTRADICTIONS : ',ANSWER)
END.
```

STRING

The type STRING is a non-standard predefined type, representing character strings with a variable length.

1
SYNTAX

1.1 String Type   Refer to paragraph 3 under this heading.

1.2 CHAR Variable Referenced as Part of a STRING.

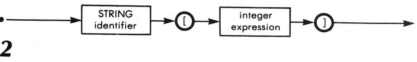

2
DESCRIPTION

2.1 Structure   The non-standard predefined type STRING is a structured type which has a current length component and packed array of CHARs. There are two ways such structures have been modeled or implemented using standard Pascal: files and records. Those Pascals which have pre-defined STRING types also have non-standard syntax and semantics for operations on STRING. The standard string constant and type (previous heading) interact with STRING types in various ways.

Note: When capitalized, "STRING" refers to the non-standard prede-fined type of this heading; lower case "string" refers to the standard type or constant.

One implementation model of a STRING is as a file of CHAR which has a maximum length. Such a file does not usually have an external counterpart; it is an "in-core" file.

The implementation model analogy used by Pascal/Z and UCSD Pascal is to consider a STRING as a record containing an integer subrange of

0..255 (the length) and a packed array of CHAR. The maximum length, which determines the storage requirements for a variable of this type, can be specified in the TYPE or VAR sections. (Refer to paragraph 3 under this heading.)

A CHAR element of a STRING can be accessed as shown in syntax diagram 1.2. In this case, the integer expression must be less than or equal to the current length (i.e., within the range of the current length).

2.2 Assignments Assignment of a value to a STRING variable can be made using the assignment statement, the STRING manipulation functions and procedures, or the READ and READLN statements.

Such assignments may affect the length of the STRING.

2.3 Relational Operators STRINGs can be compared by relational operators. When the length of the STRINGs to be compared is different and the ordering relation between the two has not been determined over the length of the shorter STRING, the comparison is done as if the shortest STRING has been extended by nulls (the lowest lexicographic character) to match the length of the longest.

Two STRINGs are equal when their contents are equal. To order unequal STRINGs, the ordinal numbers of the characters of both STRINGs are compared consecutively, as they appear in the STRINGs. The first pair of different characters determines the ordering of the STRINGs. A character string constant is treated as a STRING with its apparent length used as its current length.

3

IMPLEMENTATION-DEPENDENT FEATURES

3.1 Pascal/Z

3.1.1 Syntax

STRING type:

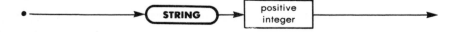

STRING is a reserved word in Pascal/Z.

STRING

3.1.2 Restrictions on the Use of STRINGs When a STRING is a *variable* parameter of a procedure or function, the *maximum size* of the *actual* parameter must be greater than or equal to the size of the *formal* parameter.

When a STRING is a *value* parameter of a procedure or a function, the size of the *actual* parameter must be less than or equal to the *maximum size* of the *formal* parameter.

When a STRING is used in relational expressions, a constant string may not appear on the left side of the expression.

3.1.3 Functions and Procedures Manipulating STRINGs APPEND: appends a STRING to another STRING. (See the APPEND heading.) The functions LENGTH and INDEX and the procedure SETLENGTH are provided in the Pascal/Z library, but are not predeclared. The SETLENGTH procedure is the only way to generate a zero-length or null string.

3.2 UCSD

3.2.1 Syntax

STRING type:

When the maximum length parameter is omitted, a length of 80 characters is assumed.

3.2.2 Functions and Procedures Manipulating STRINGs Refer to the corresponding headings for details.

CONCAT:	concatenates STRINGs.
COPY:	copies a part from one STRING to another.
DELETE:	deletes a part of a STRING.
INSERT:	inserts a STRING in another.
LENGTH:	returns the length of a STRING.
POS:	returns the position of a STRING in another string.
STR:	converts a long integer into a STRING.

3.2.3 NULL STRING A pair of single quote marks is used to represent a null or zero-length string constant.

STRING

4
EXAMPLE

```
PROGRAM STRING1;
(* UCSD ONLY *)
VAR ST1,ST2,ST3 : STRING[25];
    BEGIN
    ST1 := 'STRING ONE';
    ST2 := 'STRING TWO';
    (* STRING COMPARISONS *)
    IF ST1 = ST2
        THEN WRITELN('''',ST1,''' = ''',ST2,''', STRANGE!')
        ELSE
            IF ST1 < ST2
                THEN WRITELN('''',ST1,''' < ''',ST2,''', OK')
                ELSE WRITELN('''T'' PRECEDES ''O'' IN ALPHABET ?');
    (* STRING INPUT *)
    WRITELN('TYPE ''',ST1,'''');
    READLN(ST3);
    IF ST1 <> ST3
        THEN WRITELN('LEARN HOW TO TYPE ')
        ELSE WRITELN('GOOD');
    (* CONCATENATE STRINGS *)
    ST3 := CONCAT(ST1,',TWO');
    IF ST1 < ST3
        THEN WRITELN('''',ST1,''' < ''',ST3,''', OK !')
        ELSE WRITELN('''',ST1,''' >= ''',ST3,''', STRANGE !');
    (* DELETE A PART OF A STRING *)
    DELETE(ST3,POS('ONE',ST3),4);
    IF ST2 <> ST3
        THEN WRITELN('''',ST2,''' <> ''',ST3,''', STRANGE !')
        ELSE WRITELN('''',ST2,''' = ''',ST3,''', OK !')
END.
```

subrange

A subrange type defines a limited range of the values of an ordinal type.
The ordinal type is called the host type.

☐ SYMBOL   ■ STANDARD   ■ J & W/CDC   ■ PASCAL/Z
☐ IDENTIFIER   ■ HP 1000   ■ OMSI   ■ UCSD
■ CONCEPT

1
SYNTAX

Subrange Type:

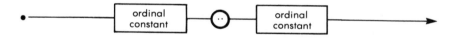

The ordinal constants must be of the same ordinal (host) type. The leftmost one must be less than or equal to the one on the right.

2
DESCRIPTION

A subrange type can be used whenever an ordinal type is legal. The use of subranges improves the clarity of the program, and allows extensive range-checking at compile or run time.

Some compilers are able to use more compact representations for subranges than for the host type.

3

IMPLEMENTATION-DEPENDENT FEATURES

3.1 HP 1000 Significant savings in memory space and execution time are obtained by declaring integer variables as subrange types with upper and lower limits UL and LL satisfying the relation:

$$-2^{15} <= \text{ LL} < \text{UL} < 2^{15}$$

subrange

3.2 J & W/CDC   None known.

3.3 OMSI   None known.

3.4 Pascal/Z   Significant savings in memory space are obtained by declaring integer variables as subrange types with upper and lower limits UL and LL satisfying the relation:

$$-2^7 <= \text{LL} < \text{UL} < 2^7$$

whenever possible. When range-checking is being done, assignments to such subrange integers can be slower than assignments to normal integers.

3.5 UCSD   None known.

4
EXAMPLE

```
PROGRAM HISTOGRAM(INPUT,OUTPUT);
CONST MAX = 100;
TYPE RANGE = 0..MAX;
VAR INDEX : RANGE;
    HISTO : ARRAY[RANGE] OF INTEGER;
    VALUE : INTEGER;
BEGIN
    FOR INDEX : = 0 TO MAX DO HISTO[INDEX] : = 0;
    WHILE NOT EOF DO
        BEGIN
            (* VALUE IS INTEGER INSTEAD OF 0..MAX TO AVOID I/O
            ERRORS WHEN DATA IS TYPED *)
            READ(VALUE);
```

```
IF VALUE IN [0..MAX]
    THEN
        BEGIN
            INDEX := VALUE;
            HISTO[INDEX] := HISTO[INDEX] + 1
        END
    ELSE
        WRITELN('VALUE OUT OF RANGE: ',VALUE)
END;
FOR INDEX :=0 TO MAX DO
    WRITELN(HISTO[INDEX],'NUMBERS HAD VALUE: ',INDEX)
END.
```

SUCC

SUCC is a standard ordinal function that returns the value following the given value in the range of all values the ordinal type can take.

□ SYMBOL ■ STANDARD ■ J & W/CDC ■ PASCAL/Z
■ IDENTIFIER ■ HP 1000 ■ OMSI ■ UCSD
□ CONCEPT

1
SYNTAX

Factor containing the function SUCC:

2
DESCRIPTION

The function SUCC has one ordinal parameter. The returned value is of the same ordinal type, and is equal to the value following the parameter's value, in the range of values that ordinal type can take. The successor of the last defined value is undefined.

3
IMPLEMENTATION-DEPENDENT FEATURES

None known.

4
EXAMPLE

```
PROGRAM SUCCTEST(INPUT, OUTPUT);
VAR C : CHAR;
BEGIN
     WRITELN('TYPE A CHARACTER');
     READLN(C);
     WRITELN('THE CHARACTER FOLLOWING ',C:1,' IS ',SUCC(C))
END.
```

TEXT

The type TEXT is a predefined file type representing a file of CHAR.

☐ SYMBOL   ■ STANDARD   ■ J & W/CDC   ■ PASCAL/Z
■ IDENTIFIER   ■ HP 1000   ■ OMSI   ■ UCSD
☐ CONCEPT

1
SYNTAX

1.1 Text Type

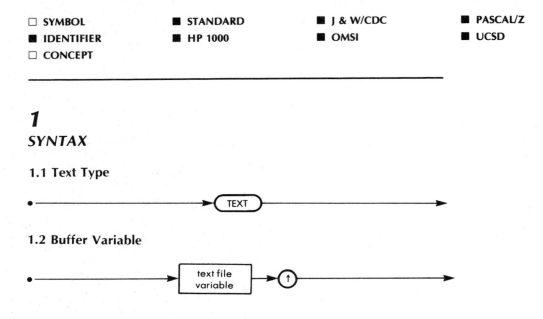

1.2 Buffer Variable

2
DESCRIPTION

The type TEXT is a file type, and as such, has all of the properties of files. A TEXT file, however, also has one important additional property: it is divided into lines.

The way in which the end of a line is recorded in a file is implementation-dependent. (In most implementations, the special characters called "carriage return" and "line feed" are used, but these characters are not available in several older character sets.)

Three standard functions are provided to handle end of lines:

WRITELN: terminates the current line of the text.

READLN: skips to the beginning of the next line of the text (the buffer variable gets the value of the first character of the next line).

EOLN: a Boolean function which is TRUE when the end of line has been reached (the buffer variable contains a blank when EOLN becomes TRUE).

More information about these functions is provided under the corresponding headings.

Note: for reasons of efficiency, several operating systems delay WRITE operations until a complete line can be written; therefore, it is a good practice to write an end of line at the end of the last line of a TEXT file.

Two standard predefined TEXT files exist, and are used to establish a dialogue between a program and its user. These files are named INPUT and OUTPUT. While they do not have to be declared, if used, INPUT and OUTPUT must appear in the program statement. In several implementations, OUTPUT must appear in the program statement (even if not used explicitly), in order to allow reporting of run time errors.

Additional information is provided under the corresponding headings.

3

IMPLEMENTATION-DEPENDENT FEATURES

3.1 HP 1000 The number of characters per line read from a TEXT file is always even. When the number of characters is odd, a trailing blank is added before the end of line.

3.2 J & W/CDC A variable number of trailing blanks is added before the end of line.

3.3 OMSI None known.

3.4 Pascal/Z None known.

3.5 UCSD Two varieties of TEXT files exist: TEXT and INTERACTIVE. The predefined files INPUT and OUTPUT are of type INTERACTIVE. See the INTERACTIVE heading for more information.

TEXT

4

EXAMPLE

```
PROGRAM LOWUP1(INP,OUT,OUTPUT);
(* THIS PROGRAM CONVERTS THE FILE INP, WHICH CONTAINS UPPER AND
LOWER CASE LETTERS AS WELL AS OTHER CHARACTERS, INTO A FILE OUT.
OUT CONTAINS ONLY UPPER CASE LETTERS AND THE OTHER CHARACTERS AS
THEY APPEARED IN INP *)
VAR INP,OUT : TEXT;
     LET : CHAR;
     OFFSET : INTEGER;
BEGIN
     RESET(INP); REWRITE(OUT);
     OFFSET := ORD('A') − ORD('a');
     WHILE NOT EOF(INP)DO
         IF NOT EOLN(INP)
         THEN
             BEGIN
                 READ(INP,LET);
                 IF LET IN['a'..'z'] THEN
                     LET := CHR(OFFSET) + ORD(LET));
                 WRITE(OUT,LET)
             END
         ELSE
             BEGIN
                 READLN(INP);
                 WRITELN(OUT)
             END;
     WRITELN(OUT)
(* THE FINAL WRITELN IS REQUIRED, SINCE THE FUNCTIONS EOF AND
EOLN BOTH BECOME TRUE AT THE END OF THE LAST LINE *)

END.
```

The reserved word THEN is a part of the IF statement.

■ SYMBOL   ■ STANDARD   ■ J & W/CDC   ■ PASCAL/Z
□ IDENTIFIER   ■ HP 1000   ■ OMSI   ■ UCSD
□ CONCEPT

1
SYNTAX

IF statement:

2
DESCRIPTION

See the IF heading.

3
IMPLEMENTATION-DEPENDENT FEATURES

None known.

TIME

TIME is a non-standard predefined function or procedure that reads the system's real time clock.

□ SYMBOL   □ STANDARD   ■ J & W/CDC   □ PASCAL/Z
■ IDENTIFIER   □ HP 1000   ■ OMSI   ■ UCSD
□ CONCEPT

1
SYNTAX

See paragraph 3 of this heading.

2
DESCRIPTION

In implementations where the operating system maintains a real time clock, TIME is a function or a procedure that provides the time of day.

3
IMPLEMENTATION-DEPENDENT FEATURES

3.1 J & W/CDC

3.1.1 Syntax

TIME procedure:

3.1.2 Description
The procedure TIME has one parameter of type ALFA. After execution of the procedure TIME, the parameter contains the time of the day in hours, minutes and seconds after midnight in the form HH.MM.SS.

3.2 OMSI

3.2.1 Syntax

TIME function:

3.2.2 Description   The real function TIME returns the time in hours after midnight. (Minutes and seconds are expressed as fractions of hours.)

3.3 UCSD

3.3.1 Syntax

TIME procedure:

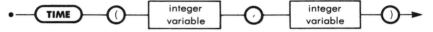

3.3.2 Description   TIME has two integer variable parameters:

TIME(HighWord, LowWord);

HighWord and LowWord form a 32-bit unsigned integer representing the current value of the system clock in 60ths of seconds. It is usually the time since last boot, and not the time of day (there are no time-of-day conventions). Because the LowWord is the low-order 16 bits of a 32-bit integer, a negative value actually represents 65536 more than its apparent value.

3.3.3 Implementation-Dependent Features   TIME is not supported by Apple or most other systems which do not have clock hardware.

4

EXAMPLES

```
PROGRAM CDCTIME(OUTPUT);
(* CDC ONLY *)
VAR T : ALFA;
BEGIN
    TIME(T);
    WRITELN(' IT IS ',T,' NOW ')
END.
PROGRAM OMSITIME;
(* OMSI ONLY *)
```

```
VAR H,M,S : INTEGER;
     T : REAL;
BEGIN
     T := TIME;
     H := TRUNC(T);
     M := TRUNC((T−H) * 60);
     S := TRUNC(((T−H) * 60 − M) * 60);
     WRITELN(' IT IS ',H:2,' : ',M:2,' : ',S:2,' NOW ')
END.
PROGRAM UCSDTIME;
(* TIME AN EMPTY NESTED FOR LOOP *)
(* UCSD ONLY *)
VAR INNER, OUTER: INTEGER;
     STARTHI, STARTLO, ENDHI, ENDLO : INTEGER;
     ELAPSEDHI, ELAPSEDLO : INTEGER;
BEGIN
     TIME (STARTHI, STARTLO);
     FOR OUTER : = 1 TO 1000 DO
          FOR INNER : = 1 TO 1000 DO
          (* NOTHING *);
     TIME (ENDHI, ENDLO);
     ENDHI : = ENDHI * 2;
     IF ENDLO < 0 THEN ENDHI : = ENDHI +1
     STARTHI : = STARTHI * 2;
     IF STARTLO < 0 THEN STARTHI : = STARTHI + 1;
     ELAPSEDLO : = ENDLO − STARTLO;
     IF ELAPSEDLO < 0 THEN BEGIN
          ELAPSEDLO : = ELAPSEDLO + MAXINT + 1;
          ENDHI : = ENDHI − 1;
          END;
     IF ENDHI − STARTHI < 0 THEN WRITELN ('ELAPSED TIME TOO BIG');
          ELSE WRITELN ('ELAPSED TIME = ', ELAPSED DIV 60, 'SECONDS');
END.
```

The reserved word TO is a part of the FOR statement, and is used when the loop parameter has to take increasing values.

■ SYMBOL   ■ STANDARD   ■ J & W/CDC   ■ PASCAL/Z
□ IDENTIFIER   ■ HP 1000   ■ OMSI   ■ UCSD
□ CONCEPT

1
SYNTAX

FOR statement:

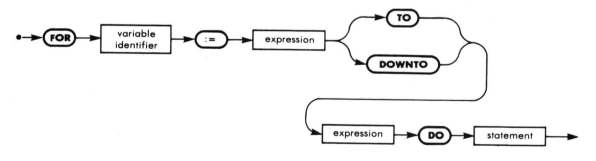

2
DESCRIPTION

See the FOR heading.

3
IMPLEMENTATION-DEPENDENT FEATURES

None known.

TO

4
EXAMPLE

```pascal
PROGRAM FORLOOP(OUTPUT);
VAR
    I : INTEGER;
BEGIN
    WRITELN('LET US COUNT');
    FOR I := 1 TO 10 DO
        WRITELN(I)
END.
```

TREESEARCH

TREESEARCH is a non-standard predefined integer function that searches binary trees.

☐ SYMBOL   ☐ STANDARD   ☐ J & W/CDC   ☐ PASCAL/Z
■ IDENTIFIER   ☐ HP 1000   ☐ OMSI   ■ UCSD
☐ CONCEPT

1
SYNTAX

TREESEARCH function:

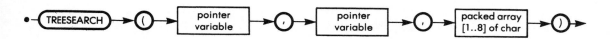

2
DESCRIPTION

TREESEARCH is a function which is used in the UCSD Pascal compiler, but is also available for user programs. It can be used to search a binary tree built out of linked records of the following type:

NODE = **RECORD**

                 NAME : **PACKED ARRAY**[1..8] **OF** CHAR;

                 LLINK, RLINK : ↑NODE;

                 ... any other fields ...

     END;

It is assumed that the names are not duplicated in the tree. It is also assumed that the names are assigned to nodes in alphabetical order

TREESEARCH

such that the left subnode's name precedes the name of the corresponding node, and that the name of the corresponding node precedes the name of the right subnode. All links which do not point to other nodes must have the value NIL.

TREESEARCH has three parameters: the first, Rootptr is a variable (of type pointer) that points to the root of the tree. The second parameter, Nodeptr, is also a variable of type pointer. Nodeptr will be set by TREESEARCH to point to the requested node. The third parameter, a packed array of CHAR, contains the name of the node to be sought:

TREESEARCH(Rootptr,Nodeptr,Array);

TREESEARCH can return three different values:

- 0: If the node has been found and Nodeptr points to it.

- 1: If the name was not found. If a node were to be added to the tree, it should be the right subnode of the node to which Nodeptr points.

- -1: If the name was not found. If a node were to be added to the tree, it should be the left subnode of the node to which Nodeptr points.

3
IMPLEMENTATION-DEPENDENT FEATURES

TREESEARCH is only implemented in UCSD Pascal.

TRUE

TRUE is a predefined Boolean constant equal to the Boolean value true.

☐ SYMBOL   ■ STANDARD   ■ J & W/CDC   ■ PASCAL/Z
■ IDENTIFIER   ■ HP 1000   ■ OMSI   ■ UCSD
☐ CONCEPT

1
SYNTAX

TRUE is a Boolean constant identifier. Refer to the CONSTant heading.

2
DESCRIPTION

TRUE is a predefined Boolean constant, equal to the Boolean value TRUE.

3
IMPLEMENTATION-DEPENDENT FEATURES

None known.

4
EXAMPLE

See the program TRUTHTABLE under the FALSE heading.

TRUNC

> **TRUNC is a standard integer function that truncates a real value to its integer part.**

☐ **SYMBOL**   ■ **STANDARD**   ■ **J & W/CDC**   ■ **PASCAL/Z**
■ **IDENTIFIER**   ■ **HP 1000**   ■ **OMSI**   ■ **UCSD**
☐ **CONCEPT**

1
SYNTAX

Factor containing the TRUNC function:

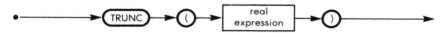

2
DESCRIPTION

The function TRUNC has one real parameter. The returned value is integer, and is equal to the integer part of the parameter. For example:

TRUNC(3.9) = 3; TRUNC(−3.9) = −3

3
IMPLEMENTATION-DEPENDENT FEATURES

3.1 HP 1000   TRUNC can be used to truncate LONGREAL expressions.

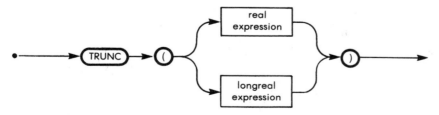

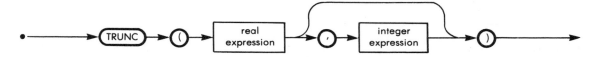

3.2 J & W/CDC A particular form of the TRUNC function with two parameters exists.

The factor TRUNC(X,N) is equivalent to the factor TRUNC(X*Y) where $Y = 2^N$.

3.3 OMSI None known.

3.4 Pascal/Z None known.

3.5 UCSD TRUNC can be used to convert long integer expressions into an integer value.

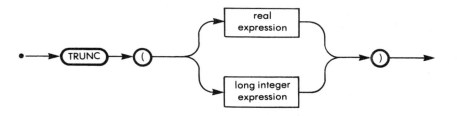

4
EXAMPLE

```
PROGRAM TRUNCTEST(INPUT,OUTPUT);
VAR R : REAL;
BEGIN
    WRITELN('TYPE A REAL NUMBER');
    READLN(R);
    WRITELN('THE TRUNCATED VALUE OF ',R:10:3,' IS ',TRUNC(R))
END.
```

TYPE

Data items are characterized by their TYPE which defines both the set of values that they can take and their internal representation.

- ■ SYMBOL
- □ IDENTIFIER
- □ CONCEPT

- ■ STANDARD
- ■ HP 1000

- ■ J & W/CDC
- ■ OMSI

- ■ PASCAL/Z
- ■ UCSD

1
SYNTAX

1.1 Type Definition

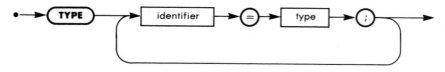

1.2 Type

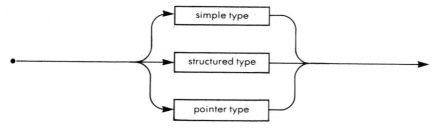

1.3 Simple Type

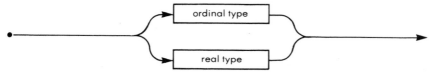

1.4 Ordinal Type

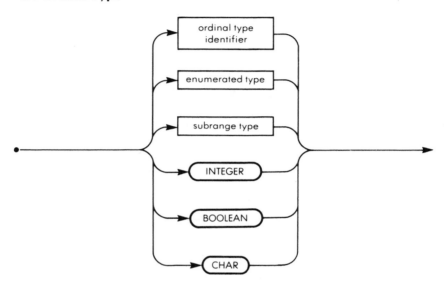

1.5 Enumerated Type

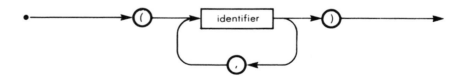

1.6 Subrange Type

1.7 Real Type

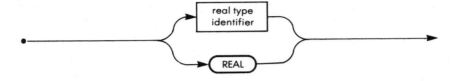

1.8 Pointer Type

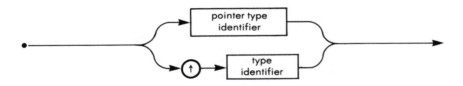

1.9 Structured Type

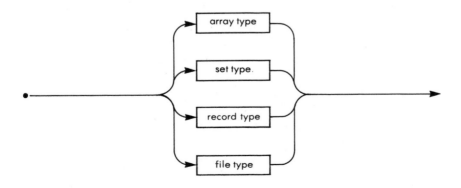

1.10 Array Type

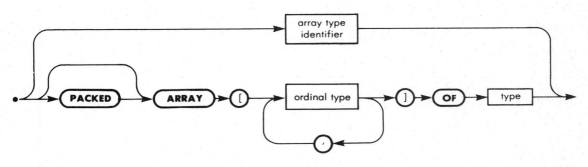

1.11 Set Type

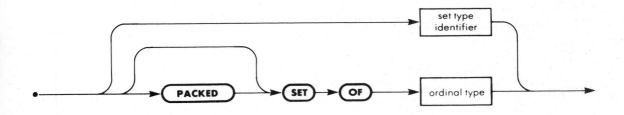

1.12 Record Type

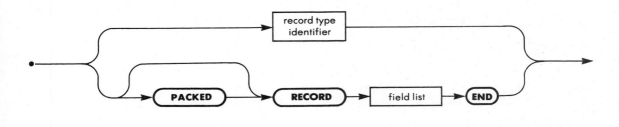

TYPE

1.13 Field List

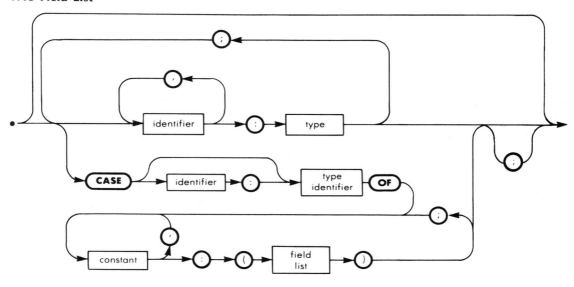

1.14 File Type

2
DESCRIPTION

To be able to handle data items, the compiler has to know the set of values they can take. Therefore it is necessary to declare the type of constants and variables used in the program. The type of constants is declared implicitly through their value. A variable's type limits the set of values that it may assume. To be compatible, types must have identical names, not just identical structures. The type of a variable must be declared through the VAR declaration.

Types can be subdivided into three categories: simple types, pointer types and structured types. The structured types are the arrays, the sets, the records and the files. Some types are predefined in the language:

— INTEGER
— REAL
— BOOLEAN
— CHARacter
— TEXT

Other types (subranges, enumerations, and structured types) can be defined by the programmer, either directly in the VAR declaration, or separately in a type declaration. In this last case the defined type gets a name which can be used in VAR declarations. A named type is needed in parameter lists.

For more information on these different types, refer to the corresponding headings.

3

IMPLEMENTATION-DEPENDENT FEATURES

3.1 HP 1000   An additional simple type LONGREAL, exists.

Simple Type:

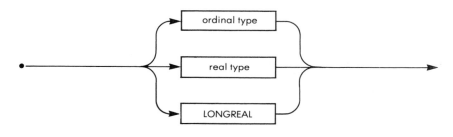

TYPE

LONGREAL Type:

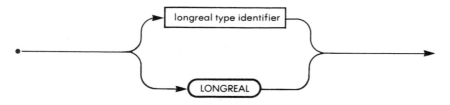

3.2 J & W/CDC An additional structured type, ALFA, exists. It is used for strings of ten characters.

Structured Type:

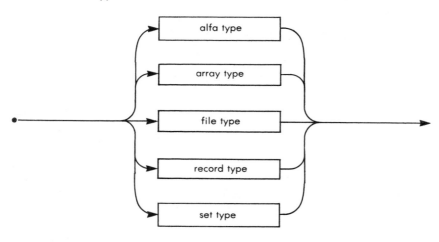

ALFA Type:

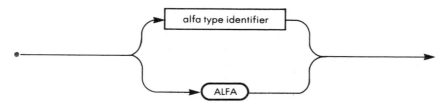

3.3 OMSI   Although the range of values for integers is −32768..+32767, it is possible to declare integers with values in the interval 0..65535 by a subrange declaration. Such integers are called unsigned integers.

3.4 Pascal/Z   None known.

3.5 UCSD   The UCSD Pascal implementation uses structural, instead of name, compatibility. Thus, "fingers = 1..10" and "toes = 1..10" are compatible types in UCSD Pascal but not in standard Pascal. The UCSD Pascal implementation has additional predeclared types.

Structured Type:

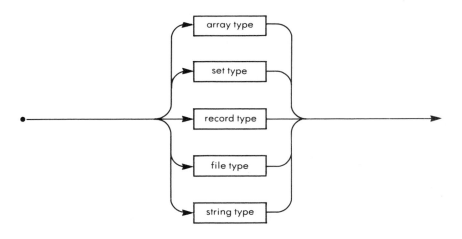

String Type:

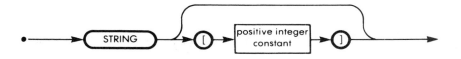

TYPE

File Type:

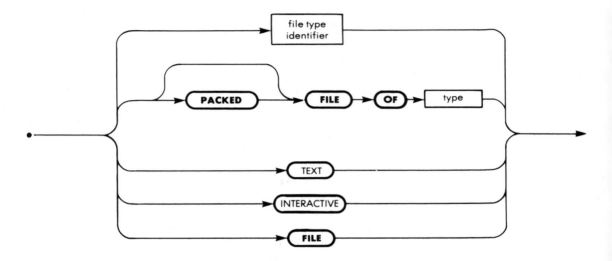

Long Integer Type:

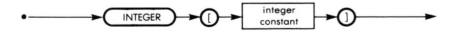

4
EXAMPLE

Examples of TYPE definitions can be found under almost all headings.

UNDEFINED

UNDEFINED is a predefined function that is TRUE when its parameter is out of range or indefinite.

☐ SYMBOL   ☐ STANDARD   ■ J & W/CDC   ☐ PASCAL/Z
■ IDENTIFIER   ☐ HP 1000   ☐ OMSI   ☐ UCSD
☐ CONCEPT

1
SYNTAX

UNDEFINED function:

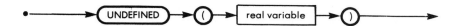

2
DESCRIPTION

The Boolean function UNDEFINED has one REAL parameter X. The function returns a TRUE value when the value of X is either "out-of-range" or "indefinite." In CDC computers, a REAL variable can have an "out-of-range" value as the result of an illegal operation such as a division by 0, and an "indefinite" value as the result of a division of 0 by 0, or the difference of two "out-of-range" terms.

3
IMPLEMENTATION-DEPENDENT FEATURES

Undefined is only implemented in J & W/CDC Pascal.

UNIT

UNIT is a non-standard reserved word that identifies a separate compilation module. A unit has a visible interface to the user but a hidden implementation, both of which are to be stored in a library.

■ SYMBOL   □ STANDARD   □ J & W/CDC   □ PASCAL/Z

□ IDENTIFIER   □ HP 1000   □ OMSI   ■ UCSD

□ CONCEPT

1
SYNTAX

1.1 Compilation

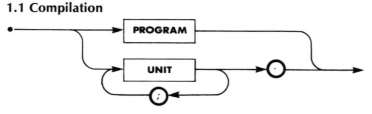

1.2 Program

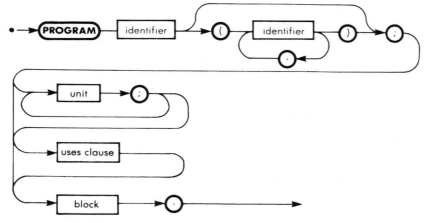

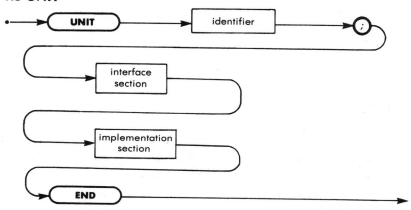

UNIT

1.3 UNIT

1.4 Interface Section

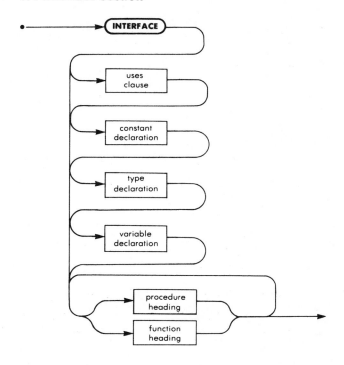

1.5 Implementation Section

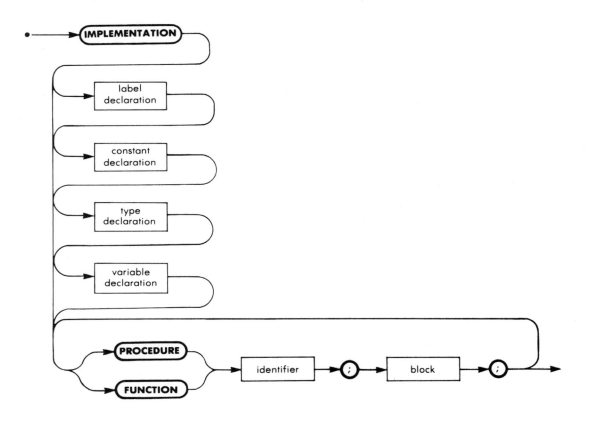

1.6 USES Clause

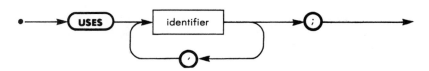

2
DESCRIPTION

Every unit must have a name, an interface section and an implementation section. A unit's name is the identifier following the reserved word UNIT. It is the name under which the unit is to be stored in the library. It is the name by which a USES directive references the unit. When a unit's name is first encountered in a USES directive, the compiler fetches the text of that unit's interface section from the library and processes it at that point. However, an in-line unit will take precedence over any unit subsequently named in a USES statement. Thus, all the constant identifiers, types, variables, procedures and functions in the interface are available to the program or other unit which is using the unit.

A compilation can be either a program or a unit. Either of these can, in turn, contain USES clauses; a program may contain in-line units, which must occur before the first USES clause of the program. After a unit is separately compiled, the text of the interface section and the p-code of the implementation section must be explicitly placed in a library before the unit can be used. If a program uses a unit which is not defined in-line, that unit's code must be linked with the main program by the linker utility to make a fully executable program.

A unit's interface section is its public part. The constant identifiers, types, variables, procedures and functions defined in the interface section are global identifiers at the outermost level, and therefore must not have the same name as any other global identifiers of the using program. These interface section identifiers can be used by a program or a unit just as though they were defined in-line. Only procedure or function headings are included in the interface section, as if they were being declared FORWARD. The types and constants are typically used to specify parameter types; the interface's variables, if any, might be used for state indicators or the bases of dynamic (list) structures. The headings of the interface section make it possible to have both type checking and separate compilation.

The implementation section of a unit is private: it is hidden from the user. It contains the bodies of the procedures and functions declared in the interface section. As with FORWARD-declared procedures, these

UNIT

procedures and functions do not have their formal parameter lists or function types repeated. They may contain nested procedures and functions. The implementation section may also have labels, constant identifiers, types, procedures and functions. These are available only to the implementation section of the unit but are in all other respects global to the program. This provides a way to keep the data structures of the unit itself hidden. Because all variables of an implementation section are in fact global to the program, they have the same lifetime as the program and can be used for preserving or passing information across invocations of procedures or functions of a unit.

When a unit uses another unit (i.e., a USES clause appears in the using unit's interface section), both units' names must appear in the USES clause of whatever program or unit is being compiled. The order of specification in the USES clause must be from the most deeply nested to the least deeply nested. Thus, if unit A used units B and C, and unit D was used by B, then the USES clause of a program using A would have to specify "USES D,B,C,A".

3
IMPLEMENTATION-DEPENDENT FEATURES

Units are only implemented in UCSD Pascal. In UCSD Pascal II.0 and Apple Pascal, the implementation section of a unit may not contain file variable declarations; and in these versions segment procedures or functions may not be declared inside an interface section.

3.1 Separate Units   Several UCSD Pascal implementations permit the use of the reserved word SEPARATE prior to the reserved word UNIT. The p-code from a separate unit is linked into the base segment of a program and not assigned to its own segment. The implementation of separate units is unreliable in some implementations, and should be used with great caution.

3.2 Labels   The ability to declare labels in an implementation section is useful only in the newer implementations of UCSD Pascal (Apple 1.1 and IV.0 from SofTech Microsystems) which have initialization and possibly termination code passages in the body of the implementation section. In II.0 UCSD Pascal, labels may be defined in the interface section, but are of no use because branching is not permitted from one procedure or function to another.

3.3 Intrinsic Units   Apple Pascal permits the user to identify a unit as intrinsic. An intrinsic unit is not combined with the p-code of a program by the linker, but left in the library until the program is loaded. At load time, the code and data segments of the unit are taken directly from the system library. The code and data segments are pre-linked to the segment numbers following the CODE and DATA directives which follow the INTRINSIC directive preceding the implementation section of the unit.

4

EXAMPLE

4.1 Program Using a Separately Compiled UNIT

```
UNIT NONDECIMAL;
(* UCSD ONLY *)
(* PROVIDE FOR HEXADECIMAL BASED NUMBERS *)
INTERFACE
    CONST
        A = 10; B = 11; C = 12;
        D = 13; E = 14; F = 15;
    TYPE
        NIBBLE = 0..15;
        BYTE = 0..255;
    FUNCTION HEX (HI,LO: NIBBLE): BYTE;
IMPLEMENTATION
```

```
FUNCTION HEX;
      BEGIN
            HEX := (HI * 16) + LO
      END;
END.
```

```
PROGRAM USESEXAMPLE;
(* UCSD ONLY *)
USES NONDECIMAL; (* FROM LIBRARY *)

BEGIN
     WRITELN('THE VALUE OF THE HEXADECIMAL NUMBER ''DE'' IS ', HEX(D,E))
END.
```

4.2 Program Using an In-Line UNIT

```
PROGRAM INLINEUNIT;
(* UCSD ONLY *)
(* 3 NIBBLE VERSION OF USESEXAMPLE *)
UNIT NONDECIMAL; (* IN-LINE *)
INTERFACE
     CONST
          A = 10; B = 11; C = 12;
          D = 13; E = 14; F = 15;
     TYPE
          NIBBLE = 0..15;
          BYTE = 0..255;
     FUNCTION HEX(HI,MID,LO: NIBBLE): BYTE;
IMPLEMENTATION
```

```
FUNCTION HEX;
    BEGIN
        HEX : = (((HI * 16) + MID) * 16) + LO
    END;
END;
USES NONDECIMAL; (* IN-LINE *)
BEGIN
    WRITELN('THE VALUE OF THE HEXADECIMAL NUMBER ''DEF'' IS ', HEX(D,E,F))
END.
```

UNITBUSY

UNITBUSY is a non-standard predefined function that tests if an I/O device is busy.

☐ SYMBOL   ☐ STANDARD   ☐ J & W/CDC   ☐ PASCAL/Z
■ IDENTIFIER   ☐ HP 1000   ☐ OMSI   ■ UCSD
☐ CONCEPT

1
SYNTAX

The UNITBUSY function:

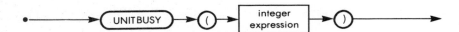

2
DESCRIPTION

The function UNITBUSY has one parameter, which is the integer name of an I/O device. UNITBUSY returns a Boolean value that is TRUE when the I/O device is busy.

Expertise and caution are required when using the UNIT procedures, since no protection against errors is provided.

3
IMPLEMENTATION-DEPENDENT FEATURES

UNITBUSY is only implemented in UCSD Pascals which support "asynchronous" I/O.

UNITBUSY

Note: UNIT procedures and functions are not available in the Intel and Z80/8080 implementations of UCSD Pascal.

4
EXAMPLE

```
PROGRAM PRINTBUSY(OUTPUT);
(* WAIT FOR THE PRINTER TO FINISH *)
CONST
    PRINTER = 6;                          {PRINTER'S INTEGER NAME}
VAR
    STR : STRING;
BEGIN
    STR := 'HELLO WORLD';
    UNITCLEAR(PRINTER);
    UNITWRITE(PRINTER,STR,5);
    WHILE UNITBUSY(PRINTER) DO
        WRITELN('I AM STILL WAITING')
END.
```

UNITCLEAR

UNITCLEAR is a non-standard predefined procedure that resets an I/O device.

- ☐ SYMBOL
- ■ IDENTIFIER
- ☐ CONCEPT
- ☐ STANDARD
- ☐ HP 1000
- ☐ J & W/CDC
- ☐ OMSI
- ☐ PASCAL/Z
- ■ UCSD

1
SYNTAX

UNITCLEAR statement:

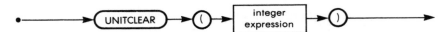

2
DESCRIPTION

The procedure UNITCLEAR has one parameter, which is the integer name of an I/O device. The execution of UNITCLEAR cancels all I/O operations on a device and resets the hardware to its power-up state.

Expertise and caution are required when using the UNIT procedures, since no protection against errors is provided.

3
IMPLEMENTATION-DEPENDENT FEATURES

UNIT procedures are only implemented in UCSD Pascal.

Note: UNIT procedures and functions are not available in the Intel and Z80/8080 implementations of UCSD Pascal.

UNITCLEAR

4
EXAMPLE

```
PROGRAM PRINTEST(OUTPUT);
(* TEST TO SEE IF THERE IS A PRINTER *)
CONST PRINTER = 6;                    {PRINTER'S INTEGER NAME}
BEGIN
     UNITCLEAR(PRINTER);
     IF IORESULT = 0
          THEN WRITELN(' THERE IS A PRINTER ')
          ELSE WRITELN(' SORRY, NO PRINTER ')
END.
```

UNITREAD

UNITREAD *is a non-standard predefined procedure that peforms low-level input operations on various devices.*

- ☐ SYMBOL
- ■ IDENTIFIER
- ☐ CONCEPT

- ☐ STANDARD
- ☐ HP 1000

- ☐ J & W/CDC
- ☐ OMSI

- ☐ PASCAL/Z
- ■ UCSD

1
SYNTAX

UNITREAD statement:

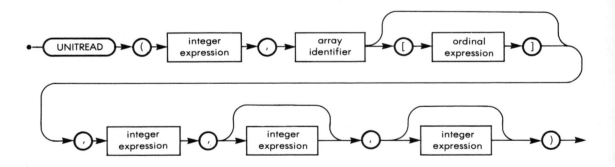

2
DESCRIPTION

The procedure UNITREAD is one of the low-level interfaces between the operating system and a Pascal program. UNITREAD reads data from a physical device.

UNITREAD

UNITREAD has six parameters:

UNITREAD,(UNITNUMBER,ARRAY[FIRST],LENGTH,BLOCKNUMBER, ASYNCFLAG).

UNITNUMBER:	is the integer name of an I/O device.
ARRAY:	is any packed array, in which the data will be stored. A subscript, FIRST, can be added to the name of the array in order to define the first element of the array in which data will be stored. If no subscript is given, 0 is assumed.
LENGTH:	is the number of bytes to be read.
BLOCKNUMBER:	is required only when the I/O device is block-structured. It is the number of the first block to be read. If omitted, BLOCKNUMBER = 0 is assumed.
ASYNCFLAG:	indicates, when equal to 1, that the transfer is to be done asynchronously. If omitted, ASYNCFLAG = 0 is assumed. This parameter is ignored on implementations which do not support asynchronous I/O.

Expertise and caution are required when using the UNIT procedures, since no protection against errors is provided.

3
IMPLEMENTATION-DEPENDENT FEATURES

UNIT procedures are only implemented in UCSD Pascal.

Note: UNIT procedures and functions are not available in the Intel and Z80/8080 implementations of UCSD Pascal.

UNITREAD

4
EXAMPLE

```
PROGRAM TOPRNT(INPUT);
(* SEND INPUT FROM CONSOLE TO PRINTER *)
CONST
     PRINTER = 6;    {PRINTER'S UNITNUMBER}
     CONSLE = 1;    {CONSOLE'S UNITNUMBER}
VAR
     STR : STRING;
BEGIN
     UNITREAD(CONSLE,STR,5);
     UNITWRITE(PRINTER,STR,5)
END.
```

UNITWAIT

UNITWAIT is a non-standard predefined procedure that waits until an I/O operation is terminated.

☐ SYMBOL
■ IDENTIFIER
☐ CONCEPT

☐ STANDARD
☐ HP 1000

☐ J & W/CDC
☐ OMSI

☐ PASCAL/Z
■ UCSD

1
SYNTAX

UNITWAIT statement:

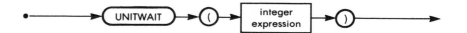

2
DESCRIPTION

The procedure UNITWAIT has one parameter, which is the integer name of an I/O device. UNITWAIT tests the status of an I/O device as long as that device is busy.

Expertise and caution are required when using the UNIT procedures, since no protection against errors is provided.

3
IMPLEMENTATION-DEPENDENT FEATURES

UNIT procedures are only implemented in UCSD Pascal.

UNITWAIT

Note: UNIT procedures and functions are not available in the Intel and
Z80/8080 implementations of UCSD Pascal.

4
EXAMPLE

```
PROGRAM PRNTWAIT;
(* SEND OUTPUT TO A PRINTER, AND WAIT FOR IT TO FINISH *)
CONST
      PRINTER = 6;                    {PRINTER'S INTEGER NAME}
VAR
      STR : STRING;
BEGIN
      STR := 'HELLO WORLD';
      UNITCLEAR(PRINTER);
      UNITWRITE(PRINTER,STR,5);
      UNITWAIT(PRINTER)
END.
```

UNITWRITE

UNITWRITE is a non-standard predefined procedure that performs low-level output operations on various devices.

□ SYMBOL　　　　　□ STANDARD　　　　　□ J & W/CDC　　　　□ PASCAL/Z
■ IDENTIFIER　　　□ HP 1000　　　　　　□ OMSI　　　　　　　■ UCSD
□ CONCEPT

1
SYNTAX

UNITWRITE statement:

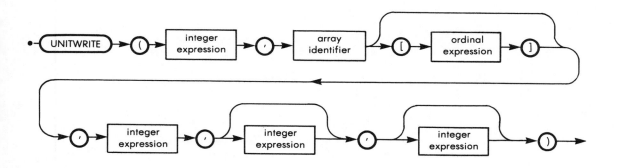

2
DESCRIPTION

The procedure UNITWRITE is one of the low-level interfaces between the operating system and a Pascal program. It writes data on a physical device.

UNITWRITE

UNITWRITE has six parameters:

UNITWRITE(UNITNUMBER,ARRAY[FIRST],LENGTH,BLOCKNUMBER,
ASYNCFLAG).

UNITNUMBER:	is the integer name of an I/O device.
ARRAY:	is the packed array, in which the data to be written is stored. A subscript, FIRST, can follow the name of the array, in order to define the first element of the array in which data is available. If no subscript is given, 0 is assumed.
LENGTH:	is the number of bytes to write.
BLOCKNUMBER:	is required only if the I/O device is block-structured. It is the number of the first block to be written. If omitted, BLOCKNUMBER = 0 is assumed.
ASYNCFLAG:	indicates, when equal to 1, that the transfer is to be done asynchronously. If omitted, ASYNCFLAG = 0 is assumed. This parameter is ignored on implementations which do not support asynchronous I/O.

Expertise and caution are required when using the UNIT procedures, since no protection against errors is provided.

3
IMPLEMENTATION-DEPENDENT FEATURES

UNIT procedures are only implemented in UCSD Pascal.

Note: UNIT procedures and functions are not available in the Intel and Z80/8080 implementations of UCSD Pascal.

4
EXAMPLE

```
PROGRAM TOPRNT(INPUT);
(* SEND INPUT FROM CONSOLE TO PRINTER *)
CONST
      PRINTER = 6;   {PRINTER'S UNITNUMBER}
      CONSLE = 1;    {CONSOLE'S UNITNUMBER}
VAR STR : STRING;
BEGIN
      UNITREAD(CONSLE,STR,5);
      UNITWRITE(PRINTER,STR,5)
END.
```

UNPACK

UNPACK is a standard procedure that transfers data from a packed array to an ordinary array.

☐ SYMBOL ■ STANDARD ■ J & W/CDC ☐ PASCAL/Z
■ IDENTIFIER ■ HP 1000 ☐ OMSI ☐ UCSD
☐ CONCEPT

1
SYNTAX

UNPACK statement:

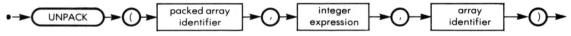

2
DESCRIPTION

If the arrays A and B are declared as follows:

A : **ARRAY**[M..N] **OF** T

B : **PACKED ARRAY**[U..V] **OF** T

with N − M >= V − U, then the statement

UNPACK(B,A,K)

is equivalent to:

FOR I := U **TO** V **DO** A[I − U + K] := B[I]

The integer expression K gives the value of the index of the first element in A to be assigned by the UNPACK procedure.

3
IMPLEMENTATION-DEPENDENT FEATURES

3.1 HP 1000 None known.

3.2 J & W/CDC None known.

3.3 OMSI The procedure UNPACK is not available; however, the FOR statement given above can be used to unpack an array.

3.4 Pascal/Z The procedure UNPACK is not available; however, the FOR statement given above can be used to unpack an array.

3.5 UCSD The procedure UNPACK is not available; however, the FOR statement given above can be used to unpack an array.

The reserved word UNTIL separates the sequence of statements which form the body of a REPEAT statement from the Boolean expression which controls the repetition of that loop.

- ■ SYMBOL
- □ IDENTIFIER
- □ CONCEPT

- ■ STANDARD
- ■ HP 1000

- ■ J & W/CDC
- ■ OMSI

- ■ PASCAL/Z
- ■ UCSD

1
SYNTAX

REPEAT statement:

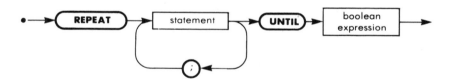

2
DESCRIPTION

UNTIL is the explicit separator used between the sequence of statements forming the body of a REPEAT statement and the Boolean expression which determines whether or not the loop should be repeated. It reduces the chances for error and misunderstanding of separation. UNTIL, together with the expression immediately following it, explicitly states the condition for termination.

UNTIL

3
IMPLEMENTATION-DEPENDENT FEATURES

None known.

4
EXAMPLE

Refer to the program RLOOP under the REPEAT heading.

The non-standard directive USES is a reserved word that makes available the algorithms and data structures of the units whose names follow.

■ SYMBOL   □ STANDARD   □ J & W/CDC   □ PASCAL/Z
□ IDENTIFIER   □ HP 1000   □ OMSI   ■ UCSD
□ CONCEPT

1
SYNTAX

1.1 USES Clause

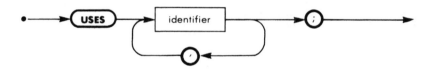

1.2 Program

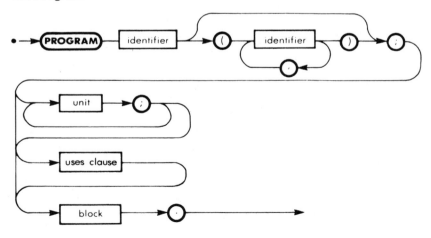

USES

1.3 Interface Section

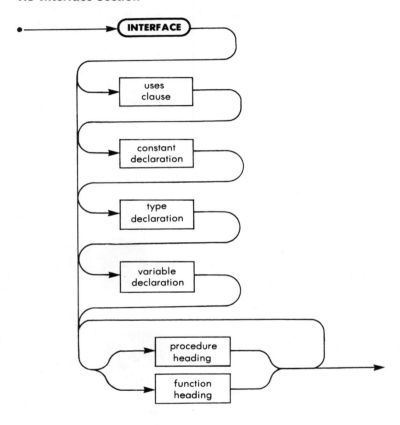

2
DESCRIPTION

The identifiers following the USES symbol inform the compiler which units' interface sections are to be used. The interface sections, if not already available, are read from a library. The contents of the interface section are treated as though they were physically part of the text of the program or unit being compiled. All of the interface information of the used

USES

unit is thus available for the remainder of the compilation, since USES clauses can only appear at the outermost declaration level of a program.

When a unit uses another unit (i.e., a USES clause appears in the using unit's interface section), both units' names must appear in the USES clause of whatever program or unit is being compiled. The order of specification in the USES clause must be from the most deeply nested to the least nested. Thus, if unit A used units B and C, and unit D was used by B, then the USES clause of a program using A would have to specify "USES D,B,C,A".

3
IMPLEMENTATION-DEPENDENT FEATURES

USES and units are only implemented in UCSD Pascal.

4
EXAMPLE

See the program USESEXAMPLE under the UNIT heading.

VARiable

VARiables are named locations in memory containing a value that can be changed during program execution.

- ■ SYMBOL
- □ IDENTIFIER
- ■ CONCEPT

- ■ STANDARD
- ■ HP 1000

- ■ J & W/CDC
- ■ OMSI

- ■ PASCAL/Z
- ■ UCSD

1
SYNTAX

1.1 Variable Declaration

1.2 Variable

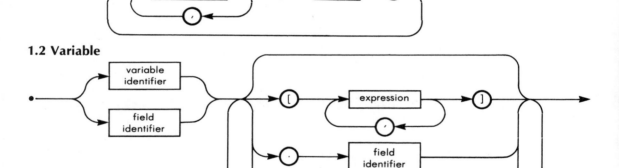

For more information about field identifiers, refer to the RECORD heading. For more information about identifiers followed by ↑, refer to the FILE or pointer headings. For more information about identifiers followed by an index expression (enclosed in [and]) refer to the ARRAY heading.

Refer to the FUNCTION heading for more information about function identifiers used to refer to the result to be returned.

For more information on variables in parameter lists and VAR parameters, refer to the PROCEDURE or FUNCTION headings.

1.3 Formal Parameter Lists

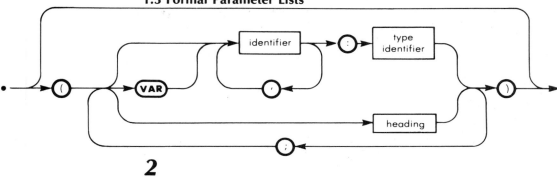

2
DESCRIPTION

Pascal uses two kinds of variables, static and dynamic. Static variables are explicitly declared by the VAR declaration, in formal parameter lists, and as function result identifiers. Static variables are denoted by their identifier. They exist (that is, typically, memory is allocated for them) during the entire execution of the block to which they are local.

Dynamic variables, on the other hand, are created dynamically during program execution by the procedure NEW. They do not occur in explicit declarations, and cannot be directly referenced by an identifier. They are referenced indirectly by a value of type pointer, which contains their address.

All variables must be declared before being referenced, either in the VAR declaration, as a function or result, or in a parameter list. VAR parameters provide a way to return values from procedures and functions.

3
IMPLEMENTATION-DEPENDENT FEATURES

3.1 HP 1000   None known.

3.2 J & W/CDC   None known.

3.3 OMSI   It is possible to associate a variable with an absolute memory address. This provides access to fixed memory addresses, such as device control registers.

Such an association is done in the VAR declaration, by writing the symbol ORIGIN and the absolute address after the name of the variable.

VARiable

VAR Declaration(OMSI):

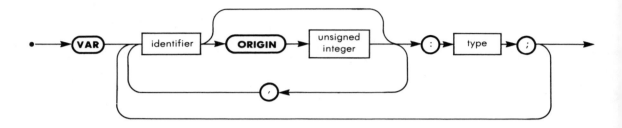

3.4 Pascal/Z   None known.

3.5 UCSD   None known.

4
EXAMPLE

Examples of static variables can be found in VAR declarations under almost all headings, as function results under the heading FUNCTION, and in parameter lists under the headings FUNCTION and PROCEDURE.

Examples of dynamic variables can be found under the heading pointer.

An example of VAR parameters can be found in the program VALVAR under the heading PROCEDURE.

WHILE

The WHILE loop allows the repeated execution of a statement. The execution depends on the value of a Boolean expression evaluated just before execution of the statement.

■ SYMBOL ■ STANDARD ■ J & W/CDC ■ PASCAL/Z
□ IDENTIFIER ■ HP 1000   ■ OMSI   ■ UCSD
□ CONCEPT

1
SYNTAX

WHILE statement:

2
DESCRIPTION

The WHILE loop can be implemented by the following flowchart.

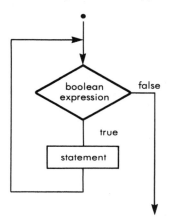

WHILE

3
IMPLEMENTATION-DEPENDENT FEATURES

None known.

4
EXAMPLE

For an example of a WHILE loop, see the program LOWUP under the CHAR heading.

WITH

The WITH statement is used to allow a shorter notation when record fields are referenced.

- ■ SYMBOL
- □ IDENTIFIER
- □ CONCEPT

- ■ STANDARD
- ■ HP 1000

- ■ J & W/CDC
- ■ OMSI

- ■ PASCAL/Z
- ■ UCSD

1
SYNTAX

WITH statement:

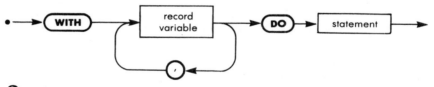

2
DESCRIPTION

When several references are made to fields of the same record in a statement, it is possible to simplify the notation by using the WITH statement. In some implementations, use of WITH statements can improve performance (execution time or code size) when the record variable has a complex specification.

The fields of a record can be referenced within a WITH statement by the field name alone, if the remaining part of the name, i.e., the record name (eventually qualified by field names) is mentioned in the WITH statement.

Example:

WITH RECORDNAME.FIELDONE **DO**
FIELDONEONE := X

WITH

is equivalent to:

RECORDNAME.FIELDONE.FIELDONEONE := X

Several WITH statements can be nested. Since field identifiers are local to the record in which they are defined, different records can have identical field identifiers. In the case of nested WITHs, the question of to which field an identifier refers is resolved by an analogy to the Pascal rules of scope: the innermost WITH statement prevails.

A short notation for nested WITH statements is provided:

WITH R1, R2, R3 **DO** S

is equivalent to:

WITH R1 **DO**
    WITH R2 **DO**
        WITH R3 **DO** S

The record to be accessed is determined prior to execution of the statement following the DO and does not change during the execution of the statement. For example, if A is an array of records whose lower bound is one, then in:

I := 1;
WITH A[I] **DO**
    BEGIN
        ...
        I := I + 1;
    END

the first array element of A is referred to implicitly throughout the WITH statement (even if I changes).

3
IMPLEMENTATION-DEPENDENT FEATURES

None known.

4
EXAMPLE

To observe the utility of WITH statements, this program should be compared with the similar program VOLUME listed under the RECORD heading.

```
PROGRAM VOLUMEW(INPUT,OUTPUT);
(* THIS PROGRAM COMPUTES THE VOLUME OF SPHERICAL OR
CYLINDRICAL CONTAINERS. TWO FORMATS OF INPUT DATA ARE
ACCEPTED:
        "SPHERE" RADIUS
        "CYLINDER" RADIUS HEIGHT
THE TWO LAST LETTERS OF THE WORD CYLINDER CAN BE OMITTED.
RADIUS AND HEIGHT ARE EXPRESSED IN METERS. *)
TYPE SHAPE = (SPHERE,CYLINDER);
    CONTAINER = RECORD
                        CASE TAG : SHAPE OF
                            SPHERE : (RADS : REAL);
                            CYLINDER : (RADC , HEIGHT : REAL)
                    END;
VAR CNTNR : CONTAINER;
PROCEDURE READSHAPE(VAR S : SHAPE);
    LABEL 1;
    VAR INP : PACKED ARRAY[1..6] OF CHAR;
        I : 1..6;
    BEGIN
    1 : FOR I := 1 TO 6 DO READ(INP[I]);
        READLN;
        IF INP = 'SPHERE'
        THEN S := SPHERE
        ELSE
            IF INP = 'CYLIND'
                THEN S := CYLINDER
```

```
            ELSE
                BEGIN
                    WRITELN('INPUT ERROR');
                    GOTO 1
                END
        END;
FUNCTION VOL(C : CONTAINER) : REAL;
    CONST PI = 3.1416;
    BEGIN
        WITH C DO
        CASE TAG OF
            SPHERE : VOL := PI * SQR(RADS) * RADS * 4.0/3.0;
            CYLINDER : VOL := PI * SQR(RADC) * HEIGHT
        END
    END;
BEGIN
    WITH CNTNR DO
        BEGIN
            READSHAPE(TAG);
            CASE TAG OF
                SPHERE : READLN(RADS);
                CYLINDER : READLN(RADC,HEIGHT)
            END
        END;
        WRITELN('THE VOLUME IS : ',VOL(CNTNR),' M3')
END.
```

WRITE

WRITE is a standard procedure that appends values to a file.

☐ SYMBOL   ■ STANDARD   ■ J & W/CDC   ■ PASCAL/Z
■ IDENTIFIER   ■ HP 1000   ■ OMSI   ■ UCSD
☐ CONCEPT

1
SYNTAX

1.1 Write Statement

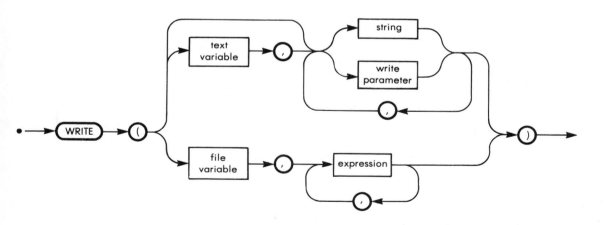

WRITE

1.2 Write Parameter

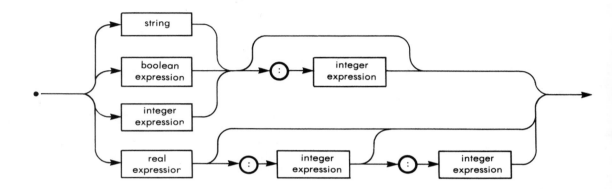

2
DESCRIPTION

2.1 Write(F,X) The exact meaning of WRITE(F,X) depends upon the types of F and X.

2.1.1 The records of F are of the same type as X.

    WRITE(F,X)

is exactly equivalent to:

BEGIN F↑ := X; PUT(F) **END**

2.1.2 The file F is of type TEXT.

2.1.2.1 X is a string.   The value of each character of the string is successively assigned to the buffer variable F↑, and appended to the file by the PUT function.

The number of characters appended to the file will be specified by a positive integer expression, which is appended to X. If this length is insufficient, the string will be truncated to the length specified. If the string is shorter than the specified length, the string will be appended to enough blanks (right-justified) to fill the specified length.

2.1.2.2 X is a Boolean expression.   Depending upon the value of X, the string 'FALSE' or 'TRUE' is generated and appended to the file (as described above).

   The number of characters appended to the file can be specified by a positive integer expression, as for strings.

2.1.2.3 X is an integer expression.   The value of X is converted to a string representing an integer number. The length of the string can be specified by a positive integer expression, appended to X. If this length is insufficient, it will automatically be increased; if it is not specified, an implementation-dependent default value will be provided.

2.1.2.4 X is a real expression.   The value of X is converted to a string representing a real number. The length of the string can be specified by a positive integer expression appended to X.

   The format of the real number representation is determined by a second optional integer expression that can be appended to X. If this second expression is missing, then the scientific format with mantissa and exponent will be used.

   The number of significant digits in the mantissa will be determined by the length of the string. If this second expression exists, a fixed-point representation will be used, and the second expression will provide the number of digits after the decimal point.

2.1.3 Other Combinations   All other combinations are illegal.

2.2 Write(F,X1,X2,X3...)   The statement WRITE(F,X1,X2,X3) is exactly equivalent to:

BEGIN WRITE(F,X1); WRITE(F,X2); WRITE(F,X3) **END**

2.3 Write(X); Write(X1,X2,X3...)   When the filename is not specified, OUTPUT is implied.

2.4 Conditions for Successful Execution of Write(F,..)   Since all forms of the WRITE statement use the PUT function, the condition for successful execution of the WRITE(F) and PUT(F) are the same. Before the first WRITE(F,..) statement is executed, F must be opened by a REWRITE(F) statement. No RESET(F), GET(F), READ(F,..), or READLN(F,..) statements may be executed between the REWRITE(F) and any WRITE(F,..) statement.

WRITE

3
IMPLEMENTATION-DEPENDENT FEATURES

3.1 HP 1000

3.1.1 Write Parameter String expressions and LONGREALs can be written as described for strings and reals respectively.

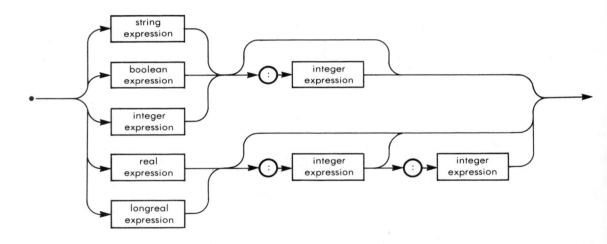

3.1.2 Prerequisites The conditions for successful execution of WRITE are changed: before a WRITE(F,..) statement can be executed, the file F must have been opened by one of the following statements:

> REWRITE(F)

> APPEND(F)

> OPEN(F)

If the file was opened by REWRITE or APPEND, the WRITE procedure behaves as described in the standard. If the file was opened by OPEN, it is not required that EOF(F) should be TRUE before a WRITE(F,..) operation is performed. WRITE simply overwrites components of F.

WRITE

Under these conditions, READ, WRITE, PUT and GET operations on the same file can be intermixed, and the file window can be arbitrarily moved by the SEEK procedure.

3.2 J & W/CDC Variables of type ALFA can be used as parameters for the WRITE procedure.

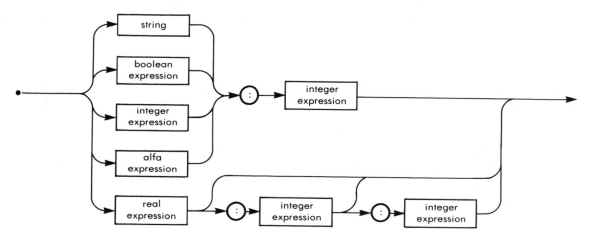

3.3 OMSI Only files of type TEXT can be written by WRITE.

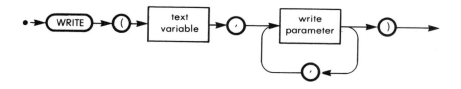

3.4 Pascal/Z Two important extensions have been made to the capabilities of the WRITE procedure: non-sequential access is possible with all files except textfiles, and enumerated types can be written on textfiles.

WRITE

3.4.1 Syntax

3.4.1.1 Write Statement

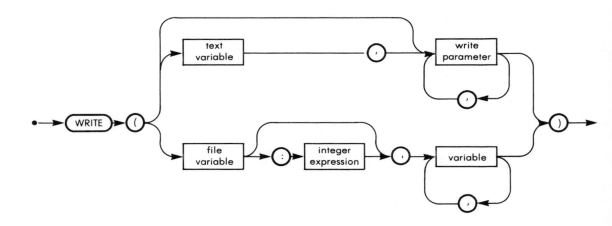

3.4.1.2 Write Parameter

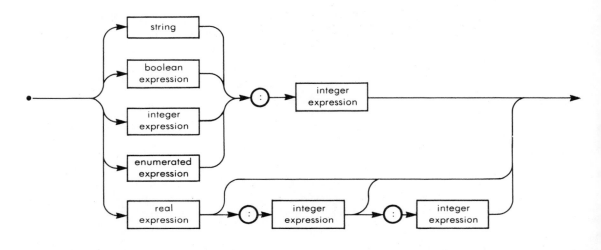

3.4.2 Direct Access to Files   By specifying a component number after the file identifier in the WRITE statement, it is possible to directly access any component of the file. If the specified record is beyond the end of the file, then the file will be extended.

The components are numbered from 1. Specifying component 0 or giving no component number causes the next sequential component to be written.

3.4.3 Enumerated Types   Variables of any enumerated type can be written on a textfile. Their value is represented by the string used in their declaration.

3.5 UCSD   Only files of type TEXT or INTERACTIVE can be written to by WRITE. UCSD Pascal does not support the output of Boolean values. The WRITE parameter can contain a string expression.

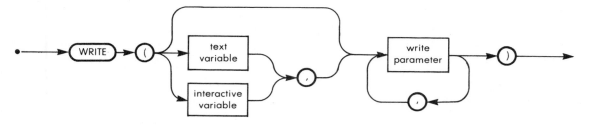

4
EXAMPLE

```
PROGRAM TESTWRITE(OUTPUT);
BEGIN
     WRITE('THIS IS THE BEGINNING');
     WRITELN('OF A LONG LINE');
     WRITELN('FOLLOWED BY A SHORT ONE')
END (* TESTWRITE *).
```

WRITEDIR

WRITEDIR *is a non-standard predefined procedure that first positions the window of a direct access file, and then performs a WRITE operation.*

☐ SYMBOL   ☐ STANDARD   ☐ J & W/CDC   ☐ PASCAL/Z
■ IDENTIFIER   ■ HP 1000   ☐ OMSI   ☐ UCSD
☐ CONCEPT

1
SYNTAX

WRITEDIR statement:

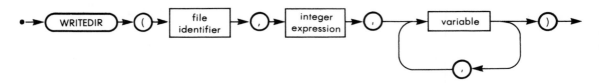

2
DESCRIPTION

The statement WRITEDIR(F,K,V1,V2,V3) is equivalent to:

BEGIN
    SEEK(F,K);
    WRITE(F,V1,V2,V3)
END.

Refer to the SEEK and WRITE headings for additional information.

Since the SEEK procedure can only be used with direct files, i.e., files opened with the OPEN statement, the same restriction applies to the WRITEDIR procedure.

WRITEDIR

3
IMPLEMENTATION-DEPENDENT FEATURES

WRITEDIR is only implemented in HP 1000 Pascal, but is very similar to the Pascal/Z implementation of WRITE.

4
EXAMPLE

See the program UPDATE SALARY under the READDIR heading.

WRITELN

WRITELN *is a standard procedure that appends zero, one or several characters, and an end of line mark to a text file.*

☐ SYMBOL   ■ STANDARD   ■ J & W/CDC   ■ PASCAL/Z
■ IDENTIFIER   ■ HP 1000   ■ OMSI   ■ UCSD
☐ CONCEPT

1
SYNTAX

1.1 Writeln Statement

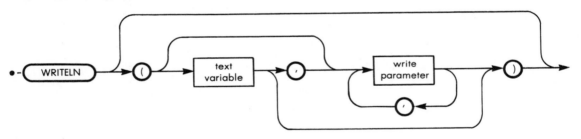

1.2 Write Parameter

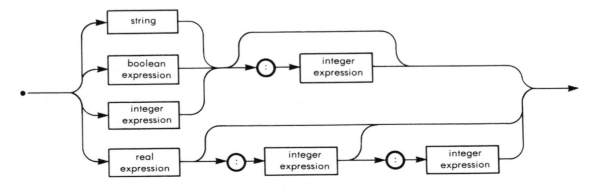

2
DESCRIPTION

2.1 Writeln(F)   The statement WRITELN(F) appends an end of line mark to the text file F. It is the only way of explicitly doing so.

2.2 Writeln(F,X1,X2,X3...)   The statement WRITELN(F,X1,X2,X3) is exactly equivalent to:

BEGIN WRITE(F,X1); WRITE(F,X2); WRITE(F,X3); WRITELN(F) **END**

2.3 Writeln; Writeln(X1,X2,X3...)   When the filename is not specified, OUTPUT is implied.

2.4 Conditions for Successful Execution of Writeln(F)   Before the first WRITELN(F) statement is executed, a REWRITE(F) statement must be executed. No RESET(F), GET(F), READ(F) or READLN(F) statements may be executed between the REWRITE(F) and any WRITELN(F) statements. (See the REWRITE heading for additional information.)

3
IMPLEMENTATION-DEPENDENT FEATURES

3.1 HP 1000

3.1.1 Write Parameter   String expressions and LONGREALs can be written as described for strings and reals respectively.

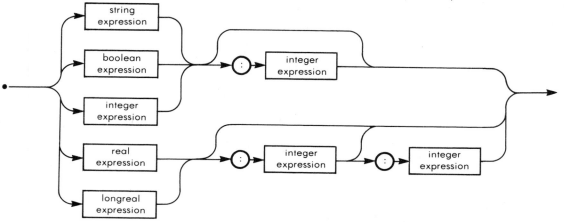

WRITELN

3.1.2 Prerequisites The conditions for successful execution of WRITELN are changed. Before the WRITELN(F,..) statement can be executed, the file F must have been opened by the REWRITE(F) or APPEND(F) statements.

3.2 J & W/CDC Variables of type ALFA can be used for the WRITELN procedure.

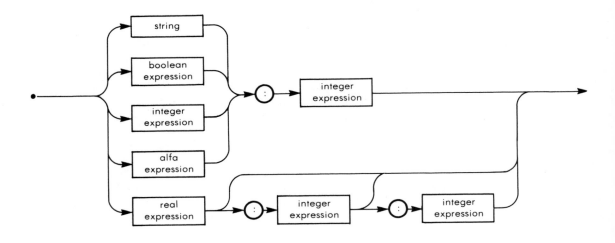

3.3 OMSI None known.

3.4 Pascal/Z Enumerated types can be written on text files. Their value is represented by the string used for their declaration.

WRITE parameter(Pascal/Z):

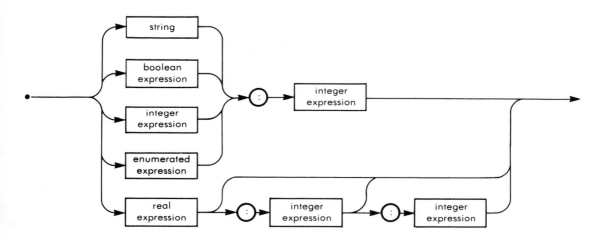

3.5 UCSD   The WRITELN statement can only be used with TEXT and INTERACTIVE files. The write parameter may contain a string expression. UCSD Pascal does not support the output of Boolean values.

WRITELN statement(UCSD):

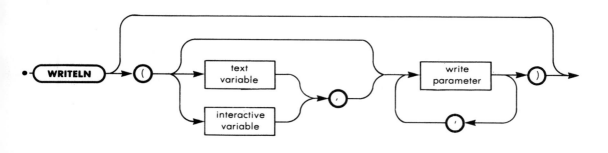

WRITELN

4
EXAMPLE

```
PROGRAM WRITELINES(OUTPUT);
VAR I,J : INTEGER;
     R : REAL;
     B : BOOLEAN;
BEGIN
     R := 123456789.123456789;
     J := MAXINT;
     B := TRUE;
     FOR I := 0 TO 69 DO WRITE((I MOD 10):1);
     WRITELN;
     WRITELN(R,R);
     WRITELN(R:20,R:10:3);
     WRITELN(J,J);
     WRITELN(J:20,J:10,J:5);
     WRITELN(B,NOT B);
     WRITELN(B: 20,NOT B:20)
END.
```

'

The single quote is used as a delimiter around character constants and strings; a pair of single quotes in a character constant or string is used to represent a single quote.

■ SYMBOL   ■ STANDARD   ■ J & W/CDC   ■ PASCAL/Z
□ IDENTIFIER   ■ HP 1000   ■ OMSI   ■ UCSD
□ CONCEPT

1
SYNTAX

1.1 Char Constant

1.2 Character

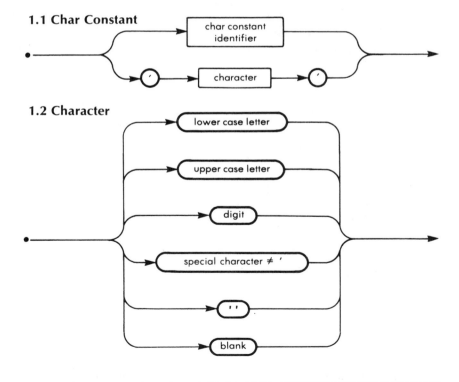

'

ASCII 39

1.3 String

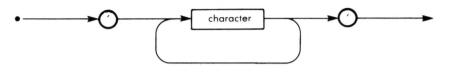

2
DESCRIPTION

The representation of single quotes as character constants or in a string is allowed; however, to avoid ambiguities, the single quotes in strings or character constants must appear twice.

3
IMPLEMENTATION-DEPENDENT FEATURES

None known.

4
EXAMPLE

Character string:

'ISOLATED SINGLE QUOTES IN STRINGS DON''T APPEAR THAT WAY'

ASCII 40 41

Parentheses can occur in various declarations, statements and expressions.

- ■ SYMBOL
- □ IDENTIFIER
- □ CONCEPT

- ■ STANDARD
- ■ HP 1000

- ■ J & W/CDC
- ■ OMSI

- ■ PASCAL/Z
- ■ UCSD

1
SYNTAX

1.1 Program

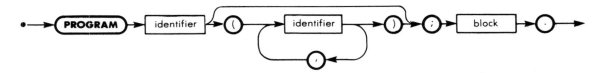

1.2 Formal Parameter List

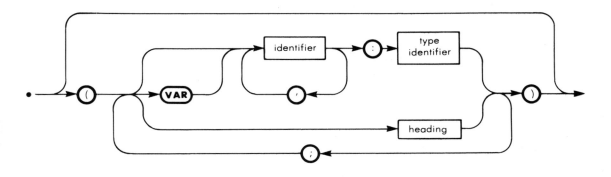

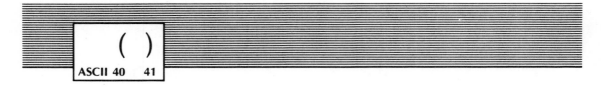

ASCII 40 41

1.3 Procedure Statement

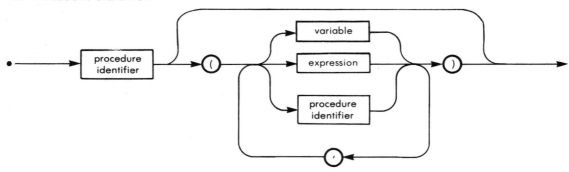

1.4 Enumerated Type

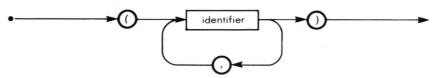

1.5 Field List

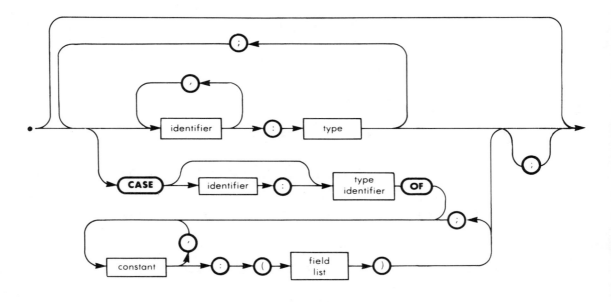

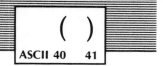
1.6 Factor

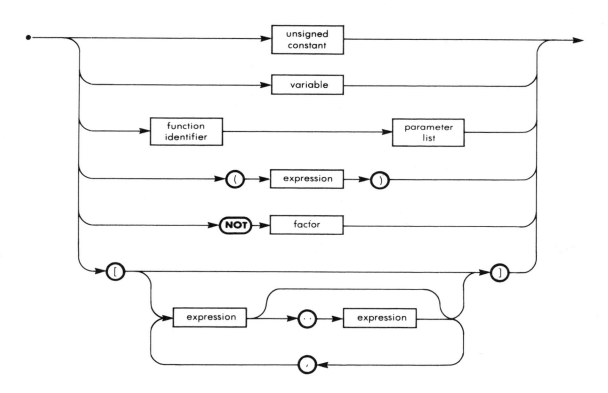

2
DESCRIPTION

Parentheses are used in program, procedure, and function headings around the list of formal parameters, in procedure and function statements around the list of actual parameters, in declarations of enumerated types around the list of possible values, in declarations of records with variants around the field lists, and in expressions to overrule the precedence rules of operators.

ASCII 40 41

For more detailed information about the use of parentheses, refer to the following headings:

      expression

      FUNCTION

      PROCEDURE

      PROGRAM

      RECORD

      ordinal

      TYPE

3
IMPLEMENTATION-DEPENDENT FEATURES

None known.

The operator * has two different uses: it is the multiplication and the intersection operator.

■ SYMBOL
□ IDENTIFIER
□ CONCEPT

■ STANDARD
■ HP 1000

■ J & W/CDC
■ OMSI

■ PASCAL/Z
■ UCSD

1
SYNTAX

Refer to the expression heading.

2
DESCRIPTION

When written between two REAL or INTEGER factors in a term, the values of these factors are first evaluated, and then multiplied. The resulting term is of type REAL, unless both factors are of type INTEGER or a subrange thereof, in which case the term is INTEGER.

When written between two factors that are sets of the same objects, the result of the operation will be a set containing only the objects common to both factors (set intersection).

3
IMPLEMENTATION-DEPENDENT FEATURES

3.1 HP 1000

Wherever REALs are allowed, LONGREALs are allowed. If one or both factors of a product are LONGREALs, then the product is a LONGREAL.

ASCII 42

3.2 J & W/CDC   None known.

3.3 OMSI   None known.

3.4 Pascal/Z   None known.

3.5 UCSD   Long integer factors are allowed in a product. If one or both factors of a product are long integers, then the product is a long integer. Long integers and REALs cannot be mixed in expressions.

4
EXAMPLE

```
PROGRAM SALESTAX(INPUT,OUTPUT);
     CONST TAXRATE = 0.06;
     VAR TAX,PRICE,TOTAL : REAL;
     BEGIN
         WRITELN('INTRODUCE PRICE');
         READLN(PRICE);
         TAX := PRICE * TAXRATE;
         TOTAL := PRICE + TAX;
         WRITELN('TOTAL IS: ',TOTAL:10:2)
     END.
```

```pascal
PROGRAM SCNDHLF(OUTPUT);
      TYPE DAYS = (MO,TU,WE,TH,FR,SA,SU);
           WEEK = SET OF DAYS;
      VAR WORKDAY,SCNDHLF,SCNWRK : WEEK;
          D : DAYS;
      PROCEDURE WRDAY(X:DAYS);
      BEGIN
          CASE X OF
               MO : WRITE(' MONDAY ');
               TU : WRITE(' TUESDAY ');
               WE : WRITE(' WEDNESDAY ');
               TH : WRITE(' THURSDAY ');
               FR : WRITE(' FRIDAY ');
               SA : WRITE(' SATURDAY ');
               SU : WRITE(' SUNDAY ')
          END
      END;
BEGIN
      WORKDAY := [MO..FR];
      SCNDHLF := [TH..SU];
      SCNWRK := WORKDAY * SCNDHLF;
      FOR D := MO TO SU DO
      IF D IN SCNWRK THEN
      BEGIN
          WRDAY(D);
          WRITELN(' IS A WORKDAY IN THE SECOND HALF',
                  ' OF THE WEEK')
      END
END.
```

ASCII 43

The + symbol has three different uses: it is a unary plus sign preceding an expression, unsigned number, or constant identifier; it is the addition operator; and it is the union operator.

■ SYMBOL ■ STANDARD ■ J & W/CDC ■ PASCAL/Z
☐ IDENTIFIER ■ HP 1000 ■ OMSI ■ UCSD
☐ CONCEPT

1
SYNTAX

For the syntax of the first use of the + symbol, refer to the NUMBER, CONSTant or expression headings. For the second and third uses, refer to the expression heading.

2
DESCRIPTION

When written in front of an expression, the + sign is ignored. When written between two REAL or INTEGER terms in an expression, the values of these terms are first evaluated, and then added; the result is of type REAL unless both terms are of type INTEGER (or a subrange thereof), in which case the result is of type INTEGER.

When written between two terms that are sets of the same base type, the result of the operation is the union of both sets.

3
IMPLEMENTATION-DEPENDENT FEATURES

3.1 HP 1000 Whenever REALs are allowed, LONGREALs are also

allowed. If one or both terms of a sum are LONGREALs, then the sum is a LONGREAL.

3.2 J & W/CDC   None known.

3.3 OMSI   None known.

3.4 Pascal/Z   None known.

3.5 UCSD   Long integer terms are allowed in a sum. If one or both terms of a sum are long integers, then the sum is a long integer. Long integers and REALs cannot be mixed in expressions.

4
EXAMPLES

```
PROGRAM SALES(INPUT,OUTPUT);
VAR PRICE,GRATUITY,TOTAL : REAL;
BEGIN
      WRITELN('INTRODUCE PRICE AND GRATUITY');
      READLN(PRICE,GRATUITY);
      TOTAL := PRICE + GRATUITY;
      WRITELN('TOTAL IS : ',TOTAL:10:2)
END.
```

ASCII 43

```
PROGRAM WEEKDAYS(OUTPUT);
TYPE DAYS = (MO,TU,WE,TH,FR,SA,SU);
     WEEK = SET OF DAYS;
VAR WORKDAY,HOLIDAY,WEEKDAY : WEEK;
    D : DAYS;
PROCEDURE WRDAY(X : DAYS);
    BEGIN
        CASE X OF
            MO : WRITE(' MONDAY ');
            TU : WRITE(' TUESDAY ');
            WE : WRITE(' WEDNESDAY ');
            TH : WRITE(' THURSDAY ');
            FR : WRITE(' FRIDAY ');
            SA : WRITE(' SATURDAY ');
            SU : WRITE(' SUNDAY ')
        END
    END;
BEGIN
    WORKDAY := [MO..FR];
    HOLIDAY := [SA..SU];
    WEEKDAY := WORKDAY + HOLIDAY;
    FOR D := MO TO SU DO
        IF D IN WEEKDAY THEN
            BEGIN
                WRDAY(D);
                WRITELN(' IS A WEEKDAY')
            END
END.
```

The comma is used as a separator between identifiers or values in lists.

■ SYMBOL   ■ STANDARD   ■ J & W/CDC   ■ PASCAL/Z
□ IDENTIFIER   ■ HP 1000   ■ OMSI   ■ UCSD
□ CONCEPT

1
SYNTAX

Refer to the relevant headings for information about the use of commas. (See below.)

2
DESCRIPTION

A comma can appear in:

— PROGRAM, PROCEDURE, and FUNCTION headings

— LABEL declarations

— Enumerated TYPE declarations

— ARRAY declarations and element accesses

— RECORD declarations

— VARiable declarations

— SET factors

— CASE statements

— actual parameter lists

— WITH statements

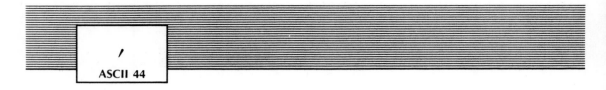

3
IMPLEMENTATION-DEPENDENT FEATURES

None known.

The – symbol has three different uses: it changes the sign of an expression, it is the subtraction operator, and it is the set-difference operator.

■ SYMBOL   ■ STANDARD   ■ J & W/CDC   ■ PASCAL/Z
□ IDENTIFIER   ■ HP 1000   ■ OMSI   ■ UCSD
□ CONCEPT

1
SYNTAX

For the syntax of the first use, refer to the NUMBER, CONSTant or expression headings. For the second and third uses, refer to the expression heading.

2
DESCRIPTION

When written in front of an expression, the – sign causes the value of the expression to be multiplied by – 1. When written between two REAL or INTEGER terms in an expression, the values of these terms are first evaluated and then the value of the right term is subtracted from the value of the left. The resulting expression is of type REAL, unless both terms are of type INTEGER, or a subrange thereof, in which case the expression is of type INTEGER.

When written between two terms that are sets of the same base type, the result of the operation will be the difference between the two sets, i.e., a set in which the elements are those belonging to the left term, but not to the right.

3
IMPLEMENTATION-DEPENDENT FEATURES

3.1 HP 1000 Wherever REALs are allowed, LONGREALs are also allowed. If one or both terms of a difference are LONGREALs, then the difference is a LONGREAL.

3.2 J & W/CDC None known.

3.3 OMSI None known.

3.4 Pascal/Z None known.

3.5 UCSD Long integer terms are allowed in a difference. If one or both terms of a difference are long integers, then the difference is a long integer. Long integers and REALs cannot be mixed in expressions.

4
EXAMPLES

```
PROGRAM ONEDOLLARDISCOUNT(INPUT,OUTPUT);
CONST DISCOUNT = 1;
VAR PRICE,TOTAL : REAL;
BEGIN
    WRITELN('INTRODUCE PRICE');
    READLN(PRICE);
    TOTAL := PRICE — DISCOUNT;
    WRITELN('TOTAL IS :',TOTAL:10:2)
END.
```

```
PROGRAM HOLIDAYS(OUTPUT);
TYPE DAYS = (MO,TU,WE,TH,FR,SA,SU);
     WEEK = SET OF DAYS;
VAR WORKDAY,HOLIDAY,WEEKDAY : WEEK;
    D : DAYS;
  PROCEDURE WRDAY(X : DAYS);
  BEGIN
     CASE X OF
          MO : WRITE(' MONDAY ');
          TU : WRITE(' TUESDAY ');
          WE : WRITE(' WEDNESDAY ');
          TH : WRITE(' THURSDAY ');
          FR : WRITE(' FRIDAY ');
          SA : WRITE(' SATURDAY ');
          SU : WRITE(' SUNDAY ')
     END
  END;
BEGIN
    WEEKDAY := [MO..SU];
    WORKDAY := [MO..FR];
    HOLIDAY := WEEKDAY - WORKDAY;
    FOR D := MO TO SU DO
       IF D IN HOLIDAY THEN
          BEGIN
             WRDAY(D);
             WRITELN(' IS A HOLIDAY')
          END
END.
```

ASCII 46

The period is used in numbers and records, and at the end of programs.

■ SYMBOL   ■ STANDARD   ■ J & W/CDC   ■ PASCAL/Z
□ IDENTIFIER   ■ HP 1000   ■ OMSI   ■ UCSD
□ CONCEPT

1
SYNTAX

1.1 Unsigned Real

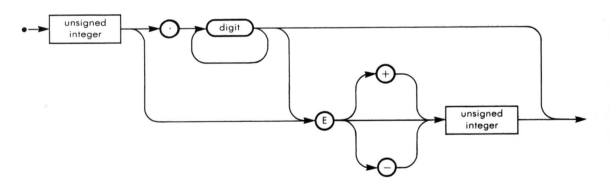

1.2 Variable Referenced as Part of a Record

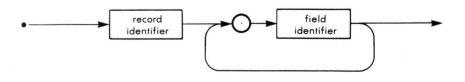

1.3 Program

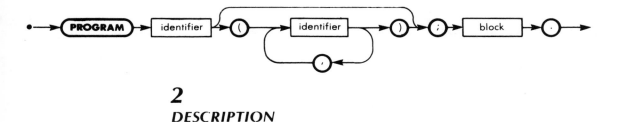

2
DESCRIPTION

Refer to the NUMBER, RECORD and PROGRAM headings.

3
IMPLEMENTATION-DEPENDENT FEATURES

None known.

ASCII 46, 46

The .. symbol is used between two ordinal expressions, to replace an enumeration of all intermediate values.

■ SYMBOL   ■ STANDARD   ■ J & W/CDC   ■ PASCAL/Z
□ IDENTIFIER   ■ HP 1000   ■ OMSI   ■ UCSD
□ CONCEPT

1
SYNTAX

1.1 Subrange Type

1.2 Integer Subrange Type

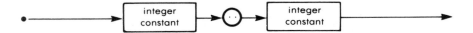

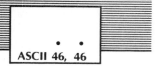

ASCII 46, 46

1.3 Set Factor

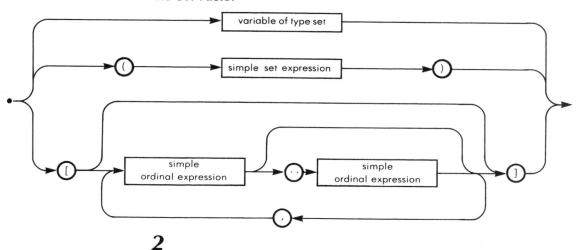

2

DESCRIPTION

In TYPE declarations and in SET definitions, it is often necessary to enumerate long sequences of consecutive values. These sequences can be replaced by the first value, the .. symbol, and the last value.

3

IMPLEMENTATION-DEPENDENT FEATURES

3.1 HP 1000

The .. symbol is also used in the definition of structured constants, and in CASE statements.

Set CONSTant:

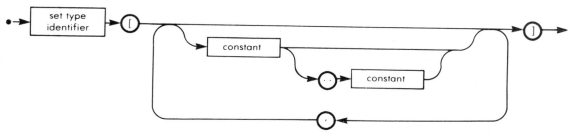

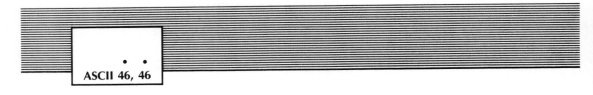

ASCII 46, 46

CASE statement(HP 1000):

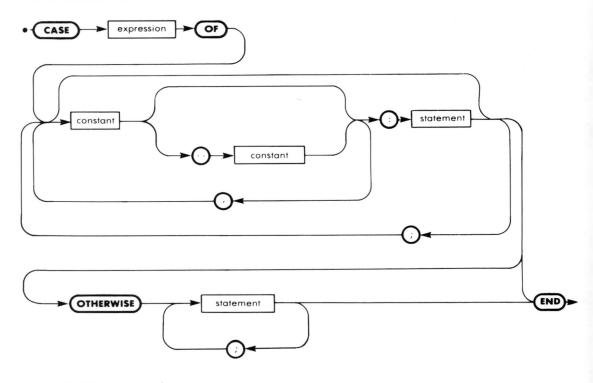

3.2 J & W/CDC   None known.

3.3 OMSI   None known.

3.4 Pascal/Z   None known.

3.5 UCSD   None known.

4
EXAMPLE

['A','B','C','D','E','F','G','H','I','J','K','L','M','N','O','P'] is
equivalent to ['A'..'P'] in the ASCII character set.

The operator / is used to compute the ratio of two REAL or INTEGER factors.

■ SYMBOL   ■ STANDARD   ■ J & W/CDC   ■ PASCAL/Z
□ IDENTIFIER   ■ HP 1000   ■ OMSI   ■ UCSD
□ CONCEPT

1
SYNTAX

Refer to the expression heading.

2
DESCRIPTION

When the / sign appears between REAL or INTEGER factors in a term, the values of these factors are first evaluated, and then the left value is divided by the right, giving a REAL result, even if both factors were INTEGER.

3
IMPLEMENTATION-DEPENDENT FEATURES

3.1 HP 1000 Wherever REALs are allowed, LONGREALs are allowed. If one or both factors of a quotient are LONGREALs, then the quotient is a LONGREAL.

3.2 J & W/CDC None known.

3.3 OMSI None known.

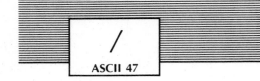

ASCII 47

3.4 Pascal/Z None known.

3.5 UCSD Long integer factors are not allowed with the / operator.

4
EXAMPLE

```
PROGRAM HALFOFF(INPUT,OUTPUT);
     CONST REDFACT = 2;
     VAR PRICE,TOTAL : REAL;
     BEGIN
          WRITELN('INTRODUCE PRICE');
          READLN('PRICE');
          TOTAL := PRICE/REDFACT;
          WRITELN('TOTAL IS : ',TOTAL:10:2)
     END.
```

	/*	*/
	ASCII 47, 42	ASCII 42, 47

The non-standard symbols / * and */ can be used instead of { and } around comments.

- ■ SYMBOL
- ☐ IDENTIFIER
- ☐ CONCEPT

- ☐ STANDARD
- ☐ HP 1000

- ☐ J & W/CDC
- ■ OMSI

- ☐ PASCAL/Z
- ☐ UCSD

1
SYNTAX

The symbol /* can be used as a delimiter at the beginning of a comment.

The symbol */ can be used as a delimiter at the end of a comment.

2
DESCRIPTION

Refer to the COMMENT heading for further details.

3
IMPLEMENTATION-DEPENDENT FEATURES

The use of /* and */ is only implemented in OMSI Pascal.

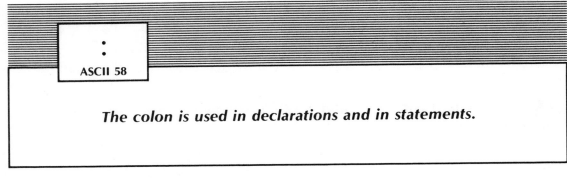

ASCII 58

The colon is used in declarations and in statements.

■ SYMBOL   ■ STANDARD   ■ J & W/CDC   ■ PASCAL/Z

☐ IDENTIFIER   ■ HP 1000   ■ OMSI   ■ UCSD

☐ CONCEPT

1
SYNTAX

Refer to the relevant headings.

2
DESCRIPTION

The different uses of the : symbol can be divided into four categories:

1. The : symbol appears between a list of variable identifiers and a type identifier. (See the VARIABLE, PROCEDURE, FUNCTION, and RECORD headings.)
2. The : symbol follows a label. (See the LABEL heading.)
3. The : symbol follows a case constant list. (See the CASE and RECORD headings.)
4. The : symbol is used as a special separator in WRITE parameters. (See the WRITE heading.)

3
IMPLEMENTATION-DEPENDENT FEATURES

None known.

The : = symbol is used to assign a value to a variable or a function. It appears in assignment statements and in FOR statements.

- ■ SYMBOL
- □ IDENTIFIER
- □ CONCEPT

- ■ STANDARD
- ■ HP 1000

- ■ J & W/CDC
- ■ OMSI

- ■ PASCAL/Z
- ■ UCSD

1
SYNTAX

Refer to the assignment or FOR headings.

2
DESCRIPTION

The variable or the function whose identifier appears to the left of the := sign is given the value of the expression on the right side.
For more details, refer to the assignment or FOR headings.

3
IMPLEMENTATION-DEPENDENT FEATURES

None known.

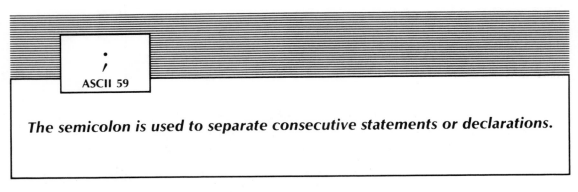

;

ASCII 59

The semicolon is used to separate consecutive statements or declarations.

■ SYMBOL   ■ STANDARD   ■ J & W/CDC   ■ PASCAL/Z
☐ IDENTIFIER   ■ HP 1000   ■ OMSI   ■ UCSD
☐ CONCEPT

1
SYNTAX

The syntax of the different uses of the semicolon can be found under the following headings:

> block
>
> CASE
>
> CONSTant
>
> PROGRAM
>
> RECORD
>
> statement
>
> TYPE
>
> VARiable

2
DESCRIPTION

Since the semicolon is a statement separator, and not a terminator (as in PL/1, for example), there is no need for a semicolon between the last statement of a compound statement and the END bracket. However, such semicolons may make editing easier and are to be encouraged.

ASCII 59

Although such a semicolon will have no effect on the meaning of a program, it can, in some less sophisticated implementations, increase the size of the object code and slow down the execution (some deviant compilers specifically disallow such semicolons).

3
IMPLEMENTATION-DEPENDENT FEATURES

None known.

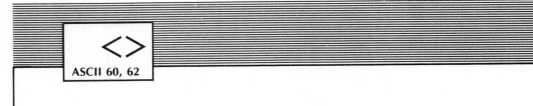

ASCII 60, 62

The relational operator **<>** *is used to check the inequality of two values.*

■ SYMBOL	■ STANDARD	■ J & W/CDC	■ PASCAL/Z
□ IDENTIFIER	■ HP 1000	■ OMSI	■ UCSD
□ CONCEPT			

1
SYNTAX

Refer to the expression heading.

2
DESCRIPTION

The operands around the <> operator must be of one of the following types: ordinal, REAL, SET, pointer, or string (PACKED ARRAY of CHAR). In general, both operands must be of identical types, but REALs, INTEGERs and subranges of INTEGERs can be mixed.

The <> relation is TRUE if the value of the left operand is not equal to the value of the right operand. Strings are equal if they are the same size and all of their components are equal.

3
IMPLEMENTATION-DEPENDENT FEATURES

3.1 HP 1000

3.1.1 Longreals   In expressions containing the <> operator, LONG-REALs are allowed wherever REALs are.

3.1.2 Structured Types   Arrays and records that do not contain files can be compared with the <> operator. Structured values are equal

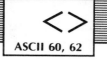

when all of their components are equal. Packed and normal structured types can also be compared.

3.1.3 Strings Strings can be compared no matter what their length. The comparison is done as if the shortest string had been extended, by trailing blanks, to match the length of the longer string.

3.2 J & W/CDC

3.2.1 Strings When strings appear in relational expression, their length should be less than ten characters, or an exact multiple of ten characters.

3.2.2 Variables of Alfa Variables of type ALFA can be compared with relational operators.

3.3 OMSI None known.

3.4 Pascal/Z Variable length STRINGs can be compared. Unless the operands are equal in length and content, $<>$ is true.

3.5 UCSD

3.5.1 Long Integers In expressions containing the $<>$ operator, one side can be a long integer expression, provided that the other side is long integer, INTEGER or a subrange of INTEGER.

3.5.2 Structured Types Arrays and records which do not contain files can be compared with the $<>$ operator. Structured values are equal when all of their components are equal. Packed and normal structured types cannot be compared.

3.5.3 STRINGs See paragraph 3.4 of this heading.

4

EXAMPLE

```
PROGRAM TESTNE(OUTPUT);
VAR I,J : INTEGER;
BEGIN
     I := 2; J := 3;
     IF I <> J THEN WRITELN('OK')
                    ELSE WRITELN('STRANGE, 2 = 3')
END.
```

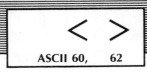

ASCII 60, 62

The relational operators $>$ and $<$ are used to compare values of simple types or strings.

■ SYMBOL   ■ STANDARD   ■ J & W/CDC   ■ PASCAL/Z
□ IDENTIFIER   ■ HP 1000   ■ OMSI   ■ UCSD
□ CONCEPT

1
SYNTAX

Refer to the expression heading.

2
DESCRIPTION

The simple expressions around the $>$ or $<$ operators must be of an ordinal or REAL type. Strings (PACKED ARRAY of CHAR) of the same length are also acceptable. The $>$ relation is TRUE when the left operand is greater than the right operand. The $<$ relation is TRUE when the right operand is greater than the left operand.

REALs, INTEGERs, and subranges of INTEGERs can be mixed in relational expressions. For enumerated types, the first value of the enumeration is said to be the smallest, and the last the largest. For Boolean expressions, the value TRUE is considered larger than the value FALSE.

To compare two strings, the ordinal numbers of the characters composing both strings are compared consecutively, in the order in which they appear in the strings. The first pair of different characters determines the ordering of the strings.

3
IMPLEMENTATION-DEPENDENT FEATURES

3.1 HP 1000

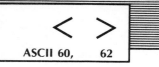
3.1.1 Longreals   In expressions containing the > or < operators, LONGREALs are allowed wherever REALs are.

3.1.2 Strings   Strings can be compared by the > or < operators. If the length of the strings is different, then the comparison is made as if the shortest string had been extended by trailing blanks to match the length of the longer string.

3.2 J & W/CDC

3.2.1 Strings   Only strings with less than ten characters, or an exact multiple of ten characters, can be compared.

3.2.2 Alfa Variables   Variables of type ALFA can be compared with other variables of type ALFA, or with strings of exactly ten characters.

3.3 OMSI   None known.

3.4 Pascal/Z   STRINGs can be compared using the > or < operators. If the lengths of the STRINGs differ and the ordering relation between the two has not been determined over the length of the shorter string, the comparison is performed as if the shorter string had been extended by nulls (the lowest lexicographic character).

3.5 UCSD

3.5.1 Long Integers   In expressions containing the > or < operators, one side can be a long integer expression, provided that the other side is a long integer, INTEGER or subrange of INTEGER expression.

3.5.2 STRINGs   See paragraph 3.4 of this heading.

4
EXAMPLE

```
PROGRAM REL1TEST(OUTPUT);
TYPE COLOR = (BLACK,BLUE,GREEN,YELLOW,RED);
VAR X,Y : COLOR;
BEGIN
      X := BLUE; Y := RED;
      IF X > Y THEN WRITELN('WRONG')
                    ELSE WRITELN('THIS IS OK')
END.
```

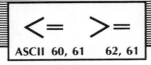

<= >=

ASCII 60, 61 62, 61

The relational operators <= and >= are used to compare values of ordinal expressions, strings or sets.

■ **SYMBOL**   ■ **STANDARD**   ■ **J & W/CDC**   ■ **PASCAL/Z**
□ **IDENTIFIER** ■ **HP 1000**   ■ **OMSI**   ■ **UCSD**
□ **CONCEPT**

1
SYNTAX

Refer to the expression heading.

2
DESCRIPTION

The simple expressions around the <= or >= operators must be of one of the following types: ordinal, REAL, SET, or string (PACKED ARRAY of CHAR).

The >= relation is TRUE when the left operand is greater than or equal to the right operand. The <= relation is TRUE when the right operand is greater than or equal to the left operand. REALs, INTEGERs, and subranges of INTEGERs can be mixed in relational expressions.

For enumerated types, the first value of the enumeration is said to be the smallest, and the last the largest. The value TRUE is considered larger than the value FALSE in Boolean expressions.

A set is considered smaller than or equal to another set when all of its elements are contained in the other set.

To compare strings, the ordinal numbers of the characters composing both strings are compared consecutively, in the order in which they appear in the strings. The first pair of different characters determine the ordering of the strings.

3
IMPLEMENTATION-DEPENDENT FEATURES

3.1 HP 1000

3.1.1 Longreals In expressions containing the >= or <= operators, LONGREALs are allowed wherever REALs are.

3.1.2 Strings. Strings can be compared by the >= or <= operators. If the length of the strings is different, then the comparison is made as if the shortest string had been extended by trailing blanks to match the length of the longer string.

3.2 J & W/CDC

3.2.1 Strings Only strings with less than ten characters, or an exact multiple of ten characters, can be compared.

3.2.2 Alfa Variables Variables of type ALFA can be compared with other variables of type ALFA, or with strings of exactly ten characters.

3.3 OMSI   None known.

3.4 Pascal/Z   STRINGs can be compared using the <= or >= operators. If the lengths of the STRINGs differ and the ordering relation between the two has not been determined over the length of the shorter string, the comparison is performed as if the shorter string had been extended by nulls (the lowest lexicographic character).

3.5 UCSD

3.5.1 Long Integers In expressions containing the >= or <= operators, one side can be a long integer expression, provided that the other side is a long integer, INTEGER or subrange of INTEGER expression.

3.5.2 STRINGs See paragraph 3.4 of this heading.

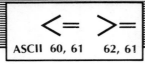

4

EXAMPLE

```
PROGRAM TESTDAY(OUTPUT);
TYPE DAYS = (MO,TU,WE,TH,FR,SA,SU);
     WEEK = SET OF DAYS;
VAR WEEKDAY,WORKDAY,HOLIDAY : WEEK;
     D : DAYS;
BEGIN
     WORKDAY := [MO..FR];
     HOLIDAY := [SA,SU];
     WEEKDAY := WORKDAY + HOLIDAY;
     IF WORKDAY <= WEEKDAY THEN WRITELN('A WORKDAY IS A WEEKDAY')
                           ELSE WRITELN('THIS IS WRONG');
     IF HOLIDAY >= WORKDAY THEN WRITELN('I DON'T WORK ON HOLIDAYS!')
                           ELSE WRITELN('A HOLIDAY IS NOT A WORKDAY')
END.
```

The = sign is used in type definitions, constant declarations, and relational expressions.

■ SYMBOL	■ STANDARD	■ J & W/CDC	■ PASCAL/Z
□ IDENTIFIER	■ HP 1000	■ OMSI	■ UCSD
□ CONCEPT			

1
SYNTAX

— For the syntax of the use of = in type definitions, refer to the TYPE heading.

— For the syntax of the use of = in constant definitions, refer to the CONSTant heading.

— For the syntax of the use of = in relational expressions, refer to the expression heading.

2
DESCRIPTION

When used in type or constant definitions, the = sign defines a type or a constant identifier. (See the TYPE and CONSTant headings.)

In relational expressions, the operands around the = operator must be of one of the following types: ordinal, REAL, SET, pointer, or string (PACKED ARRAY of CHAR). In general, both operands must be of identical types, but REALs, INTEGERs, and subranges of INTEGERs can be mixed.

The = relation is TRUE if the left operand is equal to the right operand. Strings are equal if all of their respective components are equal.

3

IMPLEMENTATION-DEPENDENT FEATURES

3.1 HP 1000

3.1.1 Longreals In expressions containing the = operator, LONG-REALs are allowed wherever REALs are.

3.1.2 Structured Types Arrays and records that do not contain files can be compared with the = operator. Structured values are equal when they are the same size and all of their components are equal. Packed and normal structured types can also be compared.

3.1.3 Strings Strings, whatever their length, can be compared. The comparison is done as if the shortest string had been extended, by trailing blanks to match the length of the longer string.

3.2 J & W/CDC

3.2.1 Strings When strings appear in relational expressions, their length should be less than ten characters, or an exact multiple of ten characters.

3.2.2 Variables of Type Alfa Variables of type ALFA can be compared with relational operators.

3.3 OMSI None known.

3.4 Pascal/Z Variable length STRINGs can be compared. If the operands are equal in current length and content, the = comparison is true.

3.5 UCSD

3.5.1 Long Integers In expressions containing the = operator, one side can be a long integer expression, provided that the other side is long integer, INTEGER, or a subrange of INTEGER.

3.5.2 Structured Types Arrays and records that do not contain files can be compared with the = operator. Structured values are equal when they are the same size and all of their components are equal. Packed and normal structured types cannot be compared.

3.5.3 STRINGs See paragraph 3.4 of this heading.

4
EXAMPLE

```
PROGRAM ALLDAYS(OUTPUT);
CONST NWORK = 5;
TYPE DAYS = (MO,TU,WE,TH,FR,SA,SU);
     WEEK = SET OF DAYS;
VAR WORKDAY,HOLIDAY,WEEKDAY : WEEK;
    NW : INTEGER;
    D : DAYS;
BEGIN
    WORKDAY := [MO..FR];
    HOLIDAY := [SA,SU];
    WEEKDAY := [MO..SU];
    IF WEEKDAY = WORKDAY + HOLIDAY
        THEN WRITELN('STILL 7 DAYS IN A WEEK')
        ELSE WRITELN('WHAT'S WRONG ?');
    NW := 0;
    FOR D := MO TO SU DO
        IF D IN WORKDAY
            THEN NW := NW + 1;
    IF NW = NWORK
        THEN WRITELN('STILL FIVE WORKDAYS')
        ELSE WRITELN('NO LONGER FIVE WORKDAYS??')
END.
```

@

ASCII 64

The @ symbol can be used instead of the ↑ symbol. In some implementations @ is also an additional operator.

- ■ SYMBOL
- □ IDENTIFIER
- □ CONCEPT

- ■ STANDARD
- □ HP 1000

- □ J & W/CDC
- ■ OMSI

- □ PASCAL/Z
- □ UCSD

1
SYNTAX

Refer to the ↑ heading for the standard use of @.

Refer to paragraph 3.1 of this heading for a description of the use of @ as an address operand.

2
DESCRIPTION

Standard Pascal allows the @ symbol to be used instead of the ↑ symbol. This has not been implemented very often.

3
IMPLEMENTATION-DEPENDENT FEATURES

3.1 OMSI   The @ symbol is an address operator.

@

ASCII 64

3.1.1 Syntax

Factor containing the @ operator:

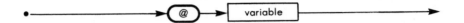

3.1.2 Description   The @ operator can be followed by a variable of any type. The resulting expression is of type pointer, and its value is the address of the variable operand.

This operator is mainly used to pass addresses of variables to low-level external procedures.

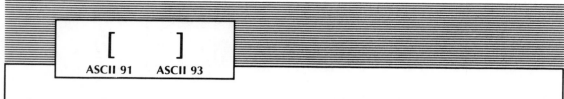

[ ]

ASCII 91   ASCII 93

The square brackets [and] are used around ARRAY subscripts and around enumerations of SET elements.

- ■ SYMBOL
- ☐ IDENTIFIER
- ☐ CONCEPT

- ■ STANDARD
- ■ HP 1000

- ■ J & W/CDC
- ■ OMSI

- ■ PASCAL/Z
- ■ UCSD

1
SYNTAX

1.1 Array Type

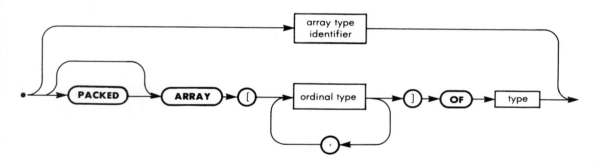

1.2 Variable Referenced as Part of an Array

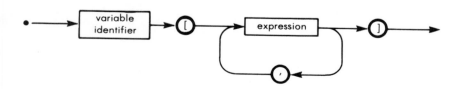

ASCII 91   ASCII 93

1.3 Set Factor

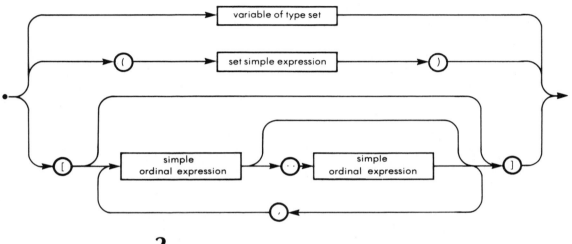

2
DESCRIPTION

See the ARRAY and SET headings.

3
IMPLEMENTATION-DEPENDENT FEATURES

3.1 HP 1000 The square brackets are also used in the definition of structured constants.

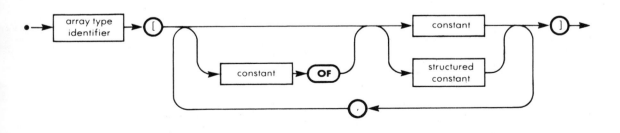

[   ]
ASCII 91   ASCII 93

3.2 J & W/CDC   None known.

3.3 OMSI   None known.

3.4 Pascal/Z   None known.

3.5 UCSD   The square brackets are also used with declarations of STRINGs and long integers, and to access an element of a STRING.

Long integer type:

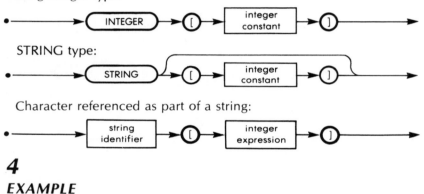

STRING type:

Character referenced as part of a string:

4
EXAMPLE

```
PROGRAM SQRBRACKETS(OUTPUT);
VAR
      ARY : ARRAY[1..12] OF CHAR;
      CHSET: SET OF 'A'..'Z'
BEGIN
      ARY[1] := 'H';
      ARY[2] := 'I';
      CHSET:=['F','G','H']
      WRITELN(ARY[1],ARY[2])
      IF ARY[1] IN CHSET THEN WRITELN('CORRECT')
                              ELSE WRITELN('ERROR');
      IF ARY[2] IN CHSET THEN WRITELN('ERROR')
                              ELSE WRITELN('CORRECT')
END.
```

ASCII 94

The ↑ symbol is used with dynamic variables and files.

■ SYMBOL   ■ STANDARD   ■ J & W/CDC   ■ PASCAL/Z
□ IDENTIFIER   ■ HP 1000   ■ OMSI   ■ UCSD
□ CONCEPT

1
SYNTAX

1.1 Pointer Type

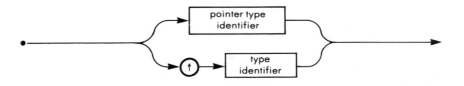

1.2 Variable Referenced Through a Pointer

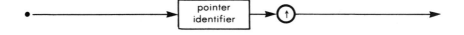

1.3 Buffer Variable

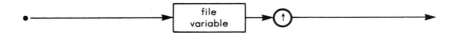

ASCII 94

2
DESCRIPTION

For more details about the role of the ↑ symbol with dynamic variables, refer to the pointer heading.

For more details about the role of the ↑ symbol with files, refer to the FILE heading.

3
IMPLEMENTATION-DEPENDENT FEATURES

None known.

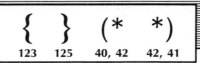

{	}	(*	*)
123	**125**	**40, 42**	**42, 41**

The symbols {, (*, *), and } are used as delimiters around comments.

■ SYMBOL ■ STANDARD ■ J & W/CDC ■ PASCAL/Z
□ IDENTIFIER ■ HP 1000 ■ OMSI ■ UCSD
□ CONCEPT

1
SYNTAX

See the comment heading.

2
DESCRIPTION

The symbols { or (* are used as delimiters at the beginning of a comment.

The symbols } or *) are used as delimiters at the end of a comment.

3
IMPLEMENTATION-DEPENDENT FEATURES

See the comment heading.

References

General:

Introduction to Pascal Including UCSD Pascal.
Rodnay Zaks. Sybex (1980).

UCSD Pascal:

Softech Microsystems, 9494 Black Mountain
Road, Building 3, San Diego, California 92126.
UCSD Pascal User Manual.
Softech Microsystems (1979).

North Star Pascal System Reference Manual,
Version 1, Revision 3. North Star Computers, Inc. (1979).
Pascal 80 Users Guide.
Intel Corporation (1979).
Apple Pascal Language Reference Manual.
Apple Computer, Inc. (1980).

Pascal/Z:

Ithaca Intersystems, Inc., 1650 Hanshaw Road,
P.O. Box 91, Ithaca, New York 14850.

Pascal/Z Implementation Manual.
Ithaca Intersystems, Inc. (1980).

Pascal 1000:

Hewlett Packard Co., Data Systems Division,
11000 Wolfe Road, Cupertino, California 95014.

Hewlett Packard Pascal 1000 Reference Manual.
#HP92832A-90001, Hewlett Packard Co. (1980).

OMSI Pascal-1:

Oregon Minicomputer Software, Inc.,
2340 SW Canyon Road, Portland, Oregon 97201.

J & W/CDC Pascal:

Pascal User Manual and Report.
Kathleen Jensen and Niklaus Wirth. Springer-Verlag
(1974-Revised Edition 1978).

ISO Standard Pascal:

Joint Pascal Committee,
CBEMA, 1800 L St. NW, Washington, D.C.

Computer Magazine, *Toward a Pascal Standard,* B. Ravenal,
pp. 68-82, IEEE Computer Society, April 1979.

Pascal User's Group, Pascal News Number 18,
P.O. Box 888524, Atlanta, GA 30338, May 1980. .

Programming in Pascal.
P. Grogono. Addison-Wesley (1980).

The SYBEX Library

BASIC PROGRAMS FOR SCIENTISTS AND ENGINEERS
by Alan R. Miller 340 pp., 120 illustr., Ref. B240
This second book in the "Programs for Scientists and Engineers" series provides a library of problem solving programs while developing proficiency in BASIC.

INSIDE BASIC GAMES
by Richard Mateosian 350 pp., 240 illustr., Ref. B245
Teaches interactive BASIC programming through games. Games are written in Microsoft BASIC and can run on the TRS-80, APPLE II and PET/CBM.

FIFTY BASIC EXERCISES
by J.P. Lamoitier 240 pp., 195 illustr., Ref. B250
Teaches BASIC by actual practice using graduated exercises drawn from everyday applications. All programs written in Microsoft BASIC.

YOUR FIRST COMPUTER
by Rodnay Zaks 260 pp., 150 illustr., Ref. C200A
The most popular introduction to small computers and their peripherals: what they do and how to buy one.

DON'T (or How to Care for Your Computer)
by Rodnay Zaks 220 pp., 100 illustr., Ref. C400
The correct way to handle and care for all elements of a computer system including what to do when something doesn't work.

INTRODUCTION TO WORD PROCESSING
by Hal Glatzer 200 pp., 70 illlustr., Ref. W101
Explains in plain language what a word processor can do, how it improves productivity, how to use a word processor and how to buy one wisely.

INTRODUCTION TO WORDSTAR
by Arthur Naiman 200 pp., 30 illustr., Ref. W110
Makes it easy to learn how to use WordStar, a powerful word processing program for personal computers.

FROM CHIPS TO SYSTEMS: AN INTRODUCTION TO MICROPROCESSORS
by Rodnay Zaks 560 pp., 255 illustr., Ref. C201A
A simple and comprehensive introduction to microprocessors from both a hardware and software standpoint: what they are, how they operate, how to assemble them into a complete system.

MICROPROCESSOR INTERFACING TECHNIQUES
by Rodnay Zaks and Austin Lesea 460 pp., 400 illustr., Ref. C207
Complete hardware and software interconnect techniques including D to A conversion, peripherals, standard buses and troubleshooting.

PROGRAMMING THE 6502
by Rodnay Zaks 390 pp., 160 illustr., Ref. C202
Assembly language programming for the 6502, from basic concepts to advanced data structures.

6502 APPLICATIONS BOOK
by Rodnay Zaks   280 pp., 205 illustr., Ref. D302
Real life application techniques: the input/output book for the 6502.

6502 GAMES
by Rodnay Zaks   300 pp., 140 illustr., Ref. G402
Third in the 6502 series. Teaches more advanced programming techniques, using games as a framework for learning.

PROGRAMMING THE Z80
by Rodnay Zaks   620 pp., 200 illustr., Ref. C280
A complete course in programming the Z80 microprocessor and a thorough introduction to assembly language.

PROGRAMMING THE Z8000
by Richard Mateosian   300 pp., 125 illustr., Ref. C281
How to program the Z8000 16-bit microprocessor. Includes a description of the architecture and function of the Z8000 and its family of support chips.

THE CP/M HANDBOOK (with MP/M)
by Rodnay Zaks   330 pp., 100 illustr., Ref. C300
An indispensable reference and guide to CP/M — the most widely used operating system for small computers.

INTRODUCTION TO PASCAL (Including UCSD PASCAL)
by Rodnay Zaks   420 pp., 130 illustr., Ref. P310
A step-by-step introduction for anyone wanting to learn the Pascal language. Describes UCSD and Standard Pascals. No technical background is assumed.

THE PASCAL HANDBOOK
by Jacques Tiberghien   490 pp., 350 illustr., Ref. P320
A dictionary of the Pascal language, defining every reserved word, operator, procedure and function found in all major versions of Pascal.

PASCAL PROGRAMS FOR SCIENTISTS AND ENGINEERS
by Alan Miller   400 pp., 80 illustr., Ref. P340
A comprehensive collection of frequently used algorithms for scientific and technical applications, programmed in Pascal. Includes such programs as curve-fitting, integrals and statistical techniques.

50 PASCAL PROGRAMS
by Rudolph Langer and Rodnay Zaks   275 pp., 90 illustr., Ref. P350
A collection of 50 Pascal programs ranging from mathematics to business and games programs. Explains programming techniques and provides actual practice.

APPLE PASCAL GAMES
by Douglas Hergert and Joseph T. Kalash   380 pp., 40 illustr., Ref. P360
A collection of the most popular computer games in Pascal challenging the reader not only to play but to investigate how games are implemented on the computer.

INTRODUCTION TO UCSD PASCAL SYSTEMS
by Charles T. Grant and Jon Butah   300 pp., 110 illustr., Ref. P370
A simple, clear introduction to the UCSD Pascal Operating System for beginners through experienced programmers.

INTERNATIONAL MICROCOMPUTER DICTIONARY

140 pp., Ref. X2
All the definitions and acronyms of microcomputer jargon defined in a handy pocket-size edition. Includes translations of the most popular terms into ten languages.

MICROPROGRAMMED APL IMPLEMENTATION

by Rodnay Zaks   350 pp., Ref. Z10
An expert-level text presenting the complete conceptual analysis and design of an APL interpreter, and actual listings of the microcode.

SELF STUDY COURSES

Recorded live at seminars given by recognized professionals in the microprocessor field.

INTRODUCTORY SHORT COURSES:
Each includes two cassettes plus special coordinated workbook (2½ hours).

S10—INTRODUCTION TO PERSONAL AND BUSINESS COMPUTING

A comprehensive introduction to small computer systems for those planning to use or buy one, including peripherals and pitfalls.

S1—INTRODUCTION TO MICROPROCESSORS

How microprocessors work, including basic concepts, applications, advantages and disadvantages.

S2—PROGRAMMING MICROPROCESSORS

The companion to S1. How to program any standard microprocessor, and how it operates internally. Requires a basic understanding of microprocessors.

S3—DESIGNING A MICROPROCESSOR SYSTEM

Learn how to interconnect a complete system, wire by wire. Techniques discussed are applicable to all standard microprocessors.

INTRODUCTORY COMPREHENSIVE COURSES:
Each includes a 300-500 page seminar book and seven or eight C90 cassettes.

SB1—MICROPROCESSORS

This seminar teaches all aspects of microprocessors: from the operation of an MPU to the complete interconnect of a system. The basic hardware course (12 hours).

SB2—MICROPROCESSOR PROGRAMMING

The basic software course: step by step through all the important aspects of microcomputer programming (10 hours).

ADVANCED COURSES:
Each includes a 300-500 page workbook and three or four C90 cassettes.

SB3—SEVERE ENVIRONMENT/MILITARY MICROPROCESSOR SYSTEMS

Complete discussion of constraints, techniques and systems for severe environment applications, including Hughes, Raytheon, Actron and other militarized systems (6 hours).

SB5—BIT-SLICE

Learn how to build a complete system with bit slices. Also examines innovative applications of bit slice techniques (6 hours).

SB6—INDUSTRIAL MICROPROCESSOR SYSTEMS

Seminar examines actual industrial hardware and software techniques, components, programs and cost (4½ hours).

SB7—MICROPROCESSOR INTERFACING

Explains how to assemble, interface and interconnect a system (6 hours).

SOFTWARE

BAS 65™ CROSS-ASSEMBLER IN BASIC

8″ diskette, Ref. BAS 65
A complete assembler for the 6502, written in standard Microsoft BASIC under CP/M®.

8080 SIMULATORS

Turns any 6502 into an 8080. Two versions are available for APPLE II.

APPLE II cassette, Ref. S6580-APL(T)
APPLE II diskette, Ref. S6580-APL(D)

FOR A COMPLETE CATALOG
OF OUR PUBLICATIONS

U.S.A.
2344 Sixth Street
Berkeley,
California 94710
Tel: (415) 848-8233
Telex: 336311

SYBEX-EUROPE
4 Place Felix Eboue
75583 Paris Cedex 12
Tel: 1/347-30-20
Telex: 211801

SYBEX-VERLAG
Heyestr. 22
4000 Düsseldorf 12
West Germany
Tel: (0211) 287066
Telex: 08 588 163